D1411097

Asian Village Economy at the Crossroads

Asian Village Economy at the Crossroads

An Economic Approach to Institutional Change

Yujiro Hayami

Masao Kikuchi

University of Tokyo Press
Tokyo
The Johns Hopkins University Press
Baltimore

First published in the United States of America in 1982 by
The Johns Hopkins University Press, Baltimore, Maryland 21218
ISBN 0-8018-2774-4
Library of Congress Catalog Card Number 81-83546

Publication of this book was supported by a grant-in-aid from the Nippon Life
Insurance Foundation.

ⓒ UNIVERSITY OF TOKYO PRESS 1981

Printed in Japan

TO
RANDOLPH BARKER AND VERNON W. RUTTAN

Contents

vii

List of Tables

List of Figures

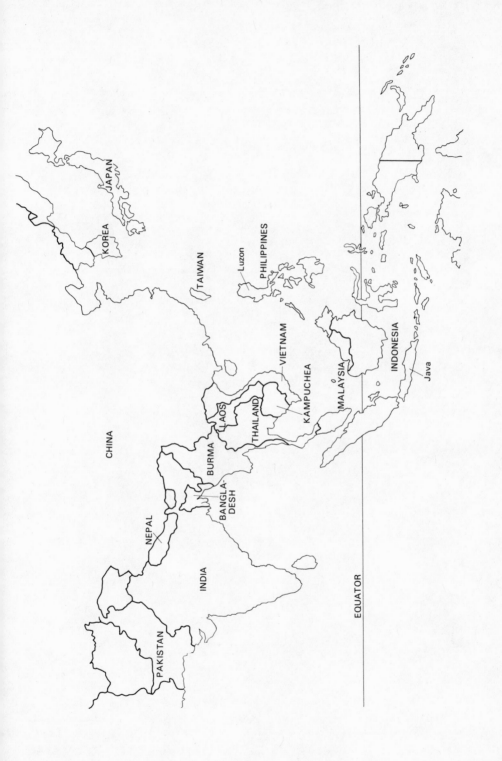

Preface

Villages in tropical Asia appear dormant in the shade of coconut and banana groves. Under the surface, however, they are experiencing a dramatic transformation in their social organization and institutions. What are the basic economic forces underlying the social and institutional changes? How are those changes affecting agricultural production and income distribution in village communities? These questions underlie the studies in this volume.

This book is the outgrowth of an experimental data collection from a small sample of households in one village in the Philippines, a survey undertaken in order to document the whole complexity of village economic activities in terms of a double-entry accounting system comparable to United Nations' system of national accounts. (The results were published in Hayami and associates, *Anatomy of a Peasant Economy: A Rice Village in the Philippines*, International Rice Research Institute, 1978.) While collecting data for that purpose, we encountered a number of intriguing phenomena in social organization and institutions in the village community. Henceforth, our investigation was redirected to focus on the institutional aspects of the village economy. In order to ascertain how unique or representative our Philippine village was, we extended our investigation to other villages, including several in Indonesia. Further, extensive surveys over wide areas of Java and Luzon were conducted in order to give a broad perspective to the intensive village studies. From the results of those extensive surveys, together with a literature review of village studies in other countries, we are convinced that the agrarian changes observed in our case-study villages are common in their basic nature throughout South and Southeast Asia, despite large variations in their appearance.

xix

A major part of the empirical research on which this book is based was conducted as a project of the agricultural economics program of the International Rice Research Institute (IRRI). Without the generous support of Director General Nyle C. Brady and the continued encouragement of Robert Herdt and other colleagues at IRRI, this study would not have been undertaken and completed. Partial support from the Agricultural Development Council, the Agro Economic Survey of Indonesia and the International Development Center of Japan were highly instrumental, especially for our research in Indonesia. A three-month visit by the senior author to the Institute of Economic Growth, Delhi, during the final stage of manuscript preparation gave us a rare opportunity to reconsider our perspective based on experience in East and Southeast Asia, in light of the reality of agrarian problems in South Asia.

We are most grateful for assistance in data collection and processing from Luisa Bambo, Violeta Cordova, Nellie Fortuna, Anwar Hafid, Sri Hartoyo, Esther Marciano, Adelaida Palacpac, Dolor Palis, Chaerul Saleh and Abrar Yusuf. Some of them are the coauthors of earlier reports, as acknowledged in the text of this volume.

Robert Bates, David Feeny, Koichi Hamada, Keijiro Otsuka and James Roumasset have read an earlier manuscript and have given us invaluable comments. We have also benefited from comments and suggestions at the various stages of research from Dale Adams, James Anderson, Hans Binswanger, Daniel Bromley, Gelia Castillo, William Collier, Robert Evenson, Shigeru Ishikawa, Motoshige Itoh, Yukihiko Kiyokawa, Konosuke Odaka, Kazushi Ohkawa, Mancur Olson, Gustav Ranis, C.H. Hanumantha Rao, Ralph Retzlaff, Theodore Schultz, Rudolf Sinaga, Akira Takahashi, Hiromitsu Umehara, Abe Weisblat, Benjamin White, Saburo Yamada and Yasukichi Yasuba. For all these benefits we express the deepest gratitude.

This book is dedicated to Randolph Barker and Vernon Ruttan, two former heads of IRRI's agricultural economics program. Their groundwork on the rice economy of tropical Asia and the research environment that they created paved the way for our studies.

May 1981   YUJIRO HAYAMI
                                                    Tokyo, Japan

                                                    MASAO KIKUCHI
                                                    Los Baños, Philippines

Asian Village Economy at the Crossroads

In many parts of Asia carabao plowing is being replaced by the use of power tillers.

Photos courtesy of the International Rice Research Institute

Chapter 1

Introduction

Waves of modernizing forces, such as commercialization, population pressure and new technology, have been pressing major change upon Asian village communities. Fears have been expressed that these forces are destroying the traditional village-community institutions based on the principles of mutual help and income sharing, and are resulting in polarization of agrarian communities and greater misery for the poor. The purpose of this book is to give a perspective on the future course of rural economy in Asia by analyzing the process by which agrarian institutions change in response to such external forces.

Focus

Asian village communities have been experiencing major changes. The land-labor ratio has been declining rapidly due to population growth at an explosive rate. In order to sustain a subsistence level of income, attempts have been made to increase land productivity; the efforts are reflected in the development and diffusion of seed-fertilizer technology and the expansion of irrigation systems. Despite such efforts, the value of labor has declined relative to the value of land.

Such changes in resource endowments and technology have been exerting strong pressure on the village institutions that have been molded under relatively stationary conditions. For example, in Java, the traditional *bawon* system, in which all community members can participate in rice harvesting with *ani-ani* (hand knives) and receive a certain share of the output, has been replaced by the *tebasan* system in which farmers sell standing crops to merchants who employ a crew of harvesting workers with sickles at a fixed wage rate (see Chapter 7). This

3

institutional change was motivated by a need to reduce the harvesting cost in correspondence with the reduction in the market wage rate due to the population pressure on land. The adoption of new varieties more susceptible to shattering increased the efficiency of harvesting rice crops by sickles relative to that of cutting panicles by *ani-ani* knives. Similarly, in the Philippines the traditional *hunusan* system, which is similar to the *bawon* system, has been replaced by the *gama* system in which employment for harvesting is limited to the workers who did weeding of the field without receiving wages (see Chapters 4 and 5). In Bangladesh, a shift from the traditional output-sharing contracts among villagers to fixed daily-wage contracts with migrant workers has been reported in a number of villages (Clay, 1976).

Those cases suggest that the distribution of income produced in the village among various resource contributors, such as landlords, tenant operators and landless laborers, responds to changing resource endowments and technology through adjustments in the institutions governing the use of land and labor.

Institutional adjustments are also required in the use of other factors of production. For example, it has been becoming more important to improve water supply and control in order to increase land productivity by introducing modern varieties and related practices. Efficient water distribution and maintenance and operation of irrigation systems require collective action in the village communities. Such institutions as water rights arrangements and obligations to participate in communal works would develop in response to the compelling need to raise land productivity. An important issue in development planning is to identify what structure in the village community is conducive to the efficient use of water resources. The same issue also applies to financial and marketing institutions.

Thus, the village institutions which control the use of labor, land and other inputs are the critical media through which population pressure and technological change influence production and income in the rural sector. They are also the media through which government policies, such as land reform and irrigation development programs, affect the welfare of rural people. Considering their strategic importance, the analysis in this book will focus on the process by which such village institutions change in response to changes in resource endowments, technology and government policies. We will also focus on how such changes influence the well-being of village people.

Approach

The focus of the book is thus on agrarian change—the term here used to denote *changes in the pattern of production and income distribution in rural communities involving major changes in institutions such as property rights and contractual arrangements.*

Since agrarian change is a multi-faceted phenomenon, a full understanding of its process will require an interdisciplinary approach using the resources and techniques of anthropology, sociology and political science. However, our approach is single-disciplinary based on economics. This does not imply that we expel political and sociocultural aspects out of the boundary of analysis by assuming them exogenous to the economic system. On the contrary, we aim to broaden the scope of economic analysis to incorporate institutional change as an endogenous variable influenced critically by political and sociocultural factors. Our approach represents an attempt to analyze by the logic of economics the process by which institutional change was dictated by noneconomic as well as economic factors. The economic approach to institutional change is elaborated in the next chapter in greater detail, but here we try to summarize its basic structure.

We define institutions as *rules sanctioned by the members of the community.*[1] The clear specification of the rules governing the rights to the use of scarce resources (property rights) and the exchange of such rights (contracts) has the effect of reducing the costs involved in negotiation, policing and enforcement of the claims and the contracts concerning the use of resources; the establishment of the socially sanctioned rules thereby facilitates the efficient allocation of resources.

The community gains from the creation of appropriate institutions. But to create, maintain and modify institutions entails costs. Time and effort are involved to obtain consensus among community members on new rules and laws as well as to enforce them. The effort to modify institutions will not be forthcoming unless the social benefit exceeds the cost. Economic factors such as changes in technology and resource endowments will induce institutional changes by making new forms of institutions more profitable to establish.

However, a high rate of social return to an institutional reform does not ensure its realization. All members of the community may gain more or less from the reform, including those who do not intend to

---

[1] This broad definition encompasses many more specific definitions, such as "regulative principles which organize most of the activities of individuals in a society into definite organizational patterns from the point of view of some of the perennial, basic problems of any society or ordered social life" (Eisenstadt, 1968, p. 409).

share the cost. If everyone wants to be a free rider, the reform will never materialize no matter how high the rate of return to the community as a whole. Here emerges the need for political entrepreneurs or leaders. A leader designs a scheme more easily acceptable to community members and obtains their sanction by persuasion and by force. He undertakes this task if he expects that he will be able to collect enough rewards from the beneficiaries, both material and non-material (such as prestige and respect), to compensate for the cost that he will have to bear. In this regard the structure of social classes or vested interest groups in the community, with which the leader may seek alliances, is a critical determinant of institutional change.

Socio-cultural environments represent another important determinant. If the social structure of a community is characterized by a high degree of cohesion and solidarity and the community places a high value on the conformity of individuals to the majority, the cost of reaching a consensus and enforcing the sanctioned rules will be lower than otherwise.

The socio-cultural environment also makes some forms of institution less costly to establish than others. In our example, the shift from the *hunusan* to the *gama* contract was motivated by a desire to reduce the real wage rate of harvesting workers. However, the same objective could have been achieved by reducing the crop share rate in the *hunusan* system or simply employing laborers at the going market wage rates in cash. In fact, it was *gama* that replaced *hunusan* because this change involved the least cost and the least resistance from the workers among the three alternatives. *Gama* was chosen because in terms of traditional moral principles in the village, such as mutual help and income sharing, the *gama* system, which maintains the traditional crop share for harvesters, appeared more legitimate and fair (see Chapters 4 and 5). Such socio-cultural factors are especially powerful in village communities where a high degree of social interaction prevails.

Our economic approach to institutional change represents an attempt to apply standard economic theories on production and exchange to human behavior involving political and socio-cultural processes. We base our analysis mainly on the data collected from the intensive surveys that we have conducted in Indonesia and the Philippines. It is our intention to identify the major current of agrarian change in developing countries in Asia today at the grass-roots level. National census data and the nationwide sample surveys could provide us useful hunches. However, because village institutions are largely customary rules, not written laws, and also because they not infrequently violate government rules and regulations, we can hardly expect to obtain deep insights into reality in village communities from such official sources alone.

The results of our village studies are supplemented by information extracted from a large number of other micro-level village studies as well as aggregative data from national- and regional-scale surveys, in order to provide a broad perspective on agrarian change in Asia. To the extent possible, we tried to compare current developments in South and Southeast Asia with historical experience in East Asia, especially in Japan.

Plan of the Book

This book consists of four major parts. Part I (Chapters 2 and 3) develops a framework of analysis. In Chapter 2, we first identify the organizational characteristics of Asian village communities and the historical process by which economic and social forces resulted in the formation of specific organizational patterns; and then specify the elements required for the construction of a relevant theory of institutional change in village communities. Chapter 3 examines external modernization forces such as population pressure, technological change and government policy that are pressing change upon agrarian communities in Asia today, and postulates a basic hypothesis on the future directions of agrarian change.

Part II (Chapters 4, 5 and 6) intends to test the hypothesis by analyzing the process of institutional changes in Philippine village communities. Chapter 4 gives a historical perspective on the evolution of land-tenure and labor-contract institutions in the central plain of Luzon, commonly refered to as the rice bowl of the Philippines. Chapters 5 and 6 report intensive investigations into two villages where highly contrasting social changes are underway. The first village represents a case of "stratification" of a relatively homogeneous peasant community into peasant sub-classes such as leasehold tenants and sub-tenants who make a sharecropping contract with the leaseholders. The second represents a case of "polarization" of a peasant community into large-scale farmers and landless laborers.

Part III (Chapters 7, 8 and 9) reports the results of Indonesian case studies. Chapter 7 identifies broad trends in the transformation of village-community institutions in Java as reflected in recent changes in rice harvesting systems. Chapters 8 and 9 attempt to supplement the broad analysis in Chapter 7 by intensive studies of two villages in West Java. The first village is characterized by stagnation in technology, whereas the second is characterized by dramatic technological progress. By comparing the two villages we try to identify the effect of technological change on agrarian structure and community institutions.

Part IV (Chapter 10) summarizes the major findings of the village studies in previous chapters and gives a perspective on the future course of agrarian change in Asia.

Part I

Village Economy and Village Institutions

Food production is increasing, but more mouths are being added.

Chapter 2

An Economic Approach to Village Community and Institutions[1]

As the first step in exploring the pattern and the source of agrarian change in Asia, we will attempt to elaborate our economic approach to the village-community organization and institutions that govern the use of resources for production and exchange in the rural sector.

Economic Organization of the Village Community

"Village" is a basic unit of rural life in Asia—it refers here to a "natural village" or hamlet where people live by family in a cluster of houses with a high degree of social and economic interdependence; it does not necessarily coincide with the local administrative unit of the modern state, though often it will. Village communities in the developing economies of Asia are, to a large extent, self-contained and subsistence-oriented, though the market linkage with the urban sector varies widely among the villages.[2] The village usually consists of peasant households in which production, consumption and investment activities are the result of a simultaneous family decision. Unlike the urban market economy in which a functional division prevails between the *firm* and the *household* in production and consumption, a peasant's production is inseparably tied to his family's consumption; his production activities are geared more to maximizing the family's total welfare than to maximizing farm profit, as suggested in the classical study of Chayanov (1966).

[1] An earlier version of this chapter is Hayami (1980).
[2] For an economic taxonomy of village communities, see Ishikawa (1975).

11

The village community governs these peasants' economic activities by coordinating the use of scarce resources through customary rules and institutions. In this section we will try to outline the organizational and institutional characteristics of the village community and identify underlying economic forces.

Village Modes of Production and Exchange

In most Asian villages, although kinship relations are important, the community tie is mainly based on the fact that villagers live together in the same location and have to cooperate for their security and survival in many ways. The need for collective action stems to a large extent from pervasive production externalities. By nature, agricultural production activities are strongly interdependent due to the ecological interdependence of biological processes. Overgrazing in a mountain pasture may increase the incidence of flooding in nearby crop fields. Diversion of irrigation water in the upstream of a river may result in a water shortage for downstream farms. Inadequate rodent management in one warehouse may trigger a village-wide outburst of rodent calamities.

An individual peasant is too small a unit of production to internalize much of such production externalities. It is imperative for the village community to organize collective action for the supply of "public goods". These public goods are both physical and institutional; the village mobilizes communal labor to construct and maintain social-overhead capital such as road and irrigation systems; it also stipulates and enforces rules and regulations to coordinate and reduce conflicts over the use of resources among villagers.

Another major factor that necessitates cooperation among peasants is strong seasonality in the demand for labor in agricultural production. At peak times a large amount of labor in excess of the family labor capacity is often required to do timely operations. The large demands for labor may also arise suddenly in an unpredictable manner owing to uncertainty in the variations of weather and other ecological conditions. Collective actions are called for to combat against production uncertainty. Mutual-help relations such as labor exchange (and exchange of other factors such as draft animals) are thus developed. When labor is hired instead of being exchanged, employment contracts in the village are usually different from impersonal market relations in the urban economy. Hiring a laborer, even if it is a casual employment by itself, tends to be part of a complex personal relationship involving a variety of exchanges. Such relationships enable employers to depend on a supply of labor from local workers for unpredictable demand peaks.[3]

It is common to observe that villagers are stratified into a spectrum of peasant sub-classes ranging from landless laborers to non-cultivating landlords according to their varying claims to land property. However, in contrast with urban industries in which laborers are alienated from the output of their labor as well as the means of production, in the peasant community even the landless have some claim to the use of land and to a share of output—typically through an arrangement such as sharecropping.

As is typical in a crop-sharing tenancy, a strong tendency exists in the village community for various transactions to be interlinked in a highly personalized relationship. A landlord does not simply receive a share rent for his contribution of land to the production process, but also bears a part of the production cost (such as that of seeds and fertilizers) and advances credits for production and consumption purposes.[4] Moreover, he often patronizes his tenant in such ways as giving gifts at the birth of a child or the death of a father and using his connections and influence to solve the tenant's problems with other villagers or outsiders. The tenant reciprocates with the loyal service of himself and his family, including voluntary domestic help at the festive occasions of his landlord.

Such a relationship is commonly called by anthropologists and sociologists a patron-client relationship—"a special case of dyadic (two-person) ties involving a largely instrumental friendship in which an individual of higher socio-economic status (patron) uses his own influence and resources to provide protection and/or benefits for a person of lower status (client) who, for his part, reciprocates by offering general support and assistance, including personal services, to the patron" (Scott, 1972, p. 8). In the patron-client relationship, exchanges are multi-stranded and the balance is cleared in the long run.

Such a mode of exchange represents a sharp contrast to that of the urban economy, where each transaction is cleared independently among anonymous agents in the market ("market" is here defined rather narrowly to refer to the concept conventionally used in the

[3] This is consistent with Bardhan's statistical finding for India that the incidence of labor-tying arrangements by use of credit and other means is smaller in areas with high unemployment rates (Bardhan, 1979a). He reasons that in slack labor markets with high unemployment rates, the employer does not bother to have labor-tying arrangements because he is sure of securing a sufficient supply of labor for peak operations.

[4] For an excellent review of issues involved in the interlinked factor markets in rural communities, see Bardhan (1980).

neoclassical economics texts—for example, Walrasian auction markets). The village mode of exchange may, to a large extent, be explained by the underdevelopment of a market in the small isolated community in which gains from the division of labor based on the market are severely limited. The potential market size is too small for specialized agents to engage profitably in the marketing of various goods and services separately. The patron-client relationship may be considered a substitute for a set of specialized markets for labor, land, credit, insurance, and so on: multiple transactions between the same parties permit the saving of transaction costs because much of the cost of information collection and contract enforcement is common to all the transactions.

In this respect the village mode of exchange is reinforced by the village mode of production. In urban industries characterized by the machine process, work is highly standardized and easy to monitor. The biological process of agricultural production, however, is subject to infinite variations in ecological conditions. Very different treatments for a crop or an animal are often required in response to slight differences in temperature and soil moisture. It matters a great deal whether a laborer performs his work with careful attention and appropriate adjustments in response to variations in plants, animals and ecology; such work quality is extremely difficult to monitor. The scattering of agricultural operations over a wide open space adds to the difficulty of monitoring.

Under such conditions quality of labor (in terms of conscientious attention and adjustments) commands a high value. A market is bound to be inefficient or vanish altogether in the absence or asymmetry of such quality information (Akerlof, 1970; Ben-Porath, 1980; Williamson, 1975). Moreover, so far as an employment relationship is limited to a spot exchange among anonymous agents in the marketplace, it is very difficult to avoid hiring workers who are dishonest or shirkers, not so much in the duration and intensity of physical work but in the work quality. The problem of moral hazard or dishonesty can be equally or more serious in other types of transaction such as credit.

The multi-faceted and enduring relationship of the patron-client type is clearly superior in the collection of quality information, because performances in past transactions comprise a reliable data set for prediction of future performance. More importantly, the chance of being cheated will be reduced, because the expected cost of committing one immoral or dishonest act is very great since its discovery by another party will endanger the whole set of transactions. The linkage between labor and land transactions in such forms as crop-sharing tenancy will enhance the morale of workers and, hence, reduce the monitoring cost because their work efforts will be rewarded by a share of the output.

The preference for the multi-faceted and enduring relationship in the village community is often extended to commodity trades. Because of his meagre resource endowments and low productivity, a peasant cannot produce much beyond his family consumption needs. Because the marketable agricultural surplus is small in volume and variable in quality, it is impractical to introduce modern marketing practices such as grading and brand names, aimed at reducing uncertainty about product quality. In the presence of severe uncertainty, coupled with the scarcity of information on the market outside of the village, regularized and entrusted transactions tied by a personal bond—"clientelization" as Clifford Geertz (1978) calls it—are much preferred to a spot exchange with strangers in the marketplace. In some cases, this preference facilitates the emergence of a trade monopoly by a big middleman who exploits poor peasants. However, the multi-faceted and enduring relationship often characterizes transactions between peasants and petty traders in a competitive environment, too (Anderson, 1969; Dewey, 1962).

The problems of quality uncertainty and moral hazard are not necessarily unique in agricultural production but are equally or more serious in some aspects of industrial production, especially when it involves management and administration. Those problems are considered to underlie the emergence of hierarchical internal organization in the form of the "firm" as a substitute for market transactions (Coase, 1937; Alchian and Demsetz, 1972; Williamson, 1975).[5] However, for the biological process of agricultural production, characterized by production uncertainty and the difficulty of delineating and standardizing production operations, it is usually not efficient to organize large-scale hierarchical units such as firm and *kolkhoz*, as the Russian experience of farm collectivization shows clearly (Schultz, 1964, pp. 122–124).[6] In the

[5] A more basic factor underlying the emergence of large-scale industrial firms is identified by Brewster (1950) as the very nature of industrial production dealing with lifeless and mobile materials, free from the time sequences and location specificities inherent to biological growth processes. Because of this nature, industrial production processes can be performed concurrently in one location, and the greater division of labor, especially the specialization of managerial and supervisory functions in separation from direct labor, becomes profitable. Of course, the extent of such division of labor is limited by the size of the market.

[6] It is relatively easy to standardize production operations in the monoculture system, compared with the more complex systems involving crop rotations and crop-livestock combinations: "In areas more suitable for multiple enterprise farms, family operations have the advantage. Increasing the number of enterprises so multiplies the number of on-the-spot supervisory management decisions per acre that the total acreage which a unit of management can oversee quickly approaches the acreage which an ordinary family can operate. The reverse is true in areas more

village environment the decentralized system of independent peasant producers tied by personalized exchanges (which may well be called a "personalized market" in contrast to the impersonal capitalist market abstracted in both neoclassical and Marxian economics) tends to work more efficiently than the markets and hierarchies of the urban type.

The institutions that govern the village economy characterized by the modes of production and exchange described above are customary rules and moral principles rather than formal laws and contracts. Because production externalities are so pervasive and possible conflicts are so numerous and variable, customs or accumulated precedents tend to be more effective means of settling the conflicts than the stipulations of formal laws. Because villagers' property, in the form of standing crops and grazing animals, is often left physically unprotected in the open fields, morals can be a more effective means of policing. Also, because the contracts implicit in the patron-client relationship are too complex to specify, rules other than general moral principles such as "mutual help and income-sharing among villagers" can hardly be applicable to the enforcement of the multi-faceted contracts.

Social Interactions

Customary rules and moral principles are enforced through social interactions in the village community. Gary Becker defines "social interactions" in terms of the utility function of a person to include other persons' reactions to his action (Becker, 1974; 1976). For example, A's welfare depends not only on his own personal income and consumption but also on how B looks at A's income and consumption levels. If A enjoys B's goodwill or fears his envy, A may transfer a part of his income to B up to a point where A's marginal loss of utility from the income transfer to B equals the marginal gain in A's utility due to the improvement in B's evaluation of A; at this point of equality A's total utility is maximized.

Because of tradition, kinship, locational affinity and the need for cooperation for the sake of minimum security and survival, a high degree of social interaction characterizes the village community. Everyone is watching everyone. Gossip about one's misconduct is circulated by word of mouth faster than any modern communication

---

suitable for single-enterprise farming" (Brewster, 1950). For this reason plantation production is limited to certain monoculture crops. Another important merit of the plantation system is that it standardizes the quality of products in large quantities; this is critically important for commercial production but not important for subsistence production.

means. In such an environment it usually entails a significant cost to violate time-honored village rules. Even if one expects large material gains from violating the rules, he may not dare to do so because of the risk of social opprobrium and perhaps ostracism.

Intricate mutual-help and patron-client relationships in village communities, as often described in sociological and anthropological literature, can be reinterpreted in terms of the theory of social interactions as resulting from the trade-off between A's own consumption of his income and the income transfer in order to buy B's goodwill. Not to behave as a good neighbor or a benevolent patron entails costs, especially when such conduct is considered inconsistent with the basic moral principles of the village.

Indeed, clear expectations of the mutual observance of reciprocal rights and duties developed from close social interactions are the basic condition for mutual-help and patron-client relationships. In the absence of such expectations, no agreement may be reached by tacit bargaining, and anarchy may prevail as the result of opportunism based on mutual distrust—a "prisoners' dilemma" or noncooperative game (Nash, 1950).

Moral Economy Approach

In terms of the emphasis on traditional moral principles and social interactions in the village community, our approach may appear to follow the "moral economy approach" of sociologists and political scientists.[7]

Moral economists hold the view that social relations in precapitalist peasant communities are geared to secure minimum subsistence for all the community members. Normally, peasants eke out their living at a near-subsistence level. They are exposed to the constant danger that their income may decline below the subsistence minimum due to external variations such as weather or internal incidents such as the sickness of family members. The compelling demand of the peasants to avoid subsistence crises is said to have resulted in a "subsistence ethic" by which the social arrangements designed to insure against such crises are considered fair and legitimate.[8]

Common features of village communities such as labor exchange, the use of communal property for the livelihood of the orphaned or the widowed, the gifts given by a patron at the birth of a child or the death

---

[7] See, among others, Migdal (1974), Scott (1972; 1976) and Wolf (1969).
[8] For a similar perspective on the laws of primitive societies, see Posner (1980).

of a father, and rent reductions in a year of crop failure are institutionalized patterns developed under this ethic. The basic principle "claims that all should have a place, a living, not that all should be equal" (Scott, 1976, p. 40). To the extent that a landlord protects the poor members in the community (tenants) against ruin in bad years, he is considered a legitimate patron.

Thus, moral economists assume a pervasive tendency in village communities to set informal social controls on the better-off members to redistribute wealth or to impose specific obligations to provide for the minimum needs of the poor. Such controls are supposed to operate through social interactions:

> The prosaic, even banal, character of these social controls belies their importance. Well-to-do villagers avoid malicious gossip only at the price of an exaggerated generosity. They are expected to sponsor more conspicuously lavish celebrations at weddings, to show greater charity to kin and neighbors, to sponsor local religious activity, and to take on more dependents and employees than the average household. The generosity enjoined on the rich is not without its compensations. It redounds to their growing prestige and serves to surround them with a grateful clientele which helps validate their position in the community. In addition, it represents a set of social debts which can be converted into goods and services if need be (Scott, 1976, pp. 41–42).

Moral economists presuppose that the cohesive community organization based on social interactions and moral principles tends to break down as the market economy or the capitalist system penetrates into the subsistence-oriented peasant economy. With the intrusion of the market economy, the moral principle of securing minimum subsistence for community members is replaced by the hard economic consideration of maximizing profit. The well-to-do members tend to rely more on external legal means to protect their property. They become more concerned about increasing their incomes in order to purchase modern goods from outside than about buying good will among their fellow villagers. The mutual-help and patron-client relationships are weakened and the poorer members are exposed to the risk of subsistence crises. Some of the small landholders are compelled to sell their land and become landless workers selling their labor in the labor market; others accumulate land to become market-oriented farmers—the process of polarization envisioned by Marx and Lenin or the process of "great transformation" more recently marshalled by Karl Polanyi (1957). The peasants stripped of the protection of traditional village institutions and patron-client bonds and faced with a subsistence crisis feel ill-treated and will eventually rise in revolt. Thus, moral economists view peasant uprisings as the desperate efforts of peasants to restore their traditional rights destroyed by capitalism (Migdal, 1974; Scott, 1976; Wolf, 1969).

The perspective of moral economists has recently been challenged by Samuel Popkin (1979). He denies the view that the pre-capitalist peasant community is moral-oriented to protect the poor. He insists that traditional village institutions and patron-client relationships have neither been motivated nor been effective to guarantee the subsistence needs of community members. It is his essential contention that even in the traditional peasant community people are predominantly motivated to seek personal gain rather than group interests; peasants rely on their families or groups smaller than the village community for their subsistence guarantees since the village-scale scheme to insure against risk is bound to be ineffective because everyone tries to claim profit from the group action without sharing the cost—the free-rider problem raised by Mancur Olson (1965); elites exploit village institutions such as community property to their own profit rather than to protect the poor and as a result village procedures reinforce, rather than level, differences in income and wealth; and the market system can be more beneficial to a majority of peasants to the extent that it emancipates them from the control of the elites and enables them to engage in transactions based on their own economic calculations.

We share Popkin's perspective that peasants in pre-capitalist society are as egoistic as any hard-calculating capitalists in seeking personal gains; that elites try to exploit village procedures to their own profit rather than to help the poor; and that market institutions can sometimes be more beneficial to a majority of peasants than non-market institutions. However, the fact that the peasants are egoists does not seem to conflict with their apparently altruistic behavior, as Becker's model predicts (Becker, 1976).

In a village community characterized by a high degree of social interaction, an elite would likely try to simulate the behavior of a benevolent patron in terms of traditional norms if he is a wise egoist. Being considered a legitimate patron by fellow villagers can be critical in avoiding malicious gossip, protecting prestige and property, and maintaining village procedures in order to maximize long-run profit. To the extent that production externalities are pervasive and that the market is characterized by high information and transaction costs, the advantage of non-market institutions is greater. A farmer may prefer to employ neighbors under the mutual-help or the patron-client relation systems rather than to employ workers in the labor market even if the nominal wage rates are the same or higher, because the cost of supervision or the cost of preventing shirking or stealing of crops may be lower for the former. Thus, conforming to village norms and institutions can be an efficient way to economize on the cost of policing and enforcement.

We do not consider that social interactions in the village are always sufficient to compel villagers to conform to traditional norms and institutions. According to Becker, a person is altruistic to the extent that the return to his altruism exceeds the cost of behaving as an altruist. The theory implies that villagers will violate the village institutions if they see opportunities where the gain from the violation exceeds the cost. Changes in production relations resulting from changes in technology, resource endowments and market structure may produce such opportunities. Whether the village institutions will be maintained depends on the balance between changes in the production relations and the solidarity of the village community.

Social Structure

From the theory of social interaction it can be predicted that village institutions are more easily enforced if the community is more cohesive and more tightly structured. In a tightly structured social system people are expected to conform closely to social norms such as reciprocal rights and duties defined clearly by tradition, whereas in a loosely structured social system the behavior is individualistic and it is easy for an individual to get away with doing something not approved by other group members.

It was John Embree, an American anthropologist, who first characterized Thailand as a loosely structured society, in contrast to his observations of a village in Japan:

> The local group in Japan, the hamlet, has a clearcut social unity with special ceremonies for entry and exit and a whole series of rights and obligations for its members. Each man must sooner or later assume the responsibility of being the representative of the local group, each must assist on occasions of hamlet cooperation such as road building or funeral preparations. In Thailand the hamlet also has its own identity and the members also have rights and duties, but they are less clearly defined and less strictly enforced. Exchange systems are less clear cut. Thus in Thailand, with its mobility of population and lack of emphasis on long term obligations, we do not find the financial

credit associations (*ko*) which extend over twenty years or so in a Japanese farm community. But they are found in China and Vietnam, areas in which we find societies similar to Japan in the sense here used (Embree, 1950, p. 185).

Embree's perspective on the basic difference in the social structure between Japanese and Thai communities has been shared by both Japanese and Thai scholars, although his original concept and terminology have been subjected to criticism.[9] Further, several comparative studies of rice villages in Japan and Southeast Asia have discovered that the villages in Southeast Asian countries such as Malaysia and the Philippines are, in general, less tightly structured than in Japan (Bauzon, 1979; Kuchiba, 1979; Kuchiba, Tsubouchi and Maeda, 1979). Of course, the degree of cohesion or tightness differs among countries. Even within Southeast Asia there are some areas that are characterized by relatively tight social structures, such as Bali in Indonesia and Ilocos in the Philippines.

A major question is what factors underlie the differences in community structures among countries and among areas. Clearly the problem defies easy generalization as it involves ecological, historical and sociological aspects. However, we will try to develop here an economic perspective.

We hypothesize that the basic force underlying the tightness in community structure is relative resource scarcity—the scarcity of non-labor resources relative to labor. So far as a resource is abundant, there is no need to coordinate its use among community members. The need arises only when the resource becomes scarce and people begin to compete for or cooperate in its use. Efficient coordination requires rules defining rights and obligations among people on the use of the resource as well as rules to settle possible conflicts. As scarcity increases and the competition is intensified, it becomes necessary to define the rules more clearly and to enforce them more rigorously.

One possible answer to the relative resource scarcity is to develop a market so that it can handle the problem of scarce resource allocations through the price mechanism; this solution is possible if property rights can be clearly specified on all resources and if transactions are costless (Coase, 1960). However, the market can solve only a part of the problem in the economy characterized by pervasive interdependence in production activities and high information costs. In order to correct market

---

[9] For examples, see Mizuno (1978) and Yamklinfung (1979). Embree's perspective has been a subject of extensive discussion among specialists on Thai society. See Evers (1969).

failures, non-market institutions should be developed to regulate villagers' behavior directly. For example, the grazing of cattle and goats in stubble and fallow should be limited to certain periods in order to avoid crop damage in neighboring fields. To economize on the use of irrigation water, water take-out along a stream should be regulated among farmers according to a time schedule.

In order to enforce such rules and regulations, reciprocal rights and duties among villagers should be clearly defined so that they can develop clear expectations of social opprobrium and perhaps ostracism against free riders or violators of the community institutions.

We hypothesize that the social structure becomes tighter and more cohesive in response to a greater need to coordinate and control the use of resources as they become increasingly more scarce—the basic perspective shared by Vernon Ruttan (1978 a and b).

Compared with Japan, Southeast Asia (with the major exception of Java) was characterized by an abundant supply of land, at least until the middle of the nineteenth century. Typically, in Thailand before the mid-nineteenth century, land had been so abundant that property rights in land had not been established (Feeny, 1977). It is natural to expect that the farming communities molded under such land-surplus conditions would be loosely structured, compared with Japanese villages that have been molded under strong population pressure for a long time (Barker, 1978).

Environmental conditions are also considered a critical variable in the formation of village structure to the extent that environment determines which resources are scarce. For example, water is a critical resource limiting rice production throughout the world. However, unless the environmental conditions are such that water can be controlled or reallocated by human effort for more efficient uses, the water cannot be considered a scarce economic resource. In the major part of Thailand's Central Plain, rice farming depends on the annual flooding of the Chao Phraya River, which is, by all means, beyond the control of peasants either individually or in local cooperative groups; the flooding water is not a scarce economic resource for which the peasants compete or cooperate among themselves. Water control of a major river delta can only be handled by a centralized unit much larger than villages.

In contrast, rice farming in Japan initially developed in fan-shaped terraces in the valley bottoms and intermountain basins. Such topography renders local cooperation effective in controlling a water supply based on small streams. The need for collective action to construct and maintain irrigation systems and to settle conflicts over the use of water at a local community level can be identified as a major force in the development of the tightly structured social system in Japanese villages (Takaya, 1977).[10] From this perspective, it is no surprise to find tightly structured villages with efficient irrigation organizations in the Ilocos region of the Philippines, characterized by mountainous topography and high population density (Lewis, 1971).

According to Yoshikazu Takaya, another ecological factor uniquely scarce in Japan is temperature adequate for rice growing (Takaya, 1975). In Southeast Asia rice can be grown almost any time throughout the year if water is available. In Japan rice culture is limited to the summer months. Therefore, Japanese farmers have been compelled to schedule production operations much more tightly. The tight schedule requires greater coordination on the timing and the sequence in the use of labor, water and other resources; the need would have added to the solidarity of village communities in Japan. This climatic difference might explain to some extent the difference in village community structure between Japan and Java despite the similarity in both high population density and mountainous topography, although sociological and political factors could well be more dominant.[11]

While we recognize the danger of sweeping generalization, it appears reasonable to identify relative resource scarcity as the basic factor in explaining the broad differences in social structure among villages in various parts of Asia. However, a perspective based on cross-sectional comparison should not blind us to the importance of the time required for social change. The cohesion and solidarity of the village community are based on the norms and moral principles sanctioned by tradition and ingrained in the minds of the villagers. They do change in response to change in the relative scarcity of resources, but the change takes a very long time, often several generations.

[10] The underlying mechanism might be as Olson describes: ". . . 'social selectives' that would enforce the provision of the local public good of irrigation works, etc. [These] would be selected by Darwinian selection: the villages without mechanisms to provide for irrigation would be unviable and some more cooperative group would take over. A village is, moreover, a 'privileged' or 'intermediate' group in the terminology of *The Logic of Collective Action*. That is, it is small enough so *some* collective action can sometimes be attained voluntarily. This smallness, I hypothesize, allows the creation of leaders and enforcement arrangements and bargaining mechanisms, which are themselves collective goods which complement social selective incentives in helping the village get the collective good of irrigation" (Olson, personal communication, November 19, 1980).

[11] Geertz (1959) traces the loose social structure in Javanese villages to the Culture System imposed by Dutch colonial rule. Kuchiba (1975) tries to explain the loose structure in Southeast Asia in general in terms of the bilateral family system (in comparison with the patrilineal system in Japan).

Towards a Theory of Institutional Change

In the previous section we identified the major role of institutions in coordinating the use of resources among people. We have developed a hypothesis that in the village community the institutions are enforced primarily through social compulsion based on close social interactions and that the cost of enforcement tends to be lower in villages with a more tightly structured social system. Further, it has been postulated that the institutions and the social system itself change in response to changes in relative resource scarcities. Relative resource scarcity in a community depends not only on the endowment of resources but also on technology and market conditions. In this section we will try to develop our basic analytical framework by elaborating the theory of institutional change.

The Process of Institutional Change

Institutions are broadly defined here as rules sanctioned by the members of the community. Such rules facilitate coordination and cooperation among people in the use of resources by helping them form expectations which each person can reasonably hold in his dealings with others. To create, maintain and modify the institutions requires collective action that entails negotiation and enforcement costs. Action for institutional change will not be organized unless the gain from the change exceeds the cost.

To perform the essential role of forming reasonable expectations in dealings among people, institutions must be stable for an extended time period. Meanwhile, resource endowments, technology and market demand change. The institutions that were efficient when created may become less efficient in facilitating resource allocation. Growing disequilibria will create profit opportunities that are sufficiently high to motivate political entrepreneurs or leaders to organize collective actions for institutional change.

Such a perspective on institutional change was forcibly marshalled in a classical statement of Marx:

> The mode of production in material life determines the general character of the social, political and spiritual processes of life. . . . At a certain stage of their development, the material forces of production in society come into conflict with the existing relations of production, or—what is but a legal expression for the same thing—with the property relations within which they had been at work before. From

forms of development of the forces of production these relations turn into their fetters. Then comes the period of social revolution. With the change of the economic foundation the entire immense superstructure is more or less rapidly transformed (Marx, 1913, pp. 11–12).

Basically we share Marx's view. However, we do not consider that institutional change is necessarily the abrupt and complete transformation of the entire institutional framework he describes. The institutional framework and property relations may change through cumulative adjustments.

Such a perspective was developed by Lance Davis and Douglass North (1970).[12] They classified institutions into two sub-categories: the basic "institutional environment" and the secondary "institutional arrangements". The former consists of a basic set of decision rules and property rights, which may be specified in formal laws or customary principles sanctified by tradition. The latter are specific forms of agreements that govern the ways in which economic units can compete or cooperate in the use of resources.

In the village community, for example, specific forms of contract to employ labor for harvesting are considered the secondary institutional arrangements, whereas traditional principles such as mutual help and income sharing among villagers comprise the basic institutional environment. Obviously, the secondary institutional arrangements are much easier to change. Davis and North argue that it is through a process of cumulative adjustments in the institutional arrangements that a change in the basic institutional environment will come about.

It is critical to understand the nature of the basic institutional environment in order to understand how a specific form of institutional arrangement emerged. The traditionally sanctified principle in a community makes a certain arrangement less costly to establish than others. As the analysis in Chapter 5 will show, in the Philippines the traditional *hunusan* contract in which all villagers can participate in harvesting and receive the one-sixth share of output has recently been replaced by the *gama* contract that gives an exclusive right of harvesting for the same share of output to the laborers who do weeding without receiving wages. The *gama* contract represents a device of employer farmers to reduce the harvesters' share corresponding to a decline in the marginal productivity of labor due to population pressure on limited land. Despite the fact that the same objective could have been achieved by other means, such

---

[12] Also see North and Thomas (1971; 1973).

as reducing the share to the harvesters or employing workers at the market wage rate, the *gama* arrangement has actually been adopted. The reason is the lower cost involved in negotiation and enforcement of the *gama* contract because it is congruent with the traditional *hunusan* system and appears legitimate to villagers in terms of traditional moral principles of mutual help and income-sharing in the village community.

We share with Davis and North the perspective that a change in the basic institutional framework will result from a cumulative process of relatively minor adjustments, while the forms of adjustment in secondary institutional arrangements are heavily influenced by the basic institutional environment. Of course, we do not rule out the possibility that in some societies the adjustments are not quite so flexible and smooth as to achieve a change in the basic institutional framework without major disruptions or revolution.

Property Rights

Property rights specify someone's rights to use resources in relation with others. They are thus "defined not as relations between men and things but, rather, as the behavioral relations among men that arise from the existence of things and pertain to their use"; therefore, the system of property-right assignments in a community represents "the set of economic and social relations defining the position of interacting individuals with respect to the utilization of scarce resources" (Pejovich, 1972).

Modern economic theorists on property rights, such as Armen Alchian and Harold Demsetz, consider the primary function of property rights to be that of guiding incentives to achieve a greater internalization of externalities.[13] If no property right is assigned, any action involving social interdependencies is a potential externality. For example, if no property right is assigned to apples, anyone can eat them without paying the price, and no one will be willing to bear the cost of growing apples. Resources can be allocated to apple production efficiently only when property rights are so assigned as to enable the growers to exclude from eating the apples those who do not pay a price equal to the marginal cost of production.

The form of property rights on a certain resource depends, to a large extent, on the cost required for the holder of the rights to exclude others from its use. It is relatively easy for a farmer to demarcate a parcel of

[13] Demsetz (1967) and Alchian and Demsetz (1973). For an excellent review of the property-rights literature, see Furubotn and Pejovich (1972).

crop land and exclude it from others' use. To use a parcel of grazing land exclusively is more difficult and costly, because one needs to build a fence to exclude others' animals from grazing in one's parcel. As a result, private ownership is commonly established for crop land, whereas communal ownership is more common for grazing land.

Thus, the form of ownership may be induced to change by an advance in the technology of exclusion. For example, the private ownership and leasing of public grazing land in the Great Plains of the United States was developed with the innovation of low-cost barbed-wire fencing (Anderson and Hill, 1975).

Likewise, an increase in the profits from an investment in achieving exclusion may induce changes in property rights. In eighteenth-century England, common pasture and open fields under communal regulation were enclosed into exclusive private units. The enclosure presented a chance to introduce a more intensive system of crop rotation in response to population growth and high food prices (Chambers and Mingay, 1966; Timmer, 1969). It is estimated that the high cost of the fencing required for enclosure yielded a high rate of return on the order of 17 percent per year (McCloskey, 1975).

In many cases, changes in property-rights relations emerge through a long cumulative process. In Japan, at the beginning of the Tokugawa period (1603–1867), peasants' rights to crop land had been limited to the right to till the soil with the obligation to pay a feudal land tax in kind.[14] As the population grew, as commercialization progressed, and as irrigation and technology were developed to make intensive farming more profitable, some peasants divided their holdings into smaller units and leased them out to ex-servants or extended family members. Some accumulated land through mortgaging arrangements and made other peasants in debt *de facto* tenants. Through the accumulation of illegal leasing and mortgaging practices, peasants' property rights on land had come close to the title in fee simple system by the end of the Tokugawa period, which was readily converted to the modern private-property system in the succeeding Meiji period.

In general, as a resource becomes relatively more scarce, the property rights to this resource become more exclusive and more clearly defined. The change often takes the form of a shift from communal to private ownership in order to minimize losses due to externalities such as over-hunting and over-grazing. However, in the case of resources characterized by a high cost of policing and scale economies, the response to

---

[14] Literature on agrarian history in the Tokugawa period is prolific, including the classic studies by Furushima (1941; 1943; 1947/49). For an excellent exposition in English, see Smith (1959).

increasing scarcity may be the tightening of control on communal properties.[15]

In Japan, although the system of private property rights was developed on crop land during the premodern period, communal ownership at the village level continued in large areas of wild and forest land which were utilized for the collection of firewood, leaves and wild grasses to fertilize rice fields. However, over time more detailed rules were stipulated on the use of communal land in order to prevent resource exhaustion. Detailed stipulations on time and place of utilization of communal land as well as rules for mobilizing village labor to maintain communal properties (such as applying fire to regenerate good grasses) were often enforced with religious taboos and rituals.

Water for irrigation is a resource characterized by scale economies and critically dependent on the community's group actions. Towards the middle of the Tokugawa period, as population grew and paddy fields were expanded, the scarcity of water became critical and water disputes increased. The response was the development of detailed rules on the allocation of water among villagers as well as among villages.[16] It appears that the solidarity and cohesiveness of Japanese villages were intensified through this process.

Changes in property rights are not purely endogenous but can be heavily influenced by external factors. For example, in Thailand the increasing scarcity of land relative to labor due to population growth and the increase in foreign demand for rice resulted in a major shift from traditional property rights in humans (corvée and slavery) to property rights in land (land ownership) in the latter half of the nineteenth century (Feeny, 1977). Besides those economic forces, two critical factors underlying the change were the introduction of the western concept of land-ownership title and a new social technology in the form of the Torrens system of land titling.

Central Luzon of the Philippines was opened up for rice production in the middle of the nineteenth century. Before then, land had been abundant and there had been no need to establish property rights on land. Yet land title had been established on this wild land through the land grants of the Spanish Crown. This "premature" establishment of land ownership explains the pervasive landlordism in the form of rice haciendas in this area (see Chapter 4).

[15] According to Hoffmann (1975), in medieval Europe traditional "individualistic" subsistence agriculture with few communal regulations antedated the common-field system, which was characterized by tight communal regulations on field operations and crop rotations. The shift was induced by the growing scarcity of grazing land due to population pressure on land.

[16] See Furushima's works and Kitamura (1950/73).

Thus, the influence of exogenous factors, through unique historical circumstances such as colonialism, as well as endogenous economic forces, have created unique agrarian structures in various parts of Asia.

Contractual Choice

Contracts stipulate the terms and conditions by which rights to use resources are exchanged. Contracts are agreements between the parties concerned. However, to the extent that certain forms of contract are sanctioned by society and are enforced by laws or customary rules, they become part of institutions. Relative to property rights, contracts are the secondary institutional arrangements, and contractual adjustments are often used to modify property-rights relations, as illustrated by the evolution of peasants' land rights in Tokugawa Japan.

In this section we will concentrate our discussion on the choice of contracts pertaining to two major factors in the village economy, land and labor. The seminal studies on share tenancy by Steven Cheung (1968; 1969a; 1969b) have established that there exists a number of contractual arrangements to achieve a social optimum in the allocation of resources under perfect market conditions with perfect information and zero transaction cost. We will begin with the abstract case of the perfect market.

A landlord can earn income from his land in one of three basic ways: (a) cultivating the land under his management by employing labor at fixed market wage rates, (b) letting someone cultivate the land and share the output, or (c) leasing out the land for a fixed amount of rent. In terms of land-tenure arrangements, the first is called "owner farming", the second "sharecropping tenancy", and the third "leasehold tenancy". If we look at them as forms of labor-employment contracts, the first may be called a "time-rate contract", the second an "output-sharing contract" or "piece-rate contract", and the third an "agency contract".

The time-rate contract is pervasive in the urban market economy, especially for factory and office workers in big corporations. The agency contract is also common. Lease of capital items such as office and shopping spaces usually takes this contractual form. The piece-rate or output-sharing contract is common in village economies, but it is also found in the urban economy, in such cases as that of travelling salesmen paid on a commission basis.

Share tenancy can be considered a special case of the output-sharing contract for labor employment. In the traditional literature on land tenure systems, it was common to blame sharecropping tenancy for its inability to achieve a socially optimum allocation of resources (Heady,

1947; Schickele, 1941). In Figure 2–1, curve DK represents a marginal product (mp $= \partial q/\partial l$) of labor applied to a given land area. If the market wage rate is given as OW, both the owner-farmer and the leasehold tenant will apply labor by OL_2 at which mp and the wage rate (measured in output) are equated and the operator's residual or profit is maximized. However, for the share tenant the marginal return to labor is lower than mp by the rate of land rent (r) that he pays to the landlord; therefore his marginal return schedule is represented by EK. The share tenant will apply his labor only up to OL_1 where $(1 - r)$mp equals the wage rate.

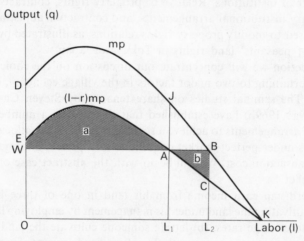

Fig. 2-1.   Model of contractual choice.

The traditional theory on the inefficiency of sharecropping has been questioned because empirical data have failed to find the significant differences in yields per hectare among tenure types predicted by the theory (Berry and Cline, 1979; Chakravarty and Rudra, 1973; Johnson, 1950; Mangahas et al., 1974; Rao, 1975; Ruttan, 1966).[17] Gale Johnson, who first cast doubt on the empirical relevance of the traditional theory, suggested that the share tenants might be induced to apply their inputs to an optimum level if the landlord monitors outputs and refuses to renew the tenure contracts of unsatisfactory tenants. A formal proof has been developed by Cheung (1968; 1969b, pp. 16–29) that under perfect market conditions with no risk and zero transaction cost, share tenancy is no less efficient than owner farming and leasehold tenancy.[18]

[17] An exceptional case supporting the traditional theory of the inefficiency of sharecropping is presented by Bell (1977) with data from Bihar, India.

[18] To look at it alternatively, with perfect information and zero transaction costs,

Cheung's arguments as reformulated by James Hsiao (1975) may be summarized in terms of Figure 2-1. If information is perfect and transaction cost is zero, the landlord will stipulate in the contract that the share tenant should apply labor up to OL_2. Such stipulation will be accepted by the tenant through bargaining if *area b*, the reduction of the tenant's income by increasing labor from OL_1 to OL_2, is smaller than *area a*, because his total income as a share tenant (*area $OECL_2$*) is still larger than the income from his alternative employment as a wage laborer (*area $OWBL_2$*). Further, if the market is perfect, the landlord will be able to bid up his share rate (r) to a level where *a* equals *b*, *i.e.*, where the sharecropper's income is equal to his potential earnings as a wage laborer.[19]

Likewise, if the market is perfect, the landlord would be able to bid up the fixed rent to a level equal to his potential income as an owner-farmer. Thus, in a perfect market with zero transaction cost, the resource allocation and the income distribution will be exactly the same among the three types of contract; the return to labor is invariably equivalent to *area $OWBL_2$* and the return to land is equivalent to *area WDB*. Both the landlord and the tenant should be indifferent as to the choice of contract in a perfect market.[20] In the real world the choice depends on the relative magnitudes of risk and the transaction cost, especially the cost of enforcing contracts.[21] From the side of the landlord,

---

the equilibrium choice of contracts to be reached from bargaining among a sufficient number of contracting parties is equivalent to the Walrasian equilibrium with universal competitive markets. In that sense, contracts are perfect substitutes for Walrasian markets (Roumasset, 1979).

[19] Cheung considers the land area held by a tenant another variable which the landlord can manipulate to maximize his rent income. His model is based on the assumption that one tenant has a constant labor endowment, implying no option for him to employ others' labor or to hire out a part of his family labor outside his farm (Cheung, 1969, pp. 16–17). This assumption is in contradiction with Cheung's assumption of the perfect labor market. If this assumption is dropped, the optimum size of the tenant's farm, for which the landlord maximizes his rent income, cannot be determined so far as the production function is linear-homogeneous.

[20] Cheung's model is incapable of dealing with the problem of the extent of tenancy incidence or how much of his land an owner cultivates by himself and how much he rents to tenants. To analyze the problem, different production and utility functions must be assumed between lessor and lessee as assumed by Bardhan (1977a; 1977b; 1979a) and Bardhan and Srinivasan (1971). However, Bardhan and Srinivasan maintain the assumption of the traditional "tax-equivalent" approach to the equality between the wage rate and $(1-r)$ mp instead of mp.

[21] Cheung (1969a; 1969b, pp. 62–87) considered that risk is the major factor underlying the incidence of sharecroppign. David Newbery (1975; 1977) and Joseph Stiglitz (1974) argued that risk cannot be the factor to explain the choice of share-cropping contract by both landlord and tenant, because the same degree of risk as for sharecropping can be achieved by an appropriate combination of fixed-rent land-lease and fixed-wage labor contracts. However, the very fact that the tenant's

the risk is the lowest for the leasehold contract with fixed rent and the highest for doing one's own farming with fixed-wage labor. The transaction cost would also be highest for the use of laborers at the fixed-wage rate because of the difficulty of preventing them from shirking.[22] The cost of enforcing a leasehold contract or of collecting fixed rent should be lower than that of enforcing a share contract especially, because the latter involves the difficulty of ascertaining how much labor is applied and how much output is produced. Thus, the preference ordering of the three contractual arrangements for landlords in terms of risk and transaction cost would be as shown in Table 2-1.

Table 2-1.   Preference ordering among alternative contracts.

Landlord side:	
Risk	$L > S > O$
Transaction cost	$L > S > O$
Tenant side:	
Risk	$L < S \gtrsim O$
Entrepreneurial opportunity	$L > S > O$

L: Leasehold tenancy with fixed rent
S: Share tenancy
O: Owner farming with fixed-rate wage labor

For the tenant, the preference ordering in terms of risk would be exactly the opposite of that for the landlord if there were no uncertainty in the labor market. However, as explained in detail in the previous section, labor demand for agricultural production is highly uncertain due to the vagaries of weather and other ecological conditions. It would be just as difficult to predict the availability of employment opportunities and the level of wage rates for next season as to predict the yield of next season's crop (Newbery, 1975; 1977). Few villagers have ready access to the stable urban labor market. Thus for them the uncertainty of future earnings from wage-labor employment would be equal to or even greater than the uncertainty of earnings from sharecropping.

---

entrepreneurial and managerial ability is indivisible would make it inefficient to allocate his time among wage employment and leasehold farming on a smaller scale, compared with a situation in which the tenant devotes his full time and effort to a larger farm operation. The inefficiency would multiply if the tenant owned other indivisible resources such as family labor and draft animals for which markets are inactive. The mixing of wage-labor and land-lease contracts does not seem a practical alternative to the cropsharing contract for reducing risk.

[22] Cheung himself considered that the transaction cost is the highest for the sharecropping contract. However, for the reasons that will be discussed below, we consider that the transaction cost required for the sharecropping contract would be rather small in the economy characterized by stagnant technology.

Another criterion for the tenant's contractual choice is the opportunity for the tenant to exploit his entrepreneurial ability, or tenant "ability to deal with disequilibria" in the sense of Theodore Schultz (1975). By this criterion the tenant will prefer leasehold tenancy to share tenancy and share tenancy to fixed-wage employment.

The actual choice of contract will be determined at a saddle point of conflicting preference orderings between landlord and tenant shown in Table 2–1. Let us first consider a near-subsistence economy with traditional agriculture as characterized by Schultz (1964), where productivity is low but resources are allocated at long-run equilibria because there is no dynamic element. In such an economy risk aversion would dominate the tenant's preference because his income is so low that he has to worry about the probability of a subsistence crisis and, also, there is little scope for him to exploit his entrepreneurial ability.[23]

On the other hand, risk should be a relatively minor consideration for the wealthy landlord. Because technology is stable, it is not so difficult to identify the optimum level of a tenant's input and the corresponding output level. Then, it is easy to specify labor input in a sharecropping contract; it is also easy to enforce the contract because the correspondence between input and output is known, and the landlord can easily detect tenant shirking by simply inspecting the share rents delivered over a period long enough to average out weather variations.[24]

Thus, the reduction in transaction cost from a shift from a share to a leasehold contract would not be large. However, the cost increase from the conversion of sharecroppers to wage laborers would likely be substantial. The cost of supervising laborers doing farmwork is usually very high, because most work is not standardized and requires personal judgments on infinite variations in plants, animals, water and soil. It is difficult to expect wage laborers alienated from the product of their labor to perform the tasks adequately.

Thus, it seems reasonable to hypothesize that the pervasive practice

[23] This does not mean that there is no scope at all to exploit the tenant's entrepreneurial ability in traditional agriculture. The fact that both leasehold and share tenancies often coexist in the same village may be explained by different entrepreneurial abilities among village workers. The contractual choice may work as a mechanism for the landlord to screen out unsuitable workers (Hallagan, 1978).

[24] Bardhan (1977a; 1977b; 1979a), Bardhan and Srinivasan (1971) and Bell and Zusman (1976) maintain the traditional assumption of inefficiency in the sharecropping contract on the grounds that the cost of enforcing tenants to apply their labor to a contractually-stipulated level is too high. However, in the traditional agriculture of Schultz's sense the cost does not seem very high, especially where landlords and tenants are tied in a patron-client relationship. In communities where the patron-client bond is weak, crop-sharing tenancy might result in efficiency as assumed by Bardhan-Srinivasan and Bell-Zusman based on their observations in India (see Postscript).

of sharecropping in traditional farming communities represented a saddle point between the tenant's strong risk aversion and the landlord's calculation of transaction cost.[25] The saddle point does change, however, in response to dynamic changes in technology and market. Such changes increase both the transaction cost of the share contract for landlords and the entrepreneurial opportunity for tenants, and induce a shift to leasehold tenancy. This prediction is supported by the study of C. H. Hanumantha Rao (1971). He found that in India the fixed-rent contract is more common for cash crops such as tobacco than for rice despite the fact that the former is more risky than the latter. The reason was identified as the higher entrepreneurial opportunity for tenants and the higher transaction cost for landlords associated with the cash crops.

Technological change may also induce a shift from share tenancy to owner farming or the conversion of sharecroppers to wage laborers. The development of large-scale farm machinery can work as a strong inducement to this change. The large machines reduce the cost of enforcement as it is easier to supervise one tractor driver than a large number of manual laborers. The possible results are clearly drawn in John Steinbeck's novel *The Grapes of Wrath*.[26]

As emphasized in the previous section, one of the major determinants of contractual choice can be identified as social interaction. If the relation between landlord and tenants is that of patron and clients bound by a multi-stranded tie involving exchanges of favors and obligations, it would be rather difficult for a tenant to cheat the landlord in the share-cropping contract. The altruism of a landlord may work effectively to minimize his enforcement cost. In a community characterized by a high degree of social interaction and where "sharing" is considered a social norm, sharecropping might be preserved despite dynamic changes in technology and market.

Collective Action

To create, maintain and modify institutions requires collective action. These collective actions are costly to organize, and the major question becomes who bears the cost. Even if a collective action produces a total

[25] There may be cases in which tenants benefit from landlords' managerial inputs under the share contract as suggested by Reid (1973; 1977). However, the cases in which such benefit is a major factor in the choice of share tenancy do not seem so common in South and Southeast Asia. In traditional agriculture in Schultz's sense the role of managerial ability in enhancing allocative efficiency is bound to be small.

[26] For an interesting analysis of the effect of cotton pickers on sharecroppers, see Day (1967). A theoretical model developed by Lucas (1979) confirms that labor-saving technological progress reduces the incidence of sharecropping.

benefit to society higher than the cost, the gain to each individual may not be large enough to cover the cost. An individual's gain is especially large when he does not participate in the collective action while all others do. A farmer can use irrigation water most abundantly and freely if all others abide by the rule on irrigation rotation and he alone does not—an extreme example of the "free-rider" problem most lucidly elaborated by Mancur Olson (1965).[27] The supply of public goods, including institutions, tends to be less than optimum because of the difficulty of preventing free rides.

As is emphasized repeatedly, a high degree of social interaction in village communities may be effective, to some extent, in preventing free riding. However, to assume a village where no serious free-rider problem exists because of social interactions is as utopian as to assume a precapitalist community where people are unselfish and consider the community good first. The over-grazed communal pasture land and silted irrigation canals commonly observed reflect difficulties in organizing collective actions at a village level.

A serious dilemma arises in that if the gain from a collective action is distributed evenly no one's gain is large enough to induce an initiative to organize the collective action; whereas if the gain is distributed unevenly, a major beneficiary may want to take the initiative but those whose benefits are small or even negative will not cooperate. Randolph Barker aptly describes this dilemma with respect to communal irrigation projects at the village level:

A major problem is that a leader who takes on both the formidable task of organizing his community for public works and convincing the government to contribute will benefit only marginally from the project if he is a small landholder. So only a rare individual dedicated to the community good will offer to organize a community project. On the other hand, if the leader is a large landholder, he will benefit substantially, but other members of the community will see the project as a means of promoting his interests rather than contributing to the common benefit. In this case, it would be extremely difficult to persuade the community members to contribute their labor (Barker, 1978, p. 149).

Theoretically it is possible to design a scheme in which all participants in collective actions bear the cost in proportion to their benefits

---

[27] For the literature on public choice, including the theory of collective action, see Mueller (1976; 1979).

and those who incur losses are compensated for them. In the real world, however, it is unrealistic to assume that such a scheme can be designed and agreed upon through voluntary negotiation and bargaining. Such a task requires the efforts of "political entrepreneurs". Olson describes the political entrepreneur's function as follows:

> A leader or entrepreneur, who is generally trusted (or feared), or who can guess who is bluffing in the bargaining, or who can simply save bargaining time, can sometimes work out an arrangement that is better for all concerned than any outcome that could emerge without entrepreneurial leadership or organization. If the entrepreneur senses that the outcome will be more efficient if each member of the group pays a share of the marginal cost of additional units of the collective good equal to his share of the benefits of each additional unit, and others do not sense this, the leader will . . . be able to suggest arrangements which can leave everyone in the group better off. If the situation before the entrepreneur arises or intervenes is not optimal, it follows that the entrepreneur may also get something for himself out of the gains he brings about. Because of this gain, and the liking some people have for being leaders, politicians, or promoters, there is often an ample supply of political entrepreneurs (Olson, 1965, pp. 176–177).

The potential availability of political entrepreneurs does not, however, ensure the optimum supply of public goods: "There is no certainty, and often not even a presumption, that an entrepreneur will be able to work out an arrangement that is agreeable to the parties concerned, and sometimes the difficulty and expense of striking the needed bargains will be too great for an entrepreneur to succeed, or even want to try" (Olson, 1965, p. 177).

In general, the task of a political entrepreneur will be easier in a community characterized by the tightly structured social system defined in the previous section. In a tightly structured community where people are less individualistic and conform to social norms more closely, it is easier to organize collective actions if the actions conform to the social norms. Thus, it is critical for village leaders to design their projects so as to be consistent with traditional norms and to appeal to villagers for cooperation on the grounds of traditional moral principles such as the *gotong-royong* (mutual help) principle in Indonesia.

Traditional norms and social interactions in village communities may be effective in organizing collective actions, but they do not necessarily promote more efficient resource allocation. In some cases traditional norms and principles may show the power of social interactions to block the efficient reallocation of resources. Whether traditional norms and principles facilitate collective action towards economic progress depends on the ability of political entrepreneurs as well as on the power structure of the community.

A political entrepreneur will undertake to organize collective actions if he believes that he will be able to collect rewards from the beneficiaries greater than the cost he will have to bear. It may be that the rewards can be collected more easily from a group within the community than from others. In that case the leader will tend to design a scheme to maximize the profit of the group while maintaining the interests of the others at a tolerable minimum. It is even possible that the resources which a certain group is ready to pay are large enough to create a power base for the leader sufficiently strong to suppress opposition from other members of the community.

The power base of a village leader will depend on his alliances with certain vested-interest groups within the community. It also depends on his alliances with outside powers such as government agencies and local politicians. Whether a certain form of institutional change will be implemented depends critically not only on how much benefit it will produce but also on how the benefit will be distributed among vested-interest groups. It is quite possible that an institutional adjustment expected to produce a large social gain may not be forthcoming under a certain power structure. It is even possible for an institutional adjustment to result in net social loss. For example, moral economists predict that if village elites' alliances with outside forces become so powerful that they no longer rely on their neighbors' good will or their clients' loyalty, they may neglect traditional institutions or profit themselves at the expense of the common good of the village.

Chapter 3

The Dynamics of Agrarian Change in Asia

In terms of the conceptual framework developed in the previous chapter, the evolution of institutions can be seen as the result of struggles among various groups in the community who seek to attain a more efficient resource allocation and to establish claims to larger income shares in response to changes in economic variables such as resource endowments and technology. This chapter aims to examine the major economic factors that are pressing change upon agrarian communities in South and Southeast Asia today, and to postulate a hypothesis on the broad trends of agrarian change.

Macro Features of Asian Agriculture

The basic force pressing change on the agrarian structure of developing countries in Asia today is the strong population pressure on land. During the past two decades the labor force engaged in agricultural production in seven countries of South and Southeast Asia increased at rates of 1.0 to 2.5% per year (Table 3–1). Meanwhile, arable land area increased at rates of about 1.0% or less except in Thailand. As a result the man-land ratio increased. More importantly, the increase in the man-land ratio accelerated from 1955–65 to 1965–75, reflecting the rapid exhaustion of land hitherto unused for cultivation. In the latter decade the man-land ratio grew rapidly, on the average, at a rate which would double the number of workers per ha within a half-century. The deterioration in the land-labor ratio has been much more serious than these data show, because cultivation frontiers have been expanded largely into marginally less productive areas, especially in Thailand.

Table 3-1. Changes in agricultural labor population, arable land area and man/land ratio in selected countries in Asia, 1955 to 1975.

	1955	1965	1975	Annual growth rate (%)		
				1955 to 1965	1965 to 1975	1955 to 1975
Agricultural labor population (million)						
Bangladesh	14.9	17.8	21.6	1.8	2.0	1.9
India	130.4	143.0	160.0	0.9	1.1	1.0
Pakistan	8.9	9.4	11.0	0.5	1.6	1.1
Sri Lanka	1.8	2.1	2.6	1.6	2.2	1.9
Indonesia	24.1	26.4	29.5	0.9	1.1	1.0
Philippines	4.8	6.3	7.8	2.7	2.2	2.5
Thailand	10.3	12.1	14.9	1.6	2.1	1.9
Arable land area (million ha)						
Bangladesh	8.1	9.0	9.5	1.1	0.5	0.8
India	158.3	162.4	167.2	0.3	0.3	0.3
Pakistan	16.3	19.3	19.5	1.7	0.1	0.9
Sri Lanka	1.5	1.9	2.0	2.4	0.5	1.4
Indonesia	16.5	17.0	18.6	0.3	0.7	0.6
Philippines	5.9	6.9	7.4	1.6	0.7	1.1
Thailand	11.1	13.2	16.6	1.7	2.3	2.0
Man-land ratio (workers/ha)						
Bangladesh	1.84	1.98	2.27	0.7	1.5	1.1
India	0.82	0.88	0.96	0.6	0.8	0.7
Pakistan	0.55	0.49	0.56	−1.2	1.3	0.2
Sri Lanka	1.20	1.11	1.30	−0.8	1.7	0.5
Indonesia	1.46	1.55	1.59	0.6	0.4	0.4
Philippines	0.81	0.91	1.05	1.1	1.5	1.4
Thailand	0.93	0.91	0.89	−0.1	−0.2	−0.1

Sources: Agricultural labor population: For the Philippines, ILO, *International Labor Statistics*, Geneva, various issues. For other countries, 1955 data are estimated by interpolation based on ILO, *Labor Force Estimates and Projection: 1950–2000*, Vol. 1, Geneva, 1977. Data for 1965 and 1975 are from FAO, *Production Yearbook*, 1977, Rome 1978.

Arable land area: For the Philippines, data are estimated by inter- and extrapolation based on 1948, 1960 and 1971 census data from National Census and Statistical Office, *1971 Census of Agriculture: Philippines*, Manila, 1974. 1955 data for Indonesia are estimated based on Biro Pusat Statistik, *Statistical Pocketbook of Indonesia*, Jakarta, various issues. For other countries, data are from FAO, *Production Yearbook*, Rome, various issues. 1950 data for Bangladesh and Pakistan are estimated by assuming the same proportion of arable land between the two regions for 1961–65.

Developing economies throughout the world began to experience explosive population growth in the second and third decades of the twentieth century; the growth rates have further accelerated since World

War II (Bairoch, 1975, pp. 5–8; Kuznets, 1966, pp. 34–40). The high rates of population growth have resulted mainly from the decline in mortality rates due to the propagation of modern public health measures and the extension of markets that prevented local crop failures from turning into famine.

A similar acceleration of population growth was experienced by Western Europe and Japan at the beginning of economic growth in those regions. However, unlike the case of those early developed economies, the population explosion in developing countries today has not been an endogenous product of growth in industrial employment and per-capita income but, rather, resulted exogenously from the importation of Western health techniques and the imposition of market economies under colonial regimes.

It is projected that the high growth rates will continue to the year 2000 (Table 3–2). Developing countries in Asia have recently recorded significant industrial development, and the relative shares of the nonagricultural sector in both national income and employment have increased. However, partly because the nonagricultural sector is still a minor sector of the total economy and partly because the industrial technology imported from developed countries has had a bias toward

Table 3-2.   Population growth and projections in the world and in selected countries.

	Population (million)			Annual growth rate (%)	
	1950	1970	2000	1950 to 1970	1970 to 2000
World	2504	3610	6257	1.8	1.9
Developed regions	857	1084	1360	1.2	0.8
Developing regions	1646	2526	4897	2.2	2.2
South Asia					
Bangladesh	41	68	144	2.6	2.5
India	353	543	1059	2.2	2.3
Pakistan	36	60	147	2.6	3.0
Sri Lanka	8	13	21	2.5	1.6
Total	438	684	1371	2.3	2.3
Southeast Asia					
Burma	18	28	55	3.0	2.3
Indonesia	75	119	238	2.3	2.3
Malaysia	6	10	22	2.6	2.7
Philippines	21	38	90	3.0	2.9
Thailand	20	36	86	3.0	2.9
Total	140	231	491	2.5	2.5

Source: ILO, *Labor Force Estimates and Projections: 1950–2000,* Vol. I and Vol. V, Geneva, 1977.

high capital intensity, the increase in nonagricultural employment has been grossly insufficient to absorb the increment of labor population in the dominant agriculture sector. The population pressure has aggravated rural poverty, with increasing fragmentation of landholdings and a growing number of landless agricultural laborers (Asian Development Bank, 1978; International Labor Organization, 1977).

There have been substantial efforts to curb birth rates. In fact, significant declines in the birth rates in developing countries have been observed for more than the past two decades (Mauldin and Berelson, 1978). These declines in birth rates have, until recently, been compensated for by declines in the death rates. But we now see real signs that population growth rates have finally begun to decelerate in the 1970s (Kirk, 1979). However, even if population growth rates decline sharply in the near furture, the growth rate of the labor force will be high for some time to come because a large percentage of the population belongs to the age group below 15 years old.

While the labor force in the rural sector will continue to increase, there is little possibility of expanding the area under cultivation. With a few exceptional spots such as the outer islands of Indonesia, Northeast Thailand, Laos and Kampuchea, the countries of South and Southeast Asia are densely populated, and cultivation frontiers have been pushed to such an extent that serious ecological decay resulting from deforestation and consequent exhaustion of soil fertility has become a common feature. Thus, in all probability farmland per worker will continue to decline for some years to come in South and Southeast Asia.

As a larger number of workers seek employment in agriculture and more labor is applied per unit of land area, the marginal productivity of labor will be reduced and the wage rate will be bid down, provided that technology (broadly defined as the production function relating output to inputs) remains constant. In fact, the production function has not remained constant. In order to sustain a subsistence level of income for agricultural workers, efforts have been made by both farmers and governments to counteract the decreasing returns to labor input by "augmenting land" or "saving land required to produce a unit of output". Land can be augmented in efficiency units by investing in irrigation and other forms of land infrastructure to improve the quality of land, and by developing "land-saving" technology such as fertilizer-responsive high-yielding varieties that facilitate substitution of fertilizers and chemicals for land in agricultural production.

Irrigation is a critical part of the infrastructure for increasing output per unit of land area. It contributes to increased yields per ha of cropping area as well as to the expansion of cropping area by facilitating multi-cropping systems. During the past two decades substantial investments have been made in this critical infrastructure in countries of South and Southeast Asia, as reflected by steady increases in the percentages of arable land and rice-crop areas under irrigation except in Thailand (Table 3–3). The percentages did not increase in Thailand not because irrigation investments were small but because the expansion of cultivation frontiers into more marginal non-irrigated areas was exceptionally fast in this country and outpaced the expansion of irrigated area.

Table 3-3.   Percentages of arable and rice areas under irrigation in selected countries in South and Southeast Asia, selected years.

(%)

	1955	1965	1975
Percentage of arable land area under irrigation[a]:			
Bangladesh	5	7	16
India	14	16	19
Pakistan	56	61	74
Sri Lanka	19	21	22
Indonesia	23	24	24
Philippines	13	14	18
Thailand	16	14	19
Percentage of rice crop area under irrigation:			
Bangladesh	5	5	12
India	35	36	38
Pakistan	100	100	100
Sri Lanka	54	60	70
Indonesia	82	80	86
Philippines	22	31	42
Thailand	25[b]	29	22[c]

[a] Figures for 1965 are as of 1966.
[b] As of 1958.
[c] As of 1974.
Sources: Arable land area and total irrigated area, see the sources in Table 3-1. Total rice crop area and rice crop area irrigated, from A. C. Palacpac, *World Rice Statistics 1980*, IRRI, Los Baños, Philippines, 1980.

The dramatic diffusion of modern semi-dwarf varieties of rice and wheat in tropical Asia since the mid-1960s, heralded popularly (and misleadingly) as the "green revolution", may be considered a major response to the rising man-land ratio in developing countries (Hayami and Ruttan, 1971). The modern varieties (MV), characterized by short and stiff stalks with pointed leaves that receive solar energy more efficiently and withstand higher application of fertilizers, have proved higher-yielding and more profitable under the conditions of adequate water control and crop care.

The initial enthusiasm for MV during the period of the "green revolution" bandwagon was later superseded by popular criticism of "the failure of miracle rice" after occasional crop failures due to pests and floods. However, the fact that MV continued to diffuse rapidly and that areas planted in MV reached as much as 20 million ha (or nearly 70%) of wheat area and 24 million ha (or nearly 30%) of rice area in South and Southeast Asia is *prima facie* evidence that MV represents an efficient and profitable technology (Table 3–4 and Figure 3–1).

Table 3-4.   Percentages of total rice and wheat areas planted to modern varieties in South and Southeast Asia, selected years.

	Rice			Wheat[a]		
	1968/69	1970/71	1975/76	1968/69	1970/71	1975/76
South Asia	6.4	12.9	29.1	34.1	42.2	73.3
Bangladesh	1.6	4.6	15.0	8.6	10.6	71.8
India	7.2	14.5	32.3	30.1	35.9	74.7
Nepal	3.6	5.7	17.3	33.5	43.0	71.0
Pakistan	19.8	36.6	38.9	43.0	52.3	69.0
Sri Lanka	1.1	4.3	63.0			
Southeast Asia	7.2	12.8	23.2[b]			
Burma	3.5	4.0	6.4			
Indonesia	2.5	11.1	31.0			
Laos	0.3	8.1	N.A.			
Malaysia (Peninsula)	20.9	31.4	37.4			
Philippines	40.6	50.3	64.2			
Thailand	—	0.4	7.1			
Vietnam (South)	1.7	20.0	N.A.			
Total	6.6	12.9	27.2[b]			

N.A.—Data not available.
[a] Area planted to modern varieties of wheat in Southeast Asia is negligible.
[b] Excludes Laos and South Vietnam.
Sources: D. Dalrymple: *Development and Spread of High-Yielding Varieties of Wheat and Rice in the Less Developed Nations,* U.S. Department of Agriculture, Washington, D.C., 1978, p. 116; and A.C. Palapac, *World Rice Statistics, 1979,* IRRI, Los Baños, Philippines, 1979.

It is important to note that the MVs propagated during the 1960s and the early 1970s were those developed by international agricultural research centers such as the International Rice Research Institute (IRRI) and the International Center for Corn and Wheat Improvement (CIMMYT); these have been replaced steadily by crosses of the international center varieties with local varieties developed by national

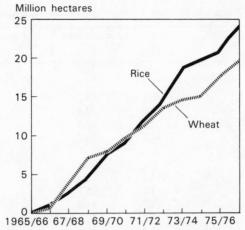

Million hectares

Fig. 3-1.   Area planted in modern varieties of rice and wheat in Asia.

Note: Rice area includes Bangladesh, Burma, India, Indonesia, Korea, Malaysia, Nepal, Pakistan, Philippines, Sri Lanka and Thailand; and wheat area includes Bangladesh, India, Nepal and Pakistan.

Source: D. Dalrymple, *Development and Spread of High-Yielding Varieties of Wheat and Rice in the Less Developed Nations,* U. S. Department of Agriculture, Washington, D.C., 1978, p. 117.

experiment stations so as to be more adaptable to local environmental conditions (Dalrymple, 1978).

Facilitated by MV and improved irrigation systems, the application of fertilizers has increased at a dramatic speed (Table 3–5). The quantity of fertilizer applied per ha (measured by the sum of nitrogen, phosphate and potash) tripled in South and Southeast Asia within a 10-year period from 1966 to 1976—a rate more than four times faster than that in the East Asian countries of Japan, Korea and Taiwan.

The development of an irrigation infrastructure and seed-fertilizer technology should have a significant effect in augmenting land and, thereby, counteracting the decreasing return to labor applied to a physically limited land area. However, land augmentation has still been insufficient to overcome the extremely strong population pressure. As a result, the marginal productivity of agricultural labor has not risen but rather has declined in many areas, as reflected by the declining or stagnant trends in real wage rates in South and Southeast Asia—except in areas where the "green revolution" had an especially strong impact, such as Punjab and Haryana in India (Table 3–6). Wage trends in South and Southeast Asia, where increases in the labor supply have been out-

Table 3-5.   Changes in fertilizer use in selected Asian countries, 1966 to 1976.

Country	kg NPK/ha arable land		% growth in NPK/ha/yr
	1966	1976	1966 to 1976
South Asia	7.1	20.9	11.4
Bangladesh	8.4	25.7	11.8
India	6.8	19.2	11.4
Nepal	1.9	7.4	14.6
Pakistan	5.7	32.3	18.9
Sri Lanka	45.0	43.7	−0.3
Southeast Asia	7.2	20.2	10.9
Burma	1.1	5.1	16.6
Indonesia	8.2	25.1	11.8
Malaysia	15.0	44.6	11.5
Philippines	15.3	33.6	8.2
Thailand	5.2	13.4	9.9
East Asia	303.1	387.4	2.5
Japan	357.1	430.5	1.9
Korea	184.6	287.4	4.5
Taiwan	276.3	395.6	3.7

Sources:
NPK consumption: India – The Fertilizer Association of India, *Fertilizer Statistics 1966 and 1977*, New Delhi, 1967 and 1978.
Bangladesh – For 1966 data, Ministry of Agriculture, *Bangladesh Agriculture in Statistics, 1970/71*, Dacca, 1973.
Other countries – FAO, *Annual Fertilizer Review 1966 and 1977*, Rome, 1967 and 1978.
Arable land: FAO, *Production Yearbook 1977*, Rome, 1978.

pacing demand, are in sharp contrast to those in East Asian countries such as Taiwan and Korea where strong demand for industrial labor has resulted in contraction of the agricultural labor force.

One consequence of population pressure on limited land resources has been the lag of food production behind rapid demand increases. During the past two decades food production in developing countries recorded relatively high rates of growth, on the order of 2 to 3% per year, comparable to the performance in developed countries (Table 3–7). However, the increase in food production was barely sufficient to keep up with population growth, and no significant increase was realized in per-capita food production in most developed countries. Meanwhile, per-capita food consumption increased due to the growth in urban income. As a result, food deficits were created which were covered by large-scale imports of grains from developed countries (Table 3–8).

Table 3-6.   Index of real wages of agricultural laborers in selected Asian countries; 1965 = 100.

| | Bangla-deshᵃ | Indiaᵇ | | | Malay-siaᵃ | Pakis-tanᵃ | Philip-pinesᵇ | Sri Lankaᶜ | Koreaᵃ | Taiwanᵈ |
		Punjab, Haryana	West Bengal	Tamil Nadu						
1960	93	—	—	—	—	—	131	98	90	—
1961	102	92	120	97	—	—	130	99	90	95
1962	96	92	99	108	—	—	121	98	92	101
1963	106	—	—	—	—	—	121	99	95	96
1964	120	79	104	102	—	103	106	98	102	95
1965	100	100	100	100	—	100	100	100	100	100
1966	86	78	99	93	100	105	137	99	153	102
1967	86	90	87	100	96	113	111	98	166	105
1968	92	108	97	104	99	113	136	107	185	119
1969	100	117	102	99	101	116	106	100	200	142
1970	101	117	98	112	100	125	93	96	215	147
1971	—	107	106	116	195	125	88	96	227	157
1972	72	—	—	—	93	130	86	110	235	164
1973	71	—	—	—	91	—	100	93	—	—
1974	64	—	—	—	—	—	—	—	—	—

ᵃ Deflated by cost of living index (for agricultural laborers).
ᵇ Deflated by consumer price index.
ᶜ Deflated by cost of living index (for male plantation workers).
ᵈ Deflated by index of prices received by farmers.
Source: Asian Development Bank, *Rural Asia: Challenge and Opportunity*, New
    York, Praeger, 1978, p. 54.

Table 3-7.   Index of food production and per-capita food production in the
world and in selected countries; 1953–57 = 100.

| | Food production | | | Per-capita food production | | |
	1953–57	1963–67	1973–77	1953–57	1963–67	1973–77
World	100	132	169	100	109	115
Developed market economies	100	133	156	100	117	127
Developing market economies	100	131	174	100	102	105
South Asia:						
India	100	121	159	100	98	102
Pakistanᵃ	100	130	170	100	97	99
Sri Lanka	100	149	180	100	116	116
Southeast Asia:						
Burma	100	134	162	100	111	105
Indonesia	100	118	169	100	94	104
Malaysia (Peninsula)	100	150	276	100	111	164
Philippines	100	139	207	100	101	107
Thailand	100	161	231	100	120	121

ᵃ Includes Bangladesh.
Sources: FAO, *The State of Food and Agriculture*, Rome, various issues.
    FAO, *Production Yearbook 1977*, Rome, 1978.

Table 3-8.   Imports of grains in developing countries.[a]   (1000 mt)

Region/Country	1953–57	1963–67	1973–77
Developing market economies	12,903	29,910	47,187
South Asia	*3,136*	*9,929*	*8,514*
Bangladesh		899	1,802
India	1,714	7,020	4,389
Sri Lanka	746	949	1,091
Pakistan	677[b]	1,062	1,233
Southeast Asia	*1,796*	*2,235*	*4,068*
Burma	32	10	20
Indonesia	611	723	2,309
Malaysia (Peninsula)	761[c]	654	803
Philippines	357	802	841
Thailand	35	47	95
South and Southeast Asia	4,933	12,165	12,582

[a] Includes wheat and wheat flour in wheat equivalent, rice, maize and barley.
[b] Includes Bangladesh.
[c] Includes Singapore.
Source: FAO, *Trade Yearbooks*, Rome, various issues.

Partly because labor supply has outpaced demand and partly because food supply has been outpaced by demand, the value of labor has declined relative to the value of food, as illustrated in the declining trends in the quantities of rice purchasable by one day's labor for the Philippines and Sri Lanka (Table 3.9).[1] These trends are in sharp contrast to the case in Japan, where the quantity of rice purchasable by one day's work nearly tripled for the past two decades despite the fact that the price of rice in Japan was raised to more than four times the world level by successive increases in government price supports during the 1960s and 1970s.

Population Pressure, New Technology and Agrarian Structure[2]

The dismal picture drawn in the previous section resembles the world of the classical economists like David Ricardo: as the growth of

[1] According to Kurien (1980), the wage rates of agricultural field laborers relative to the price of rice declined by 20 to 30% between 1951–52 and 1973–74 in Tamil Nadu, India.
[2] Some of the materials presented in this section draw on Hayami (1981a).

Table 3-9.   Farm wage/rice price ratios (kg of paddy purchasable by one day's farm work) in selected Asian countries, 1960–1977.

	Philippines	Sri Lanka		Japan	
		Male	Female	Male	Female
1960	14.0	4.5	3.7	7.2	5.9
1961	12.1	4.6	3.7	8.0	6.6
1962	12.7	4.6	3.8	9.1	7.5
1963	11.3	4.7	4.1	9.7	8.0
1964	9.5	4.8	4.0	9.7	7.9
1965	9.8	4.9	4.1	9.6	7.7
1966	9.2	4.9	4.0	9.6	7.8
1967	9.7	4.6	3.9	9.7	7.9
1968	10.4	4.9	4.1	10.9	9.1
1969	9.2	4.9	4.1	12.1	10.2
1970	8.9	5.1	4.1	13.7	11.1
1971	6.6	5.2	5.0	15.6	12.2
1972	6.2	6.3	4.5	16.5	13.0
1973	5.6	3.3	3.1	16.7	13.2
1974	7.2	3.3	2.5	16.5	13.1
1975	8.0	3.9	3.0	17.8	14.1
1976	9.3	4.3	3.3	17.7	14.1
1977	10.1			19.5	15.2

Source: Adelita C. Palacpac, *World Rice Statistics 1980*. IRRI, Los Baños, Philippines, 1980.

population presses hard on limited land resources under constant technology, cultivation frontiers are expanded to more marginal land and greater amounts of labor applied per unit of cultivated area; the marginal return to additional labor input declines and the cost of food production rises resulting in higher food prices; real wage rates measured in food grain decline and land rent increases.

In the real world technology has not remained constant. In fact, remarkable progress has been made in the development of irrigation systems and seed-fertilizer technology that should have made significant contributions to counteracting the declining return to labor applied per unit of land area. However, such efforts have failed to overcome the negative effect of strong population pressure. If this trend continues, developing economies in Asia will move towards a Ricardian stagnation, with laborers' incomes lowered to a subsistence minimum barely sufficient to maintain a stationary population and all the economic surplus captured by landlords in the form of increased land rent.

Simple Economics

In order to facilitate understanding of the effects of population pressure and technological change on income distribution, highly simplified models are developed in Figure 3–2 (for a mathematical presentation, see Appendix A).[3]

For the sake of simplicity, let us assume an agricultural production function in which output is produced from labor (L) and land (A). Output may be considered as value added after current inputs are deducted, and land as land-cum-capital. The upper diagrams in Figure 3–2 represent aggregate demand and supply of labor in the market and the lower diagrams the production function (f) that relates output per ha ($q = Q/A$) to labor input per ha of physical land area ($l = L/A$). The shape and the location of f is determined by "technology", broadly defined to include land infrastructure such as irrigation and drainage. The classical assumption of decreasing return to labor applied per unit of land is adopted.

Case I represents one polar case in which the labor demand curve

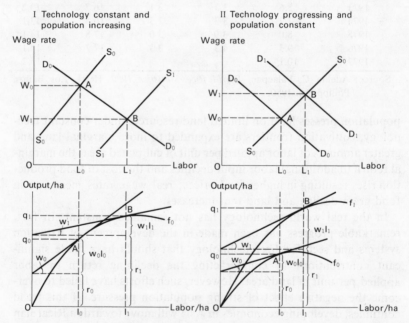

Fig. 3.2.   The effects of technological change and population pressure on income distribution among laborers and asset holders.

[3] The model to be presented below is highly simplified in order to facilitate the intuitive understanding of non-economists and non-mathematical economists rather than to provide rigorous proof. By nature, it is very partial in the sense that it deals only with the factor market. For a model that analyzes the product market effects of new technology on income distributions. see Hayami and Herdt (1977).

(the schedule of marginal products of labor) stays constant at D_0, reflecting no progress in technology (f_0), while the labor supply shifts from S_0 to S_1 due to population growth. Corresponding to a change in the market equilibrium point from A to B, the wage rate declines from w_0 (OW_0) to w_1 (OW_1) and the land rental rate rises from r_0 to r_1. If the increased labor is applied to the fixed production function (f_0) at a zone of decreasing return to labor such that the elasticity of substitution of labor for land is less than one (*i.e.*, less than a one-percent increase in the labor-land ratio results from a one-percent decrease in the wage-rent ratio), the relative income share of labor declines from ($w_0 l_0 / q_0$) to ($w_1 l_1 / q_1$).[4] If the labor application per ha continues to increase, a point will eventually be reached beyond which the elasticity of factor substitution becomes so small that labor's income declines absolutely corresponding to any further increase in labor input.

Case II represents another polar case. Let us assume that the labor supply remains constant at S_0 and the labor demand shifts from D_0 to D_1, reflecting the upward shift in the production function from f_0 to f_1. Corresponding to the change in market equilibrium from A to B, the wage rate rises from w_0 to w_1 and the absolute income of labor from ($w_0 l_0$) to ($w_1 l_1$). Whether the relative income share of labor improves or not depends on the nature of the shift in the production function. The relative share of labor (wl/q) increases if the production shifts in such a way as to increase the labor-land ratio ($1 = L/A$) for a constant rent-wage ratio (r/w) at competitive equilibrium—the "land-saving and labor-using technological change" in the Hicks definition.

In the real world both the demand for and the supply of labor shift simultaneously. However, the evidence presented in the previous section shows that the shift in the labor supply due to rapid population growth has outpaced the shift in demand due to technological progress, resulting in a decline in the real wage rate. In such a situation, income distribution would become more skewed, because the rate of return to land (r) would rise relative to that of labor (w) and an increasing share of income would be captured by the land-owning class.

Simple economics tells us that the income and the level of living of the poor in the rural sector in developing countries—landless laborers and tenants whose incomes consist mainly of earnings from their labor—will continue to decline both absolutely and relatively unless sufficient

---

[4] Evidence cited by Hanumantha Rao (1975, pp. 133–134) indicates that the elasticity of land-labor substitution in Indian agriculture for the pre-MV period was significantly lower than unity and that the elasticity was reduced further for the post-MV period; this appears common in densely populated, land-scarce economies in Asia where labor has been applied to land to such an extent that there is little room left for substitution of labor for land, at least for a given technology.

effort is made to improve technology so as to make the shift of labor demand faster than that of supply.

This does not imply that any change in technology is beneficial to the poor. There is a type of technological change which reduces labor's income by displacing labor by machinery and herbicides. Such technological change is called the "labor-saving" type in the Hicksian sense. In terms of the right-hand diagram of Figure 3–2, labor-saving (and land-using) technological change is represented by a shift in the production function in such a way as to reduce the labor-land ratio ($1 = L/A$) for a constant rent-wage ratio (r/w) in competitive equilibrium. If a technological change is of the labor-saving type, the relative income share of labor (wl/q) declines.

It is theoretically possible for the labor-saving bias to be so strong that the absolute income of labor can decline.

Does New Technology Promote Polarization?

Although not all types of technological progress contribute to greater equality in income distribution, it is very clear from the left-hand diagrams in Figure 3–2 that without technological innovations the wage rate and the income share of labor is bound to decline under the continued population pressure on land. Yet it has been common to consider that the introduction of modern technology, irrespective of its nature, results in greater inequality and a highly inequitable agrarian structure:

> Where ownership is unequally distributed, technological change is certain to result in increased income inequality and unemployment. Larger owners, through their pull with government agencies, will be able to get a disproportionate share of the new capital inputs. They will invest in tractors and displace labor. . . . Higher rates of return from the use of new capital inputs will lead them to evict tenants, in order to farm on their own account. All this will mean that the gains of technological advance will accrue mainly to the landowners and that tenants are likely to lose income and employment (Warriner, 1973, p. 129).

In much of the literature, both scientific and popular, modern rice and wheat varieties are often identified as a major force promoting polarization of agrarian communities.[5] It is argued that the new tech-

[5] The arguments that follow are mentioned by Wharton (1969), Johnston and Cownie (1969), Falcon (1970) and Palmer (1976a and b). More radical views are provided by Cleaver (1972), Fatami (1972), Frankel (1971) and Griffin (1974).

nology tends to be monopolized by large commerical farmers who have better access to new information and better financial capacity. Modern varieties can profitably use greater applications of modern inputs such as fertilizers and chemicals. Adoption of the modern varieties is said to be difficult for small subsistence farmers who have little financial capacity to purchase these inputs. If the new technology is monopolized by large farms (the argument continues), the large profits resulting from its adoption would stimulate the adopters to enlarge their operational holdings by consolidating the farms of small non-adopters through land purchase or tenant eviction. As a result, polarization of rural communities into large commercial farmers and a landless proletariat would be promoted. Further, the large commerical farms would have an intrinsic tendency to introduce large machinery for ease of labor management; this would reduce employment opportunities and wage rates for the landless population. Thus, radical and populist critics envision the polarization of Asian peasant communities into landless proletariat and *kulak* in line with the scenario of Marx and Lenin.

Indeed, such arguments are not groundless. It is not difficult to find cases in which significant trends towards polarization have developed side by side with the diffusion of modern varieties, even though these are still exceptional cases in Asian peasant economies. The point of major controversy is the causal relation between new technology and polarization phenomena. Does the adoption of new technology, in fact, tend to be monopolized by large holders because of constraints in information and credit on small holders? Does the technology make large-scale operations relatively more efficient and profitable? Is there a technical complementarity between modern varieties and labor-displacing machinery? If so, our arguments developed with reference to Figure 3–3, based on the assumption of a competitive market (or pseudo-market), will become irrelevant.[6] The issue is an empirical question and should be resolved as such.

In fact, there is little empirical evidence that the use of modern varieties has been monopolized by large farmers. Out of 36 villages selected throughout Asia for the study of the process of adoption of new rice technology, in only one village was a significant lag of small farmers behind large farmers observed in the adoption of modern varieties (MV) (International Rice Research Institute, 1975, pp. 31–39;

---

[6] The "market" in Asian village economies, unlike the Walrasian "auction market", operates through personalized relations with multi-stranded ties as discussed in Chapter 2. It is our contention that resource allocations achieved by the pseudo-market in the village system approximate those of the neoclassical impersonal market.

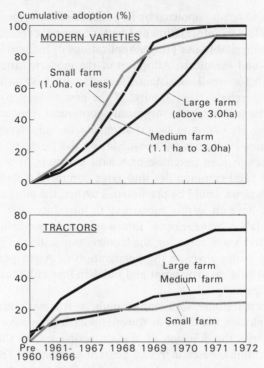

Fig. 3-3. Cumulative percentage of farms in three size classes adopting modern varieties and tractors in 30 villages in Asia.
Source: IRRI, *Interpretive Analysis of Selected Papers from Changes in Rice Farming in Selected Areas of Asia,* Los Baños, Philippines, 1978, p. 91.

and 1978, pp. 92–97). On the average, small farmers were even faster to adopt MV than large farmers (see the upper half of Figure 3–3). The pattern of MV diffusion among different farm-size classes contrasts sharply with the pattern in the diffusion of tractors, in which large farmers achieved a distinctly faster and higher rate of adoption (the lower half of Figure 3.3).

The contrasting diffusion patterns suggest differences in type of technology between MV and tractors. The latter is characterized by indivisibility or lumpiness in the use of capital and, thereby, requires a large farm size for efficient operation, whereas the former is divisible into small units at equal efficiency. In other words, the MV technology is neutral with respect to scale. The scale neutrality of MV technology was supported by an econometric test on wheat production in the Indian Punjab by Surjit Sidhu (1974).

The data collected from selected villages in Asia show that there was no significant difference in the average paddy yield per ha between large and small farmers adopting MV except for Indonesia (Table 3–10), and that there was no difference in the percentage of farmers reporting increases in profit from rice production and level of living after the introduction of MV (Table 3–11). These data are consistent with the hypothesis of scale neutrality of MV. Similar results were reported in a large body of micro-studies for various parts of Asia.[7] After a careful review of those micro-studies in Asia, Vernon Ruttan concluded that "neither farm size nor tenure has been a serious constraint to the adop-

Table 3-10. Average paddy yields on large vs. small farms adopting modern varieties (MV) in selected Asian villages, 1971/72 wet season.

| | | Paddy yield (t/ha) | | |
	No. of villages	Small farmer (S)	Large farmer (L)	Difference (L) − (S)
India	12	3.8	4.6	0.8
Pakistan	2	3.3	3.4	0.1
Indonesia	5	3.7	5.3	1.6
Malaysia	2	2.4	2.2	−0.2
Philippines	9	2.7	2.5	−0.2
Thailand	2	3.4	3.4	0
All villages	*32*	*3.3*	*3.8*	*0.5*

Source: IRRI, *Interpretive Analysis of Selected Papers from Changes in Rice Farming in Selected Areas of Asia*, Los Baños, Philippines, 1978, p. 96.

Table 3-11. Average percentage of farmers reporting increases in profit from rice and level of living after the introduction of modern varieties in selected Asian villages, 1971/72.

| | | Farmers reporting increases (%) | | | |
| | No. of villages | Profit from rice | | Level of living | |
		Small farmer	Large farmer	Small farmer	Large farmer
India	8	72	80	59	73
Indonesia	5	80	79	65	67
Malaysia	2	67	53	60	45
Philippines	12	62	64	55	62
Thailand	3	41	55	41	48
All villages	*30*	*66*	*69*	*57*	*63*

Source: IRRI, *Interpretive Analysis of Selected Papers from Changes in Rice Farming in Selected Areas of Asia*, Los Baños, Philippines, 1978, p. 108.

[7] Azam (1973) for Pakistan; Sen (1974) for India; Soejono (1976) for Indonesia; and Mangahas *et al.* (1974) for the Philippines.

tion of new high yielding grain varieties" and "neither farm size nor tenure has been an important source of differential growth in productivity" (Ruttan, 1977, p. 17).[8]

Another major issue revolves around the direction of factor-saving bias in new technology. If MV has a labor-saving bias, the income position of landless laborers and tenants will deteriorate even if the technology is neutral with respect to the scale of farm operation. The econometric test by Sidhu on Punjab wheat production, however, shows that the MV wheat represented a neutral technological change not only with respect to scale but also with respect to factor use (Sidhu, 1974). A similar study by Chandra Ranade and Robert Herdt on rice in the Philippines suggests that the MV technology is biased in the land-saving direction, though the evidence is not conclusive (Ranade and Herdt, 1978).[9]

Several micro-studies show that the income share of labor declined and the share of land increased over the period of MV diffusion. Dayanatha Jha's data indicate that the factor share to land rose in India between 1960/61 and 1970/71 (Jha, 1974). Data assembled by John Mellor and Uma Lele (1973) indicate that a disproportionately small percentage of the increased output due to MV adoption was allocated to labor. However, those data do not necessarily imply the conclusion that "landowners have gained relative to tenants and laborers from the adoption of the higher yielding grain varieties" (Ruttan, 1977, p. 18). Such a conclusion contradicts the evidence that the MV technology is neutral or biased, if any, in the land-saving direction.

Confusion stems from neglect of the fact that, while the income share of land increased, as Jha's data show, not only did technology change but labor supply increased. As our simple economics illustrate, if the labor supply increased faster than labor demand, the income share of land would have likely increased even if the technological change itself had the effect of land-saving and labor-using.

The data assembled by Mellor and Lele refer to the studies conducted at the very early stage of MV introduction. In the early stage, in which the MV adoption is of a small percentage, aggregate product

---

[8] There is one exception outside Asia. Gafsi and Roe (1979) report that the adoption of MV wheat by small farmers lagged significantly behind large farmers in Tunisia. Whether this is a common case or an exception in North Africa needs investigation.

[9] A production function study by Burke (1979) based on cross-municipal data in Mexico suggests that the technology in high fertilizer-using areas with a high average MV ratio was biased in a labor-saving and capital-using direction. It is not clear, however, whether such bias was due to MV or to other factors such as mechanization operating concurrently with the adoption of MV.

supply and aggregate factor demand do not shift significantly. In such a situation, early adopter scan capture large excess profits (Schumpeterian entrepreneurial profit) from the use of more efficient technology without bidding down product prices or bidding up factor prices appreciably. However, as the technology diffuses widely, innovators' excess profit will be lost as product and factor prices adjust to the new equilibrium. In the long run, the relative share of labor will return to the same level as before the introduction of MV if MV represents a neutral technological change, or it will become larger if it is biased in the land-saving and labor-using direction. For example, Pranab Bardhan's study (1970) for North India in an early period of MV diffusion suggests the insignificant effect of the "green revolution" on the increase in rural labor demand. However, the analysis by Deepak Lal (1976) for the same region in a later period shows clearly that, as MV use diffused more widely, the net effect of the resulting increase in labor demand was a significant rise in the real wage rates in Punjab and other parts of North India at a time when real wage rates were constant or declining in other parts of India where MV diffusion was limited.

Although more econometric investigations are required to confirm the direction of factor-saving bias in the MV technology, it is highly unlikely that the technology is heavily biased to the extent of reducing labor demand. A multiple regression analysis by C.H. Hanumantha Rao (1975, p. 227) based on cross-farm data in Ferozepur, Punjab, for 1968–69 and 1967–70 shows clearly that the contribution of MV adoption to employment was positive and highly significant. Data assembled by Randolph Barker and Violeta Cordova (1978) show that labor inputs per ha for rice production were higher for MV than for traditional varieties (TV) on the order of 10 to 50% (Table 3–12). Similar results were drawn from a review of other studies (Ahmed, 1976; Bartsch, 1973; Clay, 1976). Typically, labor application for land preparation was reduced by tractorization, but the reduction was more than compensated for by increases in labor use for weeding, other crop care and harvesting. It should also be remembered that the MV technology and the increased agricultural income resulting from its adoption have had the important effect of creating nonagricultural employment opportunities through increased demand for nonagricultural goods and services from the agricultural sector (Krishna, 1975; Mellor and Lele, 1973).

A popular argument is that, even if the MV technology is itself neutral or labor-using, it stimulates the introduction of labor-displacing machinery either through technical complementarity or through increased income for large farmers which goes to the purchase of machinery. However, such a conjecture is not supported by empirical observations.

Table 3-12.   Labor input for modern (MV) and traditional (TV) varieties of rice in rice-growing areas in Asia.

Study site	Original source	Year[a]	Season	Labor input (Man-days/ha)		$\dfrac{MV}{TV}$
				MV	TV	
Central Korea	Suh (1976)	1974	Summer	139	126	1.10
Laguna, Philippines	IRRI Survey	1975 vs. 1966	Wet	110	86	1.28
Central Thailand	Sriswasdilek (1973)	1972	Wet	117	81	1.44
Java	Sajogyo & Collier (1973)	1969/70	Wet	262[b]	235[b]	1.11
Mymensingh, Bangladesh	Muqtada (1975)	1969/70	Dry	194	137	1.42
Ferozepur, India	Mehra (1976)	1967/68 to 1969/70	Wet	92	79	1.16
Hyderabad, Pakistan	Khan (1975)	1972	Wet	58	49	1.18

[a] In all sites except Laguna, labor input for area in MV is compared with labor requirement for area in TV during the same season. In Laguna, the same farms are compared with zero MV in 1966 and 95% MV in 1975.
[b] Preharvest labor only.
Source: R. Barker and V. Cordova, "Labor Utilization in Rice Production," in IRRI, *Economic Consequences of the New Rice Technology*, Los Baños, Philippines, 1978, p. 117.

As is shown in Figure 3–3, increases in the adoption of tractors by large farmers began earlier than the introduction of MV, and there was no sign that tractor adoption was accelerated by the dramatic diffusion of MV from the late 1960s to the early 1970s.

Much of the growth in the use of tractors in South and Southeast Asia can be attributed to distortions in the price of capital by such means as overvalued exchange rates and concessional credits from national governments and international lending agencies (Barker *et al.*, 1972; Duff, 1978). Also, the ease of supervising the operation of one tractor-cum-operator relative to that of supervising a large number of laborers and bullock teams seems to have worked as a strong inducement to tractorization in large farms (Binswanger, 1978); this factor should have been especially serious where land reform regulations on land rent and tenure form depressed the incentive of large landowners to rent out their holdings in small operational units.

Conditions of Polarization

The empirical evidence fails to identify the MV technology (in combination with irrigation and fertilizer) as a factor in promoting polarization. In general, both small and large farmers adopted MV at more or less equal rates and achieved efficiency gains of the same order, except in the very early periods of its adoption. It is likely that the MV technology was neutral or biased, if anything, in the land-saving and labor-using direction and resulted in increases in labor demand, despite the concurrent progress of mechanization.

Contrary to the popular belief, we see a real danger of polarization not because of new technology but because of insufficient progress in technology. If technological progress of the land-saving type is not sufficiently rapid, the increase in labor demand will fail to keep up with the increase in labor supply arising from rapid population growth. As our simple economics predicts, the wage rate is bound to decline and the return to land to rise, and the income position of laborers and tenants to deteriorate relative to that of landowners.

A higher rate of return to land provides a strong incentive to accumulate more land, especially under conditions of an underdeveloped capital market in that alternative investment opportunities, such as stocks and securities, are not easily available. The concentration of landholding induced by the higher rate of land rental makes income distribution more skewed, which promotes the further concentration of land—a vicious circle tending towards polarization.

It is not easy to stop this process simply by instituting land reform laws and regulations or trying to protect small landholders by such means as subsidizing credit and input prices. In many cases such government interventions have the effect of promoting polarization. It is a common observation that rich farmers, through their pull with government agencies, manage to receive a disproportionate share of subsidized input and credit (Adams, 1977; Adams and Graham, 1980; Asian Development Bank 1978, pp. 90–97; Hanumantha Rao, 1970; Kurien, 1980). Land reform regulations such as rent control or land confiscation and redistribution have often resulted in the large-scale eviction of tenants in order to establish landlords' direct cultivation with the use of agricultural laborers.[10]

Polarization or Peasant Stratification?

The decreasing return to labor relative to return to land, resulting from the growing population pressure on limited land resources which

[10] This tendency seems especially pervasive in India. See Dutt (1977), Joshi (1970), Narain and Joshi (1969), Raj (1976) and Warriner (1969, pp. 136–218).

has outpaced the efforts to augment or save land by means of technological development and irrigation improvement, has been identified as the basic economic force underlying the increasing inequalities in income and asset distribution in rural Asia. Even though efforts to improve technology and land infrastructure will be intensified at both private and public levels, the rapid growth in the rural labor force may make it difficult to reverse the trend of decreasing return to labor for some years to come.

What will be the direction of change in agrarian structure under such economic conditions? One possibility would be a trend toward polarization of peasant communities into large commercial farmers and a landless proletariat, as we have discussed in detail. If rural Asia moves in this direction, personal relations between employers and employees (or landlords and tenants) which have been guided in village communities by traditional moral principles such as mutual help and income-sharing will be replaced by impersonal market relations.

Another possibility is a trend toward what we may call "peasant stratification". By this we mean increasing class differentiation in a continuous spectrum ranging from landless laborers to non-cultivating landlords, while the social mode of traditional village communities is maintained as described in the previous chapter—people are tied to one another in multi-stranded personalized relations, and all community members have some claims to the output of land (e.g., even landless workers receive a share of output after participating in the harvest). Unlike the polarization case characterized by bi-modal differentiation between *kulak* and proletariat, in the peasant stratification case semi-subsistence peasants will survive, although the majority of them may become poorer with smaller farms to cultivate.

At present, it is not certain in which direction—toward polarization or toward peasant stratification—the Asian village economy is heading. The data in Table 3–13 indicate that polarization was in progress in India during the 1960s: land was concentrated more in the hands of farmers with holdings larger than 5 ha, and the Gini coefficient increased. In Bangladesh, however, although the Gini coefficient increased, the percentage of land in the hands of larger farmers was reduced. No appreciable change in farm-size distribution was observed in the countries of Southeast Asia.

The relative stability in farm-size distribution, especially for countries in Southeast Asia, shown in Table 3–13 does not mean that economic forces have not been operating to induce polarization or peasant stratification. In some areas peasant stratification may be in progress, while in others polarization is gaining momentum. The strong

Table 3-13. Size distribution of operational landholdings in selected Asian countries.

Country	Year	Farm-size class (ha)								Gini coefficient
		0 to 1		1⁺ to 3		3⁺ to 5		Above 5		
		Farms	Area	Farms	Area	Farms	Area	Farms	Area	
		%								
Bangladesh	1960	51.6	15.2	37.7	45.7	7.3	19.1	3.5	20.0	.47
	1974	66.0	24.0	29.0	53.0	3.0	13.0	2.0	10.0	.57
India	1961	39.8	6.8	34.8	23.6	15.0	23.0	10.4	46.6	.59
	1970	50.6	9.0	28.6	22.0	9.4	15.7	11.4	53.3	.63
Pakistan	1960	32.9	3.5	28.6	13.2	15.6	15.0	22.9	68.3	.60
	1972			43.6[a]	12.2[a]	24.5	18.2	31.9	69.6	.49
Indonesia	1963	70.1	28.7	23.9	35.3	3.5	12.3	2.5	23.7	.54
	1973	70.4	29.0	24.0	37.7	3.5	12.8	2.1	20.5	.49
Philippines	1960	11.5	1.6	50.8	23.1	18.7	18.4	19.0	56.9	.52
	1971	13.6	1.9	47.5	22.2	23.7	23.7	15.2	52.2	.51
Thailand[b]	1963	18.5	2.6	29.4	13.0	27.5	26.5	24.6	57.9	.46
	1971	13.4	2.6			66.9[c]	49.2[c]	19.7	48.2	.41

[a] Size category is 0 to 3.0 ha.

[b] Size categories are 0 to .96 ha, .96 to 2.4 ha, 2.4 ha to 4.8 ha and above 4.8 ha.

[c] Size category is .96 to 4.8 ha.

Source: Asian Development Bank, *Rural Asia: Challenge and Opportunity*, New York, Praeger, 1978, p. 98.

forces pressing for change in these two opposite directions may have been in balance. To which side will the pendulum swing in the future? The Asian villge economy is at the crossroads.

Irrespective of which road is followed, income and asset distributions will become more skewed, insofar as the increase in the supply of labor outpaces the increase in labor demand. However, both efficiency and equity would likely be lower in the polarization case than in the peasant stratification case. Considering the high transaction cost of wage-labor contracts, it is expected that large commerical farms dependent on hired labor use less labor per ha than small farmers who depend more heavily on family labor. Indeed, it was established on the basis of Indian data that both output and labor input per ha were higher for smaller farms (Khusro, 1964; Mazumdar, 1963; A. P. Rao, 1967; Hanumantha Rao, 1966; Sen, 1964).[11] More recently, a detailed analysis by Albert Berry and William Cline (1979) on the relationship between farm size and productivity for six developing countries has shown not only that small farmers tend to apply more labor and produce greater output per ha of land than large farmers, but also that their production efficiency measured by the index of total productivity (the ratio of output to an aggregate of all production inputs) tends to be higher. Further, a hypothesis that rural wage levels rise corresponding to reductions in inequality in operational landholdings was confirmed by the study of Mark Rosenzweig (1978) for India.

Therefore, if small farms are consolidated into large operational units, agricultural production efficiency will be lowered and labor employment opportunities and wage rates in the rural sector will be reduced. Moreover, if the rural economy moves toward polarization, class conflicts will become more clearly visible and sharply felt. The resulting social instability in the rural sector will discourage investments in agricultural production and jeopardize efforts to overcome the population pressure on limited land resources in the long run.

The future course of agrarian change in Asia will depend most critically on the ability of village communities to develop new institutions, within the framework of the village system, that are consistent with efficient resource allocation given the growing scarcity of land relative to labor. If institutional innovations at the village level fail to meet these requirements, rural Asia will likely go the route of polariza-

[11] Alternative explanations were developed for the inverse relation between farm size and land productivity, such as zero marginal product of family labor at family farms as opposed to the positive institutional wage rate for commercial farms (see Bhagwati and Chakravarty (1969) for a critical review). However, we consider the difference in transaction cost a more reasonable explanation.

tion. Village studies reported in the rest of this book aim to investigate the nature and the process of institutional adjustments at the village level in response to changing resource endowments and technology.

Part II

Agrarian Change in Philippine Villages

In Inner Central Luzon, since the demise of the hacienda system due to land reform, farmers have been shifting from mechanical threshing using the *tilyadora* (above) to hand threshing (below).

Photos courtesy of the International Rice Research Institute

Chapter

4

The Evolution of Agrarian Institutions in the Rice Bowl

In the previous chapter we investigated the basic economic forces operating in rural Asia to induce changes in agrarian structures. A hypothesis was postulated that the strong population pressure on land has been resulting in more inequitable distribution of assets and income and that rural communities are now at the crossroads of paths leading to either polarization or peasant stratification. Which route will be followed depends on types of technological development, government policies, power structures and the basic institutional environment in village communities. The direction of agrarian change will be determined through a complex process of social interaction.

In this chapter and the two chapters which follow, we explore this process by analyzing changes in land-tenure and labor-contract relations in a major rice-growing area of the Philippines. The study covers seven provinces in Luzon—Bulacan, Nueva Ecija, Pangasinan, Pampanga and Tarlac in the region of Central Luzon, and Laguna and Rizal in the region of Southern Tagalog (Figure 4–1). Those provinces form the largest contiguous rice-producing area in the Philippines, commonly referred to as a "rice bowl". In this chapter we attempt to give a broad perspective on agrarian change in this area, which will serve as an introduction to the more intensive village case studies in the following two chapters.

Changes in Land-Tenure Systems

Needless to say, land-tenure systems are the critical determinant of resource allocation and income distribution in agrarian communities.

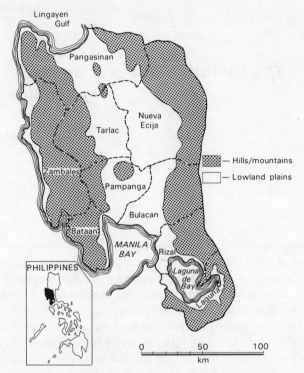

Fig. 4-1. Map of the central plain of Luzon, Philippines.

The land-tenure systems in the Philippines have recently been experiencing major changes due to land-reform programs under strong population pressure and rapid technological development. The changes have been most significant in the rice sector, because land reform efforts in the Philippines have been concentrated in rice-growing areas.

Regional Demarcation

The agrarian structures of the seven provinces under study are not homogeneous. We divide the region into two subregions: the Coastal Region and Inner Central Luzon. The Coastal Region includes Laguna, Rizal, the southern parts of Bulacan and Pampanga, and the northern part of Pangasinan. Inner Central Luzon encompasses the remaining landlocked area.

Most areas in the Coastal Region are easily accessible by sea or lake and have a long history of settlement. Laguna, southern Bulacan and Pampanga were major suppliers of rice to Manila before Inner Central

Luzon developed as a rice-producing region in the late nineteenth and early twentieth century.

Corresponding to the difference in settlement age is a major difference in the landownership pattern. Both regions are characterized by pervasive landlordism; however, landholdings in the Coastal Region are relatively small and scattered. Land accumulation here proceeded piece by piece through money-lending–mortgaging operations. In general, the landlord-tenant relationship is a paternalistic one. The landlord patronizes the tenant by advancing credit and by using his connections and influence, in return for the loyalty of the tenant (Anderson, 1964; Larkin, 1972).

In contrast, Inner Central Luzon saw the development of huge estates (*hacienda*) of from several hundred to thousands of hectares that originated from royal grants and purchases of undeveloped royal domain. The landlord-tenant relation in the large haciendas with their hundreds or thousands of tenants was inevitably less paternalistic than in the Coastal Region. Typically, the hacienda owners lived in Manila and the management was carried out by a farm manager (*encargado*) and a number of overseers (*katiwala*) (Umehara, 1974). The tenure contract was geared to economic considerations and was enforced more rigorously by legal means than by the sense of obligation based on the patron-client relationship. As a result, the haciendas became a hotbed of tenant uprisings (Dalisay, 1937; Pelzer, 1948; Rivera and McMillan, 1954). The agrarian unrest spotlighted the need for the land reform programs that have resulted in the demise of the hacienda system.

To understand the nature and the process of institutional changes in rice villages in the Philippines requires an understanding of the historical evolution of two distinct agrarian structures in the Coastal Region and Inner Central Luzon.

Pre-Hispanic Society and Hispanization

Philippine society before the Spanish conquest in the sixteenth century consisted of small communities called *barangay*—the term referred to the "boat" in which Malayan migrants voyaged to the Philippine islands. The migrants settled along the seacoasts and riverbanks and depended for their subsistence mainly on rice farming. Although no consensus has yet been established on the social structure of the *barangay*, it appears that class differentiation had already existed before the Spanish conquest; typically the *barangay* consisted of chiefs (*datu*), freemen (*timagua*), serfs or peons (*namamahay*) and slaves (*saguigilid*).[1]

[1] Some scholars assume a nobility class in addition to the chiefs, and some of them

Usually the slaves lived in quarters provided by their master and worked under his direct supervision, but the serfs, whose status was based mainly on debt peonage, lived in their own houses and turned over to the master the output of half the land that they cultivated (Pelzer, 1948, p. 88).

Land ownership was communal in the sense that the *barangay* had rights to a certain territory and that individual families had usufruct rights to specific parcels of land as long as they occupied it (Phelan, 1959, pp. 17–24). Because land was abundant and population was scarce, usufruct rights could be obtained by a community member to the amount of land that he could cultivate with the labor of his family and dependents. The source of wealth and power was the control of labor, not land. The economy was at an earlier stage than that where stipulation of private property rights in land was required for efficient resource allocation.

The Spaniards introduced, among others, one major institutional innovation—the notion of legal title to land (McLennan, 1969, p. 656). The Spaniards applied to the Philippines the same principle they applied to other new territories—that all lands except those officially proved to be private or communal possessions belonged to the Spanish crown. Thus the crown's property rights were established over vast areas of uncultivated land, including much of the *barangay* territories; that provided a basis for the establishment of large private estates later through grant and purchase of the royal domain (*realenga*). Monastic orders such as the Augustinian and Franciscan friars acquired large landholdings in the early period of the Spanish regime.

Introduction of the notion of private property rights in land opened the opportunity for the indigenous elites to encroach on communal land. The Spaniards were careful not to disturb the traditional organization of *barangay* communities and utilized them for ruling the natives. *Datu* and other leading families or *casiques*, as they were called by the Spanish, were assigned the tasks of collecting taxes, organizing compulsory labor services and administering justice at the local level. Often the *casique* advanced credit to the freemen for tax payments and, if they defaulted, established claims to both the land and labor of the indebted. In this process debt peonage, conceived as an arrangement between

---

do not distinguish two categories in the dependent class (Larkin, 1972; McLennan, 1969; Phelan, 1959). Our exposition follows Ikehata (1971) and Umehara (1976). There must have existed considerable variation in *barangay* organizations among regions.

datu and *namamahay*, shifted to a sharecropping arrangement between landlords and tenants—*kasamahan*, a Tagalog word meaning "partnership".

Such social transformation progressed only very slowly during the first 200 years of the Spanish regime. Originally the Spaniards were concerned mainly with the re-export of Chinese goods from Manila to Mexico by galleon ships and had little interest in developing domestic production within the Philippines. Outgoing cargoes of the galleons were brought to Manila by Chinese traders for transshipment to Acapulco. The galleons returned to Manila with Mexican silver. Immense profits from the monopoly of the re-export trade resulted in long neglect of the need to develop Philippine produce for the export market (Larkin, 1972, p. 42).

As both domestic and foreign demand for agricultural products were limited, land continued to be a relatively abundant resource. In such a situation the economic incentive to accumulate land would have been limited, even though the legal notion of private property rights in land had been introduced.

The Development of Landlordism in the Coastal Region

Incentives to private landholding increased sharply with the expansion in the external demand for Philippine produce due to trade liberalization in the late eighteenth century and early nineteenth century. The British occupation of Manila (1762–64) during the Seven Years' War and the subsequent opening of Manila and other ports to foreign commerce and shipments resulted in a sharp increase in the demand for commercial crops such as sugar, indigo and tobacco. Farmland became a scarce factor, which stimulated local elites to establish their exclusive rights to the use of land.

The development of landlordism was facilitated by the commercial operations of Chinese mestizos. Since before the trade liberalization, in response to the expanding consumption needs of Manila, Chinese and Chinese mestizos had developed internal trade and gained control of trade ports along the littorals of Manila Bay, the Laguna de Bay and major rivers. With the commerical wealth they accumulated, the mestizos began to acquire land by lending money to native landholders. In the money-lending arrangement called *pacto de retroventa* the lender secured control of the land as a mortgage for his loan. During the loan period, the borrower continued to cultivate the land as a sharecropper of his creditor. If unable to repay the loan at the termination of the loan period, the borrower relinquished claim to the land for a debt that usually represented only 30 to 50% of the land value (McLennan, 1969, pp. 659–660).

Land acquisitions by means of the *pacto de retroventa* arrangement increased in number in the late eighteenth century with the growth of commercial agriculture, despite Spanish attempts to prohibit the use of this device by Chinese and Chinese mestizos. In the process, not only small peasants' usufruct rights but also much of the holdings of traditional elites (*datu-casique*), characterized by those who went into debt because of their weakness for conspicuous consumption, were transferred to the hands of Chinese mestizos. Over time, the mestizos and the *casiques* intermarried and fused into a land-owning elite class called the *principalia* (Larkin, 1972, pp. 48–56).

The *pacto de retroventa* arrangement vastly expanded landlordism in the form of the sharecropping system (*kasamahan*) rooted in *barangay* communities. Because the land acquired by this device was in small parcels, the pattern of landownership molded in the eighteenth and early nineteenth century for the old settled areas of the Coastal Region was "scattered holdings" as characterized by McLennan (1969, p. 661).

In the *kasamahan* system, typically both output and production costs were shared equally by the landlord and the tenant (*kasama*). As mentioned previously, the landlord-tenant relationship was generally paternalistic in the Coastal Region. The majority of small- and medium-sized landlords lived in the *poblacion* (urban portion) and had close contacts with their tenants and their families in the *barrios* (villages) in the same municipality, often developing close personal relationships such as being godfather (*compadre*) to their children. The landlord patronized his tenants by advancing credit and utilizing his connections and social influence, in return for the loyalty of the tenants. "In a society built on patronage, having such a patron is highly valued" (Murray, 1972, p. 161). To behave like a benevolent patron was the efficient way for a landlord to establish his status as a legitimate member of the elite and the least costly way to protect his property and to enforce his contract with the tenants in the local community.

Emergence of the Hacienda in Inner Central Luzon

In contrast to the scattered holdings in the Coastal Region, huge estates (*hacienda*) of several hundreds or thousands of hectares were developed in Inner Central Luzon. According to McLennan, the *hacienda* system originated in the *inquilino* or *inquilinato* system in the friar estates located in the environs of the coastal area along Manila

Bay. Stimulated by expanding trade in rice and sugar, many of the monastic orders began to lease pasture and idle land to agricultural entrepreneurs. These lessees (*inquilino*) turned the task of cultivation over to sharecroppers, paid fixed rent to the landowners and reaped middlemen's profits:

> The *inquilinato* system, born on the friar estates in the eighteenth century, was an innovation in Philippine society and was an alternative response to the growing commercialization of the economy. Land was leased by an *inquilino* for a fixed rent. Usually the *inquilino* immediately turned the land over to a *kasama* to cultivate for shares. From its inception the *inquilinato* system had a significantly greater economic-rational emphasis. It was a means of freeing the landowner from much of the paternal relationship traditionally expected of him in Philippine society. While the monastic orders had intended that their *inquilinos* would be the cultivators, the *inquilinos*, by putting *kasamas* on the land, restored to some degree a paternal relationship to the cultivator although the tracts leased were frequently so large and occupied by so many *kasamas* that the paternal role of the *inquilino* was considerably diluted, particularly when the *inquilino* did not live on the land. Many did not, the leased land merely being a source of produce for their commercial activities. It was here on the friar lands that the hacienda system was born and it is not surprising, therefore, that the earliest tenant discontent appeared on the friar estates (McLennan, 1969, p. 666).

Private haciendas were established through royal grants and purchases of royal domain. This process of land acquisition by the Spaniards began in the eighteenth century after the removal of restrictions on Spanish residence in the provinces. The royal grants and the large-scale purchases were concentrated in the frontiers of settlement—Inner Central Luzon—"which accounts for the distribution of today's large haciendas" (McLennan, 1969, p. 668).

Until the late nineteenth century, most areas in Inner Central Luzon were covered by jungle, and the large haciendas were primarily engaged in cattle ranching. The cattle raising came to an end during the 1880s when a series of rinderpest and hoof-and-mouth disease epidemics decimated cattle herds. Subsequently, the haciendas located in the lowland areas developed a system of rice monoculture manned by the tenants who had migrated from Ilocos and Southern Tagalog, while those located in upland areas were converted into sugar plantations.

In the early stage of the development of rice haciendas, the common tenure arrangement was the fixed-rent leasehold (*canon*). The *haci-enderos* gave parcels gratis to settlers for the period of land opening, and requested only nominal rents even after the gratis period ended. However, as the population and the labor force grew, the *canon* was raised gradually, and finally it shifted into the *kasama* system (Hester and Mabbun, 1924). In many cases settlers opened new land in the belief that it was no man's land. Later, the agents of the landlords in Manila notified them that they were squatters and liable for rent payments unless they wanted to be evicted. Most of them agreed to pay because the rent requested originally was only nominal. However, the landlords' attempts to raise rent in later years met with serious resistance and disruption.

The indignation of peasants was especially great when their lands were grabbed by landlords through the registration of land titles. The Spanish government issued royal decrees in 1880 and 1894, attempting to encourage landholders to secure formal titles with the intention of promoting commerical agricultural production. Later, in 1913, the American government initiated cadastral surveys and land registration under the Torrens system. These government policies attempting to modernize land registry opened up rare opportunities for land grabbing by powerful elites. Where the majority of illiterate peasants, accustomed to unwritten rules of land tenure, were ignorant about the new laws, unscrupulous elites registered their land to claim extensive areas occupied by smallholders (McLennan, 1969, p. 673; Pelzer, 1948, pp. 89–90 and 108–110). This process occurred in the Coastal Region too, but it was more pervasive in the frontier areas of Inner Central Luzon where the power structure was more unevenly distributed and where indigenous property-rights relations were less clearly established in local communities. Agrarian unrest in Inner Central Luzon was thus deeply rooted in the historical process of land accumulation.

Furthermore, as mentioned previously, the landlord-tenant relation in the large haciendas was inevitably less paternalistic and based on more strict contracts.[2] Usually, the hacienda owner living in Manila had no personal contact with his tenant and had no concern for the tenant's personal problems. Unlike the small and the medium landlords in the Coastal Region, they were powerful enough to protect their property through the police and a private army and to enforce contracts by legal means. In general, *kasamas* were bound to the hacienda by perpetual debt which often forced them to surrender most of their

[2] It was a common practice for tenants to sign detailed written contracts with haci-endas, while written contracts were rare outside haciendas until land reform. For the hacienda tenancy contract, see Umehara (1974).

produce to the hacienda manager at harvest time. It was natural that the class confrontation between landlords and tenants was sharpest in the hacienda areas of Inner Central Luzon, as represented by the Hukbalahap (or Huk) revolt during and after World War II (Kerkvliet, 1977).

Land Reform

Pervasive landlordism in the Philippines was a heritage of colonialism resulting from the imposition of private property rights in land at a stage of the economy when technology and resource endowments were still consistent with communal ownership. Serious social unrest was inevitable because of the "deformed" agrarian structure and land-tenure relations.[3] Land reform was resorted to as a means of correcting the deformed structure for the survival of the capitalistic system.

The first step taken under the American regime was the expropriation of the friar lands. The friar estates had been confiscated and distributed among the peasants by the independent government at Malolos during the Philippine Revolution. But the Treaty of Paris (1898), which concluded the Spanish-American War, bound the United States to protect the property rights of the monastic orders. In order to avoid agrarian conflicts, the American administration decided to buy these estates. The purchase of about 200,000 ha for $6.9 million was completed in 1905 (Pelzer,1948, pp. 90–91). Government purchase of private estates for redistribution among smallholders was also undertaken during the Commonwealth period but never implemented on a large scale (Murray, 1972, p. 154).

The American colonial administration also tried to mitigate agrarian unrest through the resettlement of tenants on public lands following the precedent of homesteading on the American frontier. The homestead policy not only was unsuccessful in the socio-economic environment of the Philippines but also promoted agrarian conflicts because the cadastral surveys and land registration involved in homesteading created opportunities for land-grabbing (Pelzer, 1948, pp. 104–114).

Another measure to cope with mounting agrarian unrest was government regulation of landlord-tenant relations. In 1933, under the administration of Governor General Theodore Roosevelt, the Philippine legislature passed the Rice Share Tenancy Act (Public Act No. 4054) aimed at protecting the *kasamas* against abuses by the landlords.

---

[3] "Deformed" in the sense that the agrarian structure deviated from the one which would have been created in the absence of premature imposition of property-rights relations by the colonial power.

However, the law could go into effect "only in provinces where the majority of the municipal councils shall, by resolutions, petition for its application to the Governor General". With this provision the law was ineffective because the *principalia* controlled the municipalities. Subsequent amendments designed to make the law effective were invalidated by the resistance of the *principalia* class (Kerkvliet, 1971; Pelzer, 1948, pp. 98–101).

The need for land reform was more keenly felt with the Huk revolt in the period immediately following World War II. The United States government, seriously involved in the Cold War context, obliged the Philippines to undertake social reform as a condition for receiving aid. In this connection Robert Hardie, a land reform specialist, was brought to the Philippines by the American Mutual Security Agency. The Hardie Report (1952) recommended (a) abolition of tenancy, (b) establishment of owner-operated family-sized farms, (c) fair tenancy practices. The report created a major controversy because it denied the effectiveness of the traditional policy of land resettlement and advocated a redistributive land reform with the expropriation of holdings above 4 ha.

Although the Hardie Report was not seriously considered at the administrative and the legislative levels, it paved the way for a modified, but still "radically oriented", land reform program under President Ramon Magsaysay. Magsaysay, who had led the battle to subdue the Huk rebellion, was well aware of the social unrest that supported the Huk movement. The Magsaysay reform programs were based on the Agricultural Tenancy Act (Republic Act No. 1199) in 1954 and the Land Reform Act (Republic Act No. 1400) in 1955; the former was intended to enforce fair tenancy practices and the latter was designed to expropriate and redistribute large estates. Because of resistance from the landed interests, in the process of passage by the Congress both Acts were so watered down as to leave little of the original proposal intact (Wurfel, 1958). The Land Tenure Administration was set up for the expropriation and the redistribution of large estates. However, the estates to which the program was applicable were limited to those larger than 300 ha and petitioned by a majority of tenants. Due to landlord resistance, inefficient administration and inadequate financial backing, the total area expropriated by the Land Tenancy Administration during the first six years after its establishment was less than 20,000 ha (Takigawa, 1976, p. 23).

The Agricultural Land Reform Code, enacted in 1963 under President Diosdado Macapagal, represented a major advancement in agrarian reform legislation in line with the liberal reform tradition aimed at achieving social stability and economic progress by emancipating peasants from "feudal" bondage. The stated goal was "to establish owner-cultivatorship and the economic family-sized farm . . . to make the small farmers more independent, self-reliant and responsible citizens, and a source of genuine strength in our democracy" (Section 2, Republic Act No. 3844). Macapagal, the son of a peasant in Pampanga, saw land reform as a critical countermeasure against the latent danger of communist infiltration into the rural sector, a danger compounded by the growing tension in Southeast Asia with the spread of the Vietnam War. His idea was supported by the urban industrialist class fostered by the import-substitution industrialization policy begun in 1950 (Takigawa, 1976, pp. 31–37). The interest of urban commerce and industry was reflected in the stipulation of the Code that one of the reform goals was to "divert landlord capital to industrial development" (Section 2).

A new aspect of the Agricultural Land Reform Code distinct from earlier legislation was that the land reform was considered a major means to increase agricultural productivity—as stated in the Code, "to create a truly viable social and economic structure in agriculture conducive to greater productivity and higher farm incomes." As pointed out by Vernon Ruttan (1964), the emphasis on the role of land-tenure reform in raising agricultural productivity was based on young economist-technocrats' assumption of inefficient resource allocation under the sharecropping arrangement according to the traditional neoclassical theory (see Chapter 2). But more basically it reflected the demand of urban commerce and industry for rapid gains in agricultural productivity to ensure the supply of cheap food for urban workers in order to keep their living costs and wages low. In order to achieve the goal of high productivity, the Code made provisions to create the Agricultural Credit Administration and the Agricultural Productivity Commission to advance credit and technical extension services to small landholders.

The major thrust of the Code was the creation of owner-cultivatorship in rice and corn land. This involves two steps: first, "Operation Leasehold", which converts share tenancy to leasehold tenancy with rent fixed at the rate of 25% of average harvest for three normal years preceding the Operation; second, "Operation Land Transfer", which transfers landownership to tenants. In the latter operation government expropriates land in excess of landlords' retention limit (75 ha) with compensation to landlords of 10% of the land value in cash and the rest in interest-free redeemable Land Bank bonds. The land is resold to the tenants for annual amortization payments within 25 years.

Land reform operations based on the 1963 Agricultural Land Reform Code were limited mainly to pilot areas in Central Luzon, and its implementation at any level of intensity was confined to the pilot project in Nueva Ecija (de los Reyes, 1972). The Code was amended in 1971 under President Marcos to extend land reform to the whole nation, with automatic conversion of all share tenants to leaseholders. The 1971 Code was enforced by Presidential Decrees No. 2 and No. 27 under the Martial Law proclaimed in 1972. The landlord's retention limit was reduced successively from 75 ha to 7 ha. The period of amortization payments was shortened to 15 years.

It is easy to enumerate the shortcomings of the land reform programs in the Philippines. The retention limit is still too high compared with the average farm size, and it is often evaded by registering excess holdings in the names of relatives and friends. The land reform applies only to tenanted land planted in rice and corn. It does not apply to land under the direct administration of landlords. Nor does it apply to land used for cash crops such as sugar. Therefore, it is a widespread practice for landlords to expand the area under their direct management by evicting tenants under the guise of voluntary submission of land from tenants to landlords or in order to plant sugar in paddy land. Often collusion between landed elites and local officials invalidates the effect of the land reform programs. Operation Land Transfer has been particularly slow, and its effect has been limited.

Despite such apparent failures, it is a fact that large haciendas in Central Luzon have been broken down and that most tenants have established their status as leaseholders or amortizing owners, though sizable areas remain under landlords' direct administration. Similar to the *zamindari* system in India, the hacienda system had been the symbol of colonial exploitation in the mind of the general public. The abolition of such a system is not too difficult because large landed elites such as haciendos and zamindars are minorities, however powerful they are, and they themselves have few roots in rural communities. Extension of land reform programs to medium and small landlords is far more difficult because these landlords themselves are large in number and they make alliances with relatively wealthy peasants who are eager to expand their holdings. In developing countries in Asia in general, the strong resistance of these middle elites who have solid control over local politics and bureaucracies is the major block to the implementation of redistributive land reform beyond the expropriation of a few large estates (Joshi, 1970).

It is clear that the beneficiaries of land reform have been capturing a large economic surplus because rice yields have been increasing signiflcantly due to irrigation development and application of new varieties and fertilizers, while rent and amortization payments have been fixed. Thus, the land reform has been successful in transferring much of the economic return to land from absentee landlords to ex-sharecroppers. On the other hand, it has created serious income inequality within village communities because no gain has accrued to landless laborers, whose income did not rise or even declined because the strong population pressure on land prevented their wages from rising despite agricultural productivity increases. One consequence has been the emergence of a sub-tenancy arrangement similar to the *inquilinato* system in the friar lands during the Spanish period: the leaseholder turns the task of cultivation over to landless laborers under a sharecropping arrangement despite the land reform regulations prohibiting the practice. Such responses at the village community level to land reform, technological change and population pressure will be investigated in detail using case studies in Chapters 5 and 6.

Changes in Labor Contract Relations: The Case of Rice Harvesting[4]

Before proceeding to intensive village case studies in the next two chapters, we will try in this section to develop a broad perspective on the nature of institutional innovations at the village level through an extensive survey of the changes in rice harvesting contract and technology in the rice bowl of the Philippines.

The labor required for harvesting and threshing rice in Southeast Asia is nearly 30% of total labor and 50% of total hired labor. As a result, harvesting and threshing represent major employment opportunities for landless workers and for small farmers whose incomes from farming are insufficient to meet their subsistence need. Therefore, choice of technology and contractual arrangements with respect to the use of labor and capital for rice harvesting and threshing is a critical determinant of income distribution in village communities.

In the Philippines, the crop is usually cut by hand, but threshing methods vary from hand beating to large mechanical threshers. In general, the more mechanized the threshing operation, the smaller the laborers' share of the harvesting cost. Interacting with the choice of threshing technology are several contractual arrangements. The choice

---

[4] This section draws heavily on Kikuchi and Hayami (1980c) and Kikuchi, Cordova, Marciano and Hayami (1979).

of technology and contractual arrangement depends partly on relative prices of capital and labor and partly on technical conditions such as irrigation and seed varieties (Hayami and Ruttan, 1971). It also depends on risk, such as that of insufficient labor at the peak of harvesting, and transaction costs, such as those involved in labor recruitment, management, and work enforcement (see Chapter 2).

In addition, the mix depends on social and institutional environments in the rural community. The landlord-tenant relationship is an especially critical factor. Responsibility for the payment of harvesting costs depends on the tenure types, which range from fixed-rent lease-holding to sharecropping with costsharing arrangements. Share-tenants may not be free to choose the method of harvesting.

Thus, the choice of harvesting arrangement depends on many economic and social factors. Changes in such factors induce changes in rice harvesting arrangements. In the Philippines, dramatic changes have been occurring in response to growing population pressure; land reform; improvements in irrigation systems, land preparation and crop establishment; and the introduction of modern rice varieties.

Let us try to identify the geographic and historical patterns of change in harvesting and threshing arrangements in the seven provinces under study in relation to changes in economic and social factors.

Two Harvesting Systems

We have demarcated the rice-producing area of the central Luzon plain into the Coastal Region and Inner Central Luzon. The former was characterized by long-term settlement and scattered small landholdings, and the latter was characterized by relatively recent settlement and large estates or haciendas. Two distinct systems of rice harvesting were developed for those regions.

The harvesting system traditionally practiced in the Coastal Region was the one called the *hunusan* system. *Hunusan* is a form of contract by which, when a farmer specifies a day of harvesting, anyone can participate in harvesting and threshing, and the harvesters receive a certain share of the output.[5] The share ranges from one-fourth to one-ninth, but traditionally one-sixth was the most common. The typical land tenure arrangement before the land reform was such that the

---

[5] The *hunusan* system has a long history. Before sickles were introduced, it was a common practice in the Philippines as well as other countries in Asia to cut panicles using hand knives (*ani-ani*) with mass participation of village people. The harvested panicles were bundled, and the harvesters received one out of six bundles. For the traditional harvesting systems in the Philippines, see Africa (1920).

output was divided half and half between landlords and tenants after the share of the harvesters was deducted. In this system the crop is cut manually with sickles and the threshing is done by hand beating on wooden or bamboo plates.

A different system, which we call the *tilyadora* system, used to be practiced in Inner Central Luzon. The *tilyadora* system is characterized by the use of big threshing machines called *tilyadora* (or *trilladora*). The *tilyadora* threshers are of a McCormick-Deering design. The first few machines imported from the United States during the 1910s were run by steam engines, but these were replaced during the 1920s and 1930s by a design run by a belt pulley from a tractor of 40 to 50 horsepower. Threshing by *tilyadora* is generally done in one central location on a farm where unthreshed crops are hauled and stored in large stacks called *mandala* until the *tilyadora* arrives. Despite the mechanization of the threshing process, the crop cutting is done by hand with sickles. However, the labor contract under the *tilyadora* system is entirely different from that for *hunusan*. With *tilyadora*, crop cutting and threshing become two separate operations. It is difficult to share output at the stage of crop cutting because of the difficulty of ascertaining the quantity of grain per bundle.[6] Therefore, harvesters are employed at a fixed daily wage rate (*upahan*) or for a fixed payment for a certain area harvested (*pakyaw*). The cost of harvesting is shouldered by the tenants.[7] The threshing fee charged by the *tilyadora* operators (from 4 to 6% of output) is deducted before the output is shared between landlords and tenants.[8]

Historically, a distinct geographic distribution between the two harvesting systems was developed. In order to identify the historical pattern, we have searched for harvesting contracts in past studies and documents. Those we have found for the period from 1920 to 1964 are

[6] It is easier to standardize the grain quantity per bundle when crops are cut at the neck of panicles with hand knives than when they are cut at the bottom of the plants with sickles. Crop sharing by bundle is especially common in Indonesia where knife cutting is still common. However, even in Indonesia, crop sharing for harvesters has recently been shifting from bundle terms to threshed grain terms as sickle cutting has been introduced. See Chapter 7.

[7] In the share-tenancy contract under the *hunusan* system the cost of harvesting as well as other expenses such as seeds, fertilizers and transplanting are commonly shared half-and-half by tenants and landlords. Under the *tilyadora* system, the crop-cutting cost is shouldered by tenants and the transplanting cost is shouldered by landlords, while the other costs are shared half and half.

[8] In reality, wide variations existed for each category of harvesting system. There were cases where the fixed wage contract was used together with animal treading instead of *tilyadora*. There were also cases where the *hunusan* harvesters used mechanical threshers; in this case, the harvesters usually paid for the machine rental from their share of output.

Fig. 4-2. Traditional pattern in the regional distribution of different harvesting systems, based on past studies.

Note: The names of persons conducting the surveys and the survey years are placed outside and inside parentheses, respectively.

Sources: Africa (1920), Anderson (1964), Hester and Mabbun (1924), Rivera and McMillan (1954), Takahashi (1969).

plotted in Figure 4–2, which clearly shows a demarcation between the Coast Region and Inner Central Luzon.

Historical Perspective

A major question is why the two different systems of rice harvesting with respect to the use of technology and type of contract were developed in two regions within a geographically contiguous and ecologically homogeneous area.[9] The answer should be sought in the different agrarian structures of the two regions.

[9] The two regions have similar climatic patterns subject to the influence of the southwest monsoon and have the same farming systems except for harvesting and threshing. On the average, irrigation systems are better developed in the Coastal Region than in Inner Central Luzon. But there are a number of districts in Inner Central Luzon where the irrigation systems are equally well established.

The introduction of *tilyadora* in Inner Central Luzon can be partly explained by a relative shortage of labor in a newly settled area. However, a more important reason appears to be that *tilyadora* was used by hacienda owners to collect share rent. Under the sharecropping system the first requirement for collecting the right amount of rent was to ascertain the quantity of output.

In the Coastal Region, where paternalistic relations between landlords and tenants were highly developed, the landlords could largely trust the honesty of their tenants in their report on the crop harvested (Anderson, 1964); to look at it in another way, the tenants would not have dared to cheat the landlords so much as to risk the patron-client relationship with their landlords, who usually lived in the same municipalities and had fairly accurate ideas of the crop yields in respective years. Thereby the transaction cost involved in the collection of share rent was relatively modest, even if the traditional *hunusan* system was used for harvesting.

Such conditions did not exist in the large haciendas in Inner Central Luzon. In order to manage the sharecropping system in a hacienda, it was critical to develop a method of ascertaining output on a large number of tenant farms. The *tilyadora* was the answer. In the haciendas, the tenants were requested to store their harvested crops in certain locations. *Tilyadoras* hired by the haciendas for a custom-service contract went around to those locations for threshing operations under the supervision of overseers. The quantities threshed were measured at the threshing sites, and landlords' shares were taken away after the threshing fees were deducted. No chance of cheating was left for the tenants. Of course, there were alternative ways to collect share rents. But, given the socioeconomic and technical conditions in those days, especially with the general hostility among tenants against haciendedros, *tilyadora* would have represented the most efficient way to collect the share rents.[10]

It appears possible that *tilyadora* was the factor underlying the emergence of the sharecropping system in the haciendas. Sharecropping (*kasama*) had been a common form of tenancy in Inner Central Luzon until the recent land reform. However, in the earlier stage of the development of rice haciendas, the common tenure arrangement was the leasehold at a fixed rent (*canon*). As explained previously, in the beginning of settlement, the haciendedros charged settlers only nominal rents. As population and labor force grew, the *canon* rose gradually, and

---

[10] For sharecroppers' resistance to hacienda management in the form of cheating and shirking, which gave the haciendedros an incentive to mechanize, see Kerkvliet (1977).

finally shifted into the *kasama* system).[11] The shift from leasehold to share tenancy can be understood as based on the preference of hacienderos to raise the average rate of land rent at the expense of shouldering a part of the risk involved in rice production (see Chapter 2).

The shift in tenure status took place largely during the 1920s and 1930s. The census of 1903 indicates that there were 2,215 cash tenants and only 290 share tenants in Nueva Ecija. The 1918 census reveals a transition, with 2,796 cash tenants and 1,798 share tenants. By 1939, the transition was complete in Nueva Ecija with only 867 cash tenants and 50,831 share tenants. The 1920s and 1930s were also the years when the *tilyadora* became the common method of threshing.[12]

This concurrent growth in the share tenancy system and the use of *tilyadora* suggests that the major factor underlying the diffusion of the *tilyadora* system in Inner Central Luzon was the motivation of hacienderos to reduce the transaction cost required for the collection of share rent and that the *tilyadora* facilitated the conversion of the land tenure system from one of leasehold to one of share tenancy.[13] The *tilyadora* was not adopted in the Coastal Region because the scope of reduction in the transaction cost expected from its introduction was much smaller where paternalistic relations between landlords and tenants applied.

Changing Patterns

The best data to test our hypothesis (suggested from historical observations) were those on the recent changes in the harvesting system in Inner Central Luzon. We should expect, if the introduction of *tilyadora* was mainly based on the motivation of hacienderos to reduce the transaction cost involved in the collection of share rent, that the *tilyadora* system was abandoned when the land reform programs broke the hacienda system and abolished the share tenancy system.

[11] Although the shift from *canon* to the *kasama* system was found widely in Nueva Ecija where large haciendas were pervasive, it was also observed in other areas in Inner Central Luzon such as Northeastern Pampanga.

[12] Data on the number of *tilyadora* threshers are not available. However, according to the sales records of the International Harvester Company, the number of threshers shipped to the Philippines increased from only 3 in 1926 to 37 in 1939 (data are available only for those two years before 1940) (personal communication from Mr. Greg Lennes, Corporate Archivist, International Harvester, Chicago, August 31, 1978).

[13] The results of our personal interviews with aged people, including the ex-manager of a hacienda, who witnessed the process of tenure change are consistent with the hypothesis that the sharecropping system could not have been adopted in the haciendas without *tilyadora*.

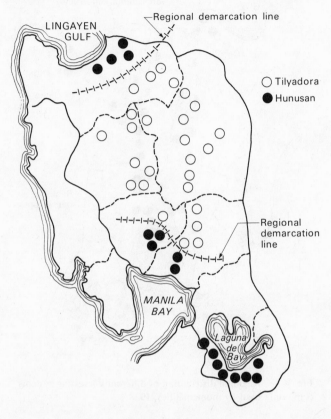

Fig. 4-3. Regional distribution of different harvesting systems commonly used by municipalities, 1968.

In order to test the hypothesis, we conducted a two-stage survey, with the first round in February 1978 and the second in July 1978, covering 100 farms in 43 municipalities (data are summarized in Appendix B). The sample consisted of the farms covered by the Central Luzon/Laguna Loop Surveys conducted by the International Rice Research Institute in 1966, 1970 and 1974. Historical information was supplemented from those earlier surveys.

The result of the survey was highly consistent with our hypothesis. The land reform operations resulted in the demise of rice haciendas, mostly within the 1968–75 period. Correspondingly, major changes in harvesting systems occurred. Our survey data show that the regional distribution of harvesting systems in 1968 was essentially the same as

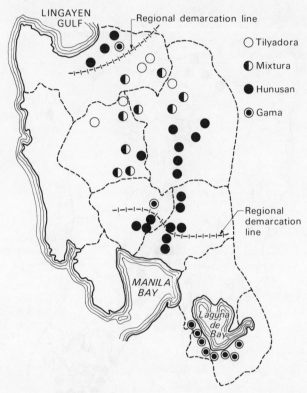

Fig. 4-4.   Regional distribution of different harvesting systems commonly used by municipalities, 1978.

the traditional pattern (compare Figure 4–3 with Figure 4–2).[14] However, by 1978 an entirely different pattern had emerged (Figure 4–4).

The most dramatic change was, as expected, a shift from the *tilyadora* system to the *hunusan* system. In 1968, 96% of the sample farmers in Inner Central Luzon used the *tilyadora* system. However, the percentage declined sharply to 33% by 1978 (Table 4–1), even though the services of *tilyadoras* for hire with operators continued to be available as before. The majority of the farmers shifted completely to the *hunusan* system with hand threshing for both wet and dry seasons or adopted the new system partially for the wet season while using the traditional system for the dry season ("mixture").

[14] The marks in Figures 4–3 and 4–4 represent municipalities. There were variations in harvesting systems within each municipality. Systems as marked in the figures were the ones most commonly practiced in the municipalities.

Table 4-1.   Changes in rice harvesting arrangements in seven provinces in the central plain of Luzon, 1968 to 1978.[a]

	Coastal Region		Inner Central Luzon		Total	
	No.	(%)	No.	(%)	No.	(%)
1968						
Tilyadora system	0	(0)	68	(96)	68	(72)
Output sharing system:						
Hunusan	20	(83)	3	(4)	23	(24)
Gama	4	(17)	0	(0)	4	(4)
Mixture	0	(0)	0	(0)	0	(0)
Total	24	(100)	71	(100)	95	(100)
1978						
Tilyadora system	0	(0)	25	(33)	25	(25)
Output sharing system:						
Hunusan	11	(44)	36	(48)	47	(47)
Gama	14	(56)	8	(11)	22	(22)
Mixture	0	(0)	6	(8)	6	(6)
Total	25	(100)	75	(100)	100	(100)

[a] The *tilyadora* system is the system in which harvesting is done by hired labor with fixed wages (either *upahan* or *pakyaw*) and threshing is done by *tilyadora*. In the output-sharing system, harvesters get a certain percentage of total rice output as wages in kind. If a farmer adopts the output-sharing system in the wet season and the *tilyadora* system in the dry season, he is classified under "Mixture". The total number of farmers in 1968 is less than that in 1978 because five sample farmers began farming after 1968.

Another major change was the rapid diffusion of a new contractual arrangement called *gama* in the Coastal Region. *Gama* is an output-sharing arrangement similar to *hunusan* except that employment for harvesting and threshing is limited to workers who worked on the weeding of the field without receiving wages; in other words, in the *gama* system weeding labor is a free service of workers to establish a right to participate in harvesting and threshing and to receive a certain share, usually one-sixth, of the harvest.[15] In 1968, 83% of sample farms in the Coastal Region used the *hunusan* system; the ratio declined to less than 50% due to the spread of the *gama* system by 1978.

[15] This system originated in the province of Laguna and was called *gama* from a Tagalog word, *gamas*, meaning "weeding". A variation of the system, called *atorga* in Pampanga, is to request free service of pulling of seedlings to establish a right to be employed as harvesters (Bautista, 1977). Another variation in Pangasinan is to give the harvesting right to the workers who provided free transplanting service. In this study, these variations are grouped together under the name of *gama*. A system similar to the *gama* system is also found outside of Luzon; in Iloilo it is called *sagod* (Ledesma, 1980).

From Tilyadora to Hand Threshing

The shift from the *tilyadora* system to the *hunusan* system was not uniform within Inner Central Luzon. The shift was most complete in the eastern part of the region, especially northern Bulacan and south-to-central Nueva Ecija, where the *hunusan* system was adopted by most farmers for both wet and dry seasons (Figure 4–4).

In the western part of Inner Central Luzon (Southern Pangasinan, Tarlac and Northern Pampanga), the diffusion of the new system was slower and its adoption is partial in the sense that the *hunusan* system is used for the wet season only. In Figure 4–5 the years of shift of sample farmers from the *tilyadora* system to the *hunusan* system are compared with the years of shift in their tenure status from sharecroppers to leaseholders or amortizing owners. The fact that no observation lies below the 45-degree line is consistent with the hypothesis that *tilyadora* was introduced in order to facilitate hacienda management under the sharecropping system and that, therefore, a change in tenure status was a precondition for a shift in the harvesting system. In the figure, almost all the observations in our sample from northern Bulacan and south-central Nueva Ecija are located on the 45-degree line, im-

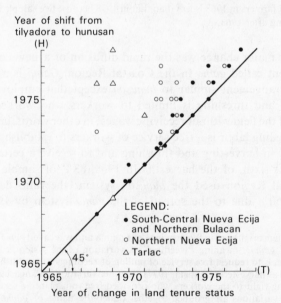

Fig. 4-5. Relation between the year of shift in the harvesting system and the year of change in land tenure status.

plying that most farmers shifted from the *tilyadora* system to the *hunusan* system in the years of their tenure change.

Sample observations from northern Nueva Ecija and Tarlac are located above the 45-degree line in Figure 4-5 indicating that time lags were involved in the shifts from the *tilyadora* to the *hunusan* system. A regression equation was estimated with the year of the adoption of *hunusan* (H) as a dependent variable and with the year of tenure change (T) and regional dummies (D_n for northern Nueva Ecija and D_t for Tarlac) as independent variables. The least-square estimation with the sample of 40 farmers for which data are available resulted in

$$H = 4.78 + 0.94T + 1.64D_n + 4.61D_t, \qquad R^2 = 0.683$$
$$\quad (8.43) \quad (0.12) \quad (0.59) \quad (0.92)$$

where the figures in parentheses are the standard errors of the estimated parameters, and R^2 is the coefficient of determination.

The results of the regression analysis show that the intercept is not significantly different from zero and that T's coefficient is not significantly different from one at conventional levels. These results support the hypothesis that the relation between H and T is the 45-degree line. In other words, the estimated relation between H and T implies that the shift from *tilyadora* to *hunusan* occurred as soon as the tenure status changed, except for regional time lags. The coefficients of D_n and D_t indicate that the shift in the harvesting system lagged behind the tenure change, 1.6 years on average for farmers in northern Nueva Ecija and 4.5 years in Tarlac.

Such time lags seem to reflect the geographic route and direction of the diffusion of the *hunusan* system. According to the information obtained from the interviews in our survey, the concept of the *hunusan* system that diffused in Inner Central Luzon during the past decade came from Laguna and southern Bulacan.

The medium of diffusion of the concept was primarily seasonal migrant workers. Most farmers that we interviewed replied that workers from the south who migrated to their farms at harvesting season or workers in their villages who returned from harvesting work in the south asked the farmers to adopt the *hunusan* system.

Because of the geographical affinity to the origin, the diffusion of the *hunusan* system first began in the eastern part of Inner Central Luzon and then moved to the north and the west, as illustrated in Figure 4–6. It appears that direct diffusion from southern Pampanga to Tarlac was blocked by the wide sugar cane belt covering both sides of the two provinces. The diffusion from the coastal area of Pangasinan to the

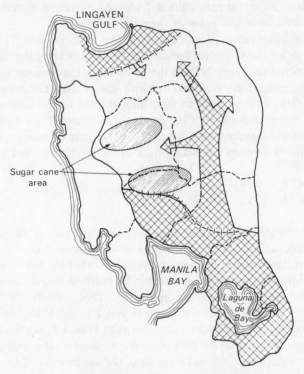

Fig. 4-6. The pattern of diffusion of the *hunusan* system.

south was not very significant, perhaps because of the lack of large-scale migration for harvesting workers.

The speed with which farmers in Bulacan and Nueva Ecija shifted from the *tilyadora* system to the *hunusan* system after the land tenure change may partly be explained by the revulsion against *tilyadora* as a symbol of the exploitative hacienda system. It must be recognized, however, that although the land-tenure reform was the basic condition for the shift from the *tilyadora* to the *hunusan* system, technological developments in rice production had made the use of *tilyadora* less efficient before the reform. First, during the 1960s the area under irrigation expanded greatly, especially in Nueva Ecija with the construction of the Upper Pampanga River System. Second, in the late 1960s a dramatic diffusion began of modern rice varieties (MV) with short-maturing and non-photosensitive characteristics. Those developments made the double-cropping of rice a common practice.

In the single-cropping system with traditional photosensitive varieties, rice crops mature after November when the day becomes shorter and the rainy season is over. Because the weather is dry, harvested crops can be stored in the fields without the danger of spoilage until the *tilyadora* arrives. However, in the double-cropping system, the modern varieties mature before the rainy season is over. Since heavy *tilyadora* cannot enter wet fields, the harvested crops must be hauled for long distances to available dry spots. The risk of crop damage is also large due to a possible delay in the arrival of the *tilyadora*.

Despite such conditions, the farmers were not able to abandon the *tilyadora* system as long as the regulations of the haciendas were still in force. It seems reasonable to hypothesize that the farmers' accumulated frustration resulted in an overnight switch to hand threshing when they were emancipated by the land-tenure reform.

As a test of this hypothesis, we estimated a regression equation: the dependent variable is the time interval between the years of shift from *tilyadora* to hand threshing (H) and of change in the tenure status (T), and the independent variable is the time interval between T and the year of introduction of the rice double-cropping system (M). We expect that the longer the interval between T and M, the more clearly farmers can recognize the inefficiency of the *tilyadora* system and, therefore, the shorter the interval between H and T will be.

The least-square estimation based on the sample of 26 farmers for which data were available resulted in

$$(H - T) = 0.39 - 0.66 \ (T - M), \qquad R^2 = 0.582$$
$$(0.33) \quad (0.12)$$

where the figures in parentheses are the standard errors of the coefficients and R^2 is the coefficient of determination. The results are consistent with our hypothesis, showing the significant effect of the time interval between the tenure change and the introduction of double-cropping in reducing the time lag between the tenure change and the shift in the harvesting arrangement.

From Hunusan to Gama

While the *hunusan* system has been newly adopted in Inner Central Luzon, it has been replaced rapidly by the *gama* system in the Coastal Region. The shift from *hunusan* to *gama* was already completed in Laguna by 1978. In other areas, however, *hunusan* is still a common practice.

The *gama* can be considered an institutional innovation to reduce the wage rate under the traditional *hunusan* system in which the harvesters receive one-sixth of the output. In earlier days, when the rice yield per hectare was low and labor was scarce, the one-sixth share of output under the *hunusan* system would have been a wage rate fairly close to the marginal productivity of labor for harvesting work. However, as the yield per hectare increased and the labor supply became more abundant, the one-sixth share could have become substantially higher than the marginal productivity of labor, because much less than a one-percent increase in labor is normally required to harvest a one-percent increase in yield per ha.

In such a situation, farmers could increase their incomes by replacing the *hunusan* with the labor of daily fixed-wage workers (*upahan*). However, it would involve substantial friction to change a long-established custom in the village community such as the one-sixth share. Also, although labor is normally abundant, there is a risk involved for an individual farmer who may not be able to find a sufficient number of daily wage workers at the right time.

The *gama* system is another way to reduce the wage rate, because the one-sixth share covers the costs of both weeding and harvesting; it involves less social friction because it is in harmony with long-established custom. In addition, *gama* has the merit of saving the cost of monitoring weeding labor because an incentive scheme is incorporated in the output sharing. Also, the availability of labor at the harvesting time is guaranteed by contract. From the employee's side, the *gama* is more secure; it involves less risk of being left without employment.

New rice technology also underlay the development of the *gama* system. The increased fertilizer application and use of young seedlings associated with the adoption of MV increased the weed population in the highly fertilized soil. With the use of young seedlings, it became difficult to control weeds by flooding fields because of the danger of drowning the short seedlings in their early growth stage.[16] A large amount of weeding work had to be completed in a short period of time—a task the family was unable to handle (Smith and Gascon, 1979, pp. 5–6). Thus, underlying the farmers' choice of weeding as a supplementary job to request of the harvesters was the increased demand for weeding labor. The *gama* system developed and spread very rapidly in Laguna where increases in rice yields were especially large due to an improved irrigation system and earlier and more complete diffusion of modern rice technology. The system seems to be still in an early stage of diffusion in southern Bulacan and Pampanga.

[16] Young seedlings 9 to 14 days after seeding are commonly used in Laguna, according to the seedbed preparation method called the *dapog* method. In this method seeds are sown on a bed made of banana leaves placed on cemented or dry clay ground.

Calculus of Technological and Contractual Choice

It appears that the dramatic changes in rice harvesting technology and contract in the Philippines not only reflect the farmers' desire to maximize private profit but also result from the social interactions in village communities, especially those among farmers and landless workers. A system was chosen not simply because it was economically profitable for individual farmers but also because it was acceptable in terms of the social and institutional environment of the village communities.

In the village community, where traditional customs often overrule formal laws and police forces, the cost of enforcing a contract could be very high if the contract is of a type which violates the sense of fairness or justice based on community principles of mutual help and income sharing (see Chapter 2). Also, in the village community that is characterized by a high degree of social interaction, a strong preference would exist for the well-to-do farmers to choose a contractual form which promotes the patron-client relation with the poor. At least, they would try to avoid the use of a contract that created antagonism among the poorer members of the community.

Such considerations would not have been so important for very powerful elites like hacienda owners who lived outside the community and could rely on private armies as well as public police and courts for the enforcement of contracts. However, for small elites within the village community, like the farmers who gained the status of leaseholder or amortizing owner in the recent land reform, the choice of a specific system of harvesting cannot be independent of the reaction of the landless workers in the same community.

It seems reasonable to hypothesize that the changes in harvesting technology and contract for the past decade have been based, to a significant extent, on the sense of obligation of those new, small elites in the rural communities to increase labor employment in order to maintain the income of the poor.[17] Such a consideration may be based partly on altruism but probably is even more strongly motivated by the desire of the new village elites to protect their property and status. In any case, this kind of altruism, if that is what it is, has the effect of economizing on the cost of policing and enforcing laws and contracts (see Chapter 2).

In order to test the hypothesis, we tried to compare the costs of harvesting and threshing by the three systems among which substitu-

---

[17] In fact, there was a case where a meeting of *barrio* captains (village headmen) in a municipality in Nueva Ecija made a resolution to abandon the use of *tilyadora* in order to increase the employment and income of landless workers.

tions have occurred (Table 4–2). In the wet season of 1970, which was an early stage of a shift in the harvesting method, there was no significant difference between the costs for the *tilyadora* system and for the *hunusan* system at the output-sharing rate of one-sixth. In the early stage of diffusion of the *hunusan* system in Inner Central Luzon, the one-sixth share was brought in from the Coastal Region as part of the new system. But, probably because the system was new and not sanctified by tradition as in the Coastal Region, the share rates were allowed to decrease in Inner Central Luzon to one-seventh and one-eighth in response to yield increases. As a result, despite the yield increases, *hunusan* cost was about the same as *tilyadora* cost in 1978.

In our calculation, we could not incorporate such costs as crop damage in the wet season due to the late arrival of *tilyadora*. Therefore, the advantage for the *hunusan* over the *tilyadora* system for the wet

Table 4-2.   The costs of harvesting and threshing for different systems.

	1970	1978	
		wet	dry
Rice yield (kg/ha)	2200	3100	3600
Rice price (₱/kg)	0.42	1.15	1.15
Tilyadora system			
Labor requirement for harvesting[a] (man-days/ha)	20	24	24
Wage rate for harvesting[b] (₱/man-day)	4.5	11	11
(1) Harvesting cost (₱/ha)	90	264	264
(2) Threshing cost[c] (₱/ha)	46	178	207
(3) = (1) + (2) Total cost (₱/ha)	*136*	*442*	*471*
Hunusan system			
(4) Output share of 1/6 (₱/ha)	*154*	*594*	*690*
(5) Output share of 1/8 (₱/ha)	*116*	*446*	*518*
(4) − (3)	18	152	219
(5) − (3)	−20	4	47
Gama system			
Labor requirement for weeding (man-days/ha)	10	20	20
Wage rate for weeding (₱/man-day)	3	8	8
(6) Imputed wage for weeding (₱/ha)	30	160	160
(7) = (4) − (6) Imputed costs for harvesting and threshing (₱/ha)	*124*	*434*	*530*
(7) − (4)	−30	−160	−160
(7) − (5)	8	−12	12

[a] Includes labor for reaping, bundling, hauling and stacking.

[b] Includes food served to workers.

[c] Assumes the *tilyadora* threshing fee of 5% of paddy threshed. The fee includes wages for machine operators.

season was probably much larger than this calculation shows. However, it does not appear that the *hunusan* system has much advantage over the *tilyadora* system for the dry season. It appears necessary to consider the social interactions within the village community and the pressures of the landless in order to understand the introduction of the *hunusan* system, at least for the dry season.

From Table 4–2, it is clear that adoption of the *gama* system resulted in a large cost saving where the one-sixth share was maintained, as was the case in Laguna. But if the share rate could have been lowered to one-eighth, as in Inner Central Luzon, there would have been no merit for the Laguna farmers in adopting the *gama* system. The calculation shows clearly that the major merit of *gama* for farmer employers was its reduction of hired wage rates without involving social frictions and promotion of patron-client relations with landless workers in the communities in which a one-sixth share had been established as a traditional norm. The possible advantage of saving the cost of monitoring weeding labor because of the incentive mechanism built into the output-sharing system appears to be minor, if any, in view of the fact that the *gama* system was rarely adopted in Inner Central Luzon where the share rate was allowed to decrease.

The possible effects of a choice of harvesting system on the income

Table 4-3. The shares of labor and capital in the costs of harvesting and threshing, at 1978 prices.[a]

	Tilyadora system	Mixture[b]	Hunusan system
			₱/ha/year
Labor:			
Family	176 (19)	88 (10)	0 (0)
Hired	352 (39)	622 (68)	963(100)
Machine operators	90 (10)	49 (5)	0 (0)
Total	618 (68)	759 (83)	963(100)
Capital	295 (32)	158 (17)	0 (0)
Total	913(100)	917(100)	963(100)

[a] Figures in parentheses are percentages.
The assumptions made in the computation are as follows:
1) Farmers grow two crops of rice in a year. 2) Yield: 3100 kg/ha for wet season, 3600 kg/ha for dry season. 3) Labor requirement for harvesting activities: reaping = 16 man-days/ha (hired), bundling, hauling and stacking = 8 man-days/ha (family and exchange labor) for both wet and dry season. 4) Wage rate for the harvesting activities: ₱11.00/man-day. 5) Price of rice: ₱1.15/kg. 6) Rental rate for threshing machine: 5% of paddy threshed. 7) Wage rate for threshing machine operators: ₱13.50/ton of paddy threshed. 8) Harvesters' share for *hunusan* system: 1/8.
[b] *Hunusan* for wet season and *tilyadora* for dry season.

distribution in the village community are demonstrated in Table 4–3. In the *tilyadora* system, about 30% of the total harvesting and threshing cost is paid to capital (machinery) and about 70% to labor. With the adoption of the *hunusan* system for the wet season alone the share of labor increases to more than 80%; with complete adoption for two seasons the share goes up to 100%.

An equally important effect is the change in the composition of labor's share. In the *tilyadora* system, family labor is commonly used for bundling and making stacks, and machine operators' labor is also required; only 40% of the total cost consists of the earnings of hired workers. In contrast, the earnings of hired harvesters under the *hunusan* system comprise the whole cost of harvesting and threshing.[18]

In an economy where strong population pressure on limited land resources is resulting in an increase in the number of landless agricultural workers and in a decrease in their wage rates, a "regressive" shift from the machine system to the manual system in rice harvesting and threshing may be the best choice for farmers wishing to establish themselves as legitimate members of the elite in the community by patronizing landless workers. In the process the cost of labor-contract enforcement would be reduced substantially.

Interplay between Technological and Institutional Changes

The process of change in rice harvesting systems in the Philippines illustrates the complex interactions among economic and social forces which result in a specific choice of technology and contract. It is important to recognize that a certain type of contract (such as output sharing) is preferred for a certain technology (such as hand cutting and hand threshing) because it minimizes the transaction cost. It is also important to recognize that a specific system or combination of technology and contract is chosen under a certain institutional environment through a dynamic process of social interaction. The combination of

---

[18] In the *hunusan* system, family members do not usually work at harvesting. In the old *tilyadora* system they worked only at carrying bundled stalks and stacking them in a certain location. However, they worked neither at crop cutting (done by hired laborers) nor at threshing (done by professional machine operators). Therefore, the reduction of family labor due to the shift from the *tilyadora* to the hand threshing was not so great. The marginal reduction in family labor may be explained by the income effect of the reform or by the social obligation of relatively wealthy people to give working opportunities to the poor. It is important to note that, though the family members do not cut crops or thresh in their own fields, they do work in neighbors' fields and receive output shares. Under the *tilyadora* system before the reform, they usually did not cut their own crops by themselves but were employed by the neighbors for crop-cutting work for cash wages.

tilyadora thresher and fixed-wage labor contract was chosen under the hacienda system because it reduced the enforcement cost involved in collection of share rent. As the basic institutional environment changes, the transaction cost involved may also change, thus necessitating a change in the choice of technology and contract. An example of such a process is the shift from the *tilyadora* system to the *hunusan* system in Inner Central Luzon, corresponding to the demise of the hacienda system as a result of recent land reform programs. On the other hand, changes in technological opportunities may influence the institutional framework of a society, as evidenced by the conversion from the leasehold to the share tenancy system in haciendas due to the introduction of *tilyadora* threshers during the 1920s and 1930s. Recent shifts to the *hunusan* system and to the *gama* system under the guise of the patron-client relations between employer farmers and landless workers in village communities might, in the future, be reversed by technological innovations, such as the development of more efficient portable threshers suited to small-scale family farming.

The historical change in harvesting technology and contract in the Philippines should not be considered a unique experience. A detailed analytical review by Hans Binswanger (1978) of tractorization studies for the Indian subcontinent in recent years shows that the profitability of tractorization is usually not so great as to induce farmers to adopt tractors, if reductions in labor and bullock costs and increases in crop yield and intensity alone are counted as benefits from tractorization. He concludes that, besides direct and indirect subsidies from governments and aid agencies, a major factor underlying tractorization has been the lower cost of labor management required for large farmers to supervise a smaller number of workers with a tractor than with many bullock teams. In other words, tractors have been adopted mainly for the purpose of saving labor enforcement costs. New land reform regulations such as rent control and the prospective confiscation of tenanted land, which increased the incentive for large landowners to cultivate their holdings under direct administration rather than rent them out in smaller operational units, seem to be an important institutional condition under which tractors were resorted to as a major means of saving labor transaction costs.

Prediction of the future form of social and economic systems and the setting of policy to guide them appropriately will require better understanding of the dynamic interactions of technological and institutional changes which alter the transaction costs involved in alternative forms of contractual arrangements.

Chapter 5

A Village en Route to Peasant Stratification[1]

The broad observations in the previous chapter on the changes in agrarian institutions in wide areas of the rice bowl in the Philippines do not suffice to identify the direction of agrarian change at the village community level. The land reform was successful in breaking down large estates or haciendas. Ex-sharecroppers who were converted into leaseholders or amortizing owners can now capture a sizable fraction of economic rent or economic return to the service of land.

The land reform contributed to a reduction in the portion of income produced in village communities which flows out to absentee landlords. Thus, the reform contributed to an increase in village income and a reduction in urban-rural disparity. However, inequality within the village community increased because the larger tenants were the ones to capture major benefits, and no gain accrued to landless laborers. Inequality was further aggravated as the return to labor declined relative to the return to land due to strong population pressure.

The major question is whether the growing inequality will take the form of polarization or peasant stratification. Will the new rural elites—large leaseholders and amortizing owners—try to expand the scale of their operations in a capitalistic mode of production using large-scale machinery and wage laborers? Or will they prefer to play the role of "legitimate" patrons in traditional village communities, protecting the subsistence of landless clients or subordinates in return for their "loyal" services? In the latter case, village employment may continue to take the traditional forms of work-sharing and income-sharing arrangements under the patron-client relationship, and class

[1] This chapter draws heavily on Kikuchi and Hayami (1980a).

differentiation will take the form of stratification of peasant sub-classes instead of polarization into capitalist and proletariat classes.

In this chapter and the next we present intensive case studies of two villages—one characterized by the progress of peasant stratification and another characterized by the polarization process. By comparing the two cases, we try to identify the economic and social forces underlying the two different types of agrarian change. First, in this chapter, a village in which the growing disparity has been resulting in peasant stratification is investigated.

The study is based on a survey conducted from November 1976 to January 1977 in a *barrio* (village) in the province of Laguna. This is the village for which somewhat similar surveys were conducted in 1966 by Hiromitsu Umehara (1967) and again in 1974 by the International Rice Research Institute (Hayami *et al.*, 1975). Those previous studies provide the benchmark information with which historical changes can be ascertained. The survey was based on interviews with the heads of all households in the *barrio*. The data collected are primarily for 1976. However, to the extent possible we tried to collect data for 1956 and 1966 as well. In the following, unless otherwise stated, the data for 1976 and 1956 are based on our survey; those for 1974 are based on the previous IRRI survey; and those for 1966 are based on the Umehara survey supplemented by our survey.

Dynamics of the Village Economy

Village Profile

The village under study is located about 90 kilometers south of Manila on the east coast of the Laguna de Bay—henceforth we call it the "East Laguna Village" (Figure 5–1). The *barrio* is connected by a narrow unpaved road of about 2 kilometers to the *poblacion* (urban district) of the municipality to which this *barrio* belongs.

The *poblacion* of this municipality has been developed since the early Spanish period. Within the municipality, this *barrio* represents a newly developed area, inhabited only since the late nineteenth century. The major area in this *barrio* had been left uncultivated and used as a common pasture for grazing carabaos until the beginning of this century.

However, the largest area in the *barrio* is now a well-developed paddy field in which rice double-cropping is commonly practiced. There is little difference in elevation between the paddy fields and the Laguna

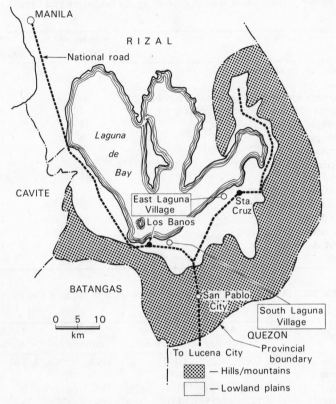

Fig. 5-1.   Map of the Province of Laguna, Philippines.

de Bay demarcating the northeastern border of the barrio. The fields are often flooded during the rainy season. Houses are located in the coconut grove which is slightly higher than the paddy fields.

As in other areas in the Philippines, absentee landlordism is pervasive in this village. Only 2.4 hectares out of the total 108 hectares of paddy fields are owned by villagers (Table 5–1).[2] The landownership pattern is typical of the Coastal Region, characterized by small scattered holdings of small landlords. A majority of landlords live in the *poblacion* of the same municipality or in other nearby municipalities. Usually they have close personal contacts with their tenants.

Rice farming is by far the most important source of income in this East Laguna Village (Table 5–2). Duck and hog raising are the common sideline enterprises. Coconuts are a very minor source of income for

[2] The areas refer to those cultivated by villagers.

Table 5-1.   Distribution of landlords owning rice land in the East Laguna Village, 1976.

	Number of landlords	Area owned (ha)
Distribution by residence:		
This *barrio*	4	2.4
The same municipality (except this *barrio*)	34	56.6
Laguna province (except this municipality)	7	11.7
Batangas province	14	17.6
Rizal province	5	15.7
Manila	1	2.2
Baguio	1	2.0
Total	*66*	*108.2*
Distribution by ownership size:		
Less than 1 ha	20	10.2
1 to 2.9 ha	34	46.2
3 to 6.9 ha	11	38.2
More than 7 ha	1	13.6
Total	*66*	*108.2*

Table 5-2.   Average household incomes by sources in the East Laguna Village, 1976.

Source	All households		Large farmers[b]		Small farmers[c]		Landless workers	
	US $[a]	%	US $	%	US $	%	US $	%
Farming								
Rice	412	(49)	1414	(70)	385	(48)	0	(—)
Other	127	(15)	131	(6)	217	(27)	73	(20)
Total	539	(64)	1545	(76)	602	(75)	73	(20)
Non-farm enterprise	50	(6)	38	(2)	53	(7)	54	(15)
Wage earning:								
Farm	143	(7)	56	(3)	101	(13)	205	(56)
Non-farm	110	(13)	388	(19)	40	(5)	34	(9)
Total	253	(30)	444	(22)	141	(18)	239	(65)
Total	842	(100)	2027	(100)	796	(100)	366	(100)

[a] Based on the exchange rate of 1 U.S. dollar to 7 pesos.
[b] Operational holding above 2 ha.   [c] Operational holding below 2 ha.

the villagers. Except for a few wealthy farmers who own housing lots, villagers reside under the coconut trees only with the implicit consent of the coconut owners who live outside the *barrio*. By custom, they are allowed to utilize the space below the trees for planting fruits and vegetables or raising livestock and poultry. In return, they serve as caretakers, clearing away the undergrowth. Farm wage earnings are another major income source, especially for landless laborers. Relatively few non-farm employment opportunities are open for villagers.

The rate of commercialization is rather high. On the average, about 40% of rice produce in a farm is sold, 20% submitted to landlords as rent, and 10% paid as wages in kind to hired labor. Only about 20% is retained for home consumption, including seed and feed uses.

Population Pressure

The population growth rate in the East Laguna Village was very high, as much as 2.6% per year for 1903–76 (Table 5–3). Moreover, the rate accelerated from 2.3% for 1903–60 to 4.9% for 1966–76. Meanwhile, cultivated land area (paddy field area) increased by 1.2% per year for 1903–60 and its expansion virtually stopped after then. As a result, the man/land ratio has deteriorated dramatically since 1960.

Table 5-3. Changes in population, cultivated land area and man/land ratio in the East Laguna Village.

	Population	Land area[a]	Man/land ratio	Source
	(1)	(2)	(1)/(2)	
	persons	ha	persons/ha	
1903	94	52	1.8	Census
1960	349	104	3.4	Census
1966	393	104	3.8	Umehara survey (as of Dec.)
1974	549	111	4.9	IRRI survey (as of Nov.)
1976	644	108	6.0	This survey (as of Dec.)
Growth rate (%/year)				
1903 to 1960	2.3	1.2	1.1	
1960 to 1976	3.8	0.2	3.6	
1966 to 1976	4.9	0.4	4.5	
1903 to 1976	2.6	1.0	1.6	

[a] Paddy-field area.

Since the population growth rate in this *barrio* for 1966–76 was substantially higher than in the Philippines as a whole (about 3% per annum), it seems reasonable to expect that there was a net migration into the *barrio* in addition to a high natural reproduction rate. From 1966 to 1976 the pyramid of population distribution by age groups widened its base distance, indicating a sharp rise in the birth rate

(Figure 5-2). By comparing the distribution of 1976 for the population above 10 years old with the distribution of 1966, we can infer that there were relatively large net inflows of the male population 20–24, 25–29 and 45–49 years old, and of the female population 25–29 and 45–49 years old. The inflow occurred partly because the population density used to be relatively low since this *barrio* represented a frontier within the municipality and partly because labor demand increased with the development of irrigation systems and new rice technology.

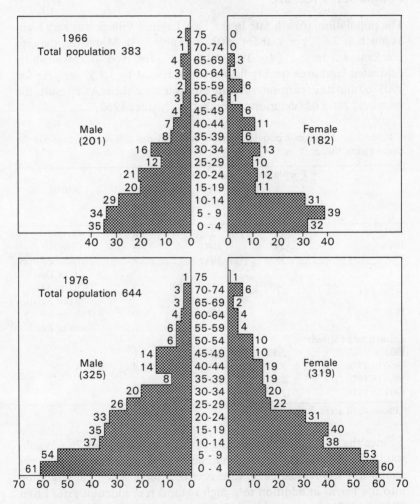

Fig. 5-2. Age distribution of population in the East Laguna Village, 1966 and 1976.

One consequence of the strong population pressure on land was an increase in the number of landless laborers. The increase in the number of households from 1966 to 1976 paralleled the growth in the population (Table 5–4). The total number of households increased from 66 to 109. The number of landless worker households increased dramatically faster than the number of farmer households. All the new households formed from 1974 to 1976 belonged to the landless class. As a result, the share of landless households in the total number of households increased from 30% to 50%.

The process of increase in the number of landless laborers can be seen from the data on the formation of households (Table 5–5). Households

Table 5-4.   Changes in the number of households in the East Laguna Village.

	Farmers	Landless workers	Total
1966	46	20	66
	(70)	(30)	(100)
1974	55	40	95
	(58)	(42)	(100)
1976	55	54	109
	(50)	(50)	(100)
Growth rate (%/year)			
1966 to 1976	1.8	9.9	5.0

Table 5-5.   Formation of households in the East Laguna Village (number of households).[a]

Date of household formation	Farmer households			Landless laborer households			Total (7)= (3)+(6)
	Independence (1)	Migration (2)	Total (3) = (1) + (2)	Independence (4)	Migration (5)	Total (6)= (4)+(5)	
Before 1939	9	2	11	2	0	2	13
	(70)	(15)	(85)	(15)	(0)	(15)	(100)
1940–49	5	4	9	3	1	4	13
	(38)	(31)	(69)	(23)	(8)	(31)	(100)
1950–59	9	2	11	6	1	7	18
	(50)	(11)	(61)	(33)	(6)	(39)	(100)
1960–69	10	5	15	12	2	14	29
	(35)	(17)	(52)	(41)	(7)	(48)	(100)
1970–76	3	6	9	16	11	27	36
	(8)	(16)	(24)	(45)	(31)	(76)	(100)
Total	36	19	55	39	15	54	109
	(33)	(17)	(50)	(36)	(14)	(50)	(100)

[a] Figures inside the parentheses are percentages.

were created either by the children of parents within the *barrio* who founded their own families or through migration from outside of the *barrio*. In both cases the ratio of landless worker households increased over time. Due to the limited cultivated area within the *barrio*, the opportunities for children to become independent farm operators grew scarcer over time. Likewise, in earlier years people migrated into this *barrio* as farmers by acquiring land through marriage or some other means, whereas in later years more people in-migrated only because employment was available for landless farm workers.

The growing relative scarcity of land due to population pressure is also reflected in changes in farm-size distribution (Table 5-6). Average farm size declined from 2.3 hectares in 1966 to 2.0 hectares in 1976. The number of farms below 2 hectares increased from 43% to 61%. It is important to note that the size distribution of operational holdings in this village was relatively equal and uni-modal. Even the largest operational holding was only 8 ha.

Table 5-6.   Farm-size distribution in the East Laguna Village.[a]

	1966		1976	
	Number of farmers No. (%)	Rice area Ha (%)	Number of farmers No. (%)	Rice area Ha (%)
Below 1 ha	6 (13)	3 (3)	13 (24)	6 (6)
1 ha–1.9 ha	14 (30)	18 (17)	20 (37)	28 (26)
2 ha–2.9 ha	10 (22)	21(20)	8 (15)	18 (17)
3 ha–4.9 ha	13 (28)	46 (44)	11 (20)	41 (38)
5 ha and above	3 (7)	17 (16)	2 (4)	14 (13)
Total	46(*100*)	105(*100*)	54(*100*)	107(*100*)
Average rice area per farm (ha)	2.3		2.0	

[a] Farm size in terms of the operational holding of paddy field.

Technological Change

One of the most significant changes in the village economy for the past two decades was the extension of a national irrigation system to this *barrio* in 1958. The irrigation made double-cropping of rice possible in all the paddy fields in the *barrio*, thereby doubling the rice yield per unit of physical area. It also made possible the conversion of land used for upland crops into paddy fields, establishing a complete rice monoculture pattern.

Another major change was the introduction of modern semi-dwarf varieties of rice developed at the International Rice Research Institute and the University of the Philippines College of Agriculture, located in the same province. According to the Umehara survey, no one in the *barrio* had tried the modern varieties in 1966. In 1976, 100% of the farmers planted the modern varieties. The diffusion of modern varieties has been accompanied by the application of fertilizers and chemicals and by the adoption of improved cultural practices such as intensive weeding and straight-row planting.

As a result of the improvements in irrigation and technology, the average paddy yield per hectare of planted area in this village increased as follows:

	Wet season	Dry season	Total
	—m.ton/ha—		
1956	2.2	—	2.2
1966	2.4	3.1	5.5
1976	3.2	3.6	6.8

Another aspect of technological innovation in agriculture is reflected in changes in the holdings of productive assets (Table 5–7). From 1966 to 1976, the number of hand tractors increased from 14 to 24. In contrast, the number of carabaos declined from 21 to 8, indicating the process of substitution of automotive power for animal power. Corresponding to the introduction of seed-fertilizer technology, the numbers of sprayers and rotary weeders increased dramatically.

Table 5-7. Changes in the holdings of productive assets in the East Laguna Village.

		1966				1976		
		Large	Small	Landless		Large	Small	Landless
	Total	farmers	farmers	workers	Total	farmers	farmers	workers
Hand tractor	13	8	5	n.a.	24	17	7	0
Sprayer	0	0	0	n.a.	26	18	8	0
Rotary weeder	45	20	25	n.a.	127	41	43	43
Carabao	21	11	10	n.a.	8	6	2	0

Farm Wage Rates

In terms of the simple economic model in Chapter 3, rapid population growth implies a rightward shift in the labor supply curve, which, *ceteris paribus*, reduces the wage rate. The declining wage rate can be counteracted by a rightward shift in the labor demand curve resulting from technological change of a labor-using or land-saving type. According to our previous observations in Chapter 3, the shift in labor supply for the Philippines as a whole seems to have outpaced the demand shift, with the result a decline in real wage rates for agricultural laborers (Tables 3–6 and 3–9).

However, in this East Laguna Village the real wage rates (as measured by daily wages in paddy terms) stayed, on the average, fairly stable for 1966–76, though the wage trends differed for different tasks (Table 5–8). The data suggest that the increase in labor demand due to the intensification of rice farming resulting from both the improvement of irrigation systems and the diffusion of seed-fertilizer technology was sufficiently rapid to compensate for the downward pressure from the growth of the labor force on agricultural wage rates. However, the stable wage rate during the period of significant increases in rice yields per ha implies that the return to land increased relative to the return to labor.

Table 5-8.   Changes in wage rates in the East Laguna Village.

	1966	1976	Rate of change 1966 to 1978
Nominal wage rates:[a]	₱/day	₱/day	%
Land preparation	4.5	13.0	189
Transplanting	3.4	8.4	147
Weeding	3.0	8.0	167
Paddy prices	₱/kg	₱/kg	
	0.40	1.02	155
Real wage rates:[b]	kg/day	kg/day	
Land preparation	11.3	12.7	12
Transplanting	8.5	8.2	−4
Weeding	7.5	7.8	4
Average	9.1	9.5	4

[a] Include cost of meal.
[b] Nominal wage rates divided by paddy prices.

Stratification in Land Tenure Relations

In this village a major share of the increased return to land has been captured by the tenant farmers who were converted to leaseholders by recent land reform programs and whose rent has been fixed despite the significant rise in rice yields. The surplus of economic rent over the actual rent paid to landlords has been captured as a part of the mixed income of tenant farmers. At the same time, a new institutional arrangement has emerged under which tenant farmers sub-rent their leasehold land. Thus, a multistage landlordism has been created despite the land reform regulations.

Changes in Land Tenure Relations

Traditionally, the common form of land tenure contract in this village was the cropsharing tenancy with both output and cost shared equally by landlords and tenants. However, the cost sharing was not exactly 50:50. The most common arrangement was: 100% of the cost for land preparation borne by tenants; 100% of the irrigation fee borne by landlords; and other costs, including seeds, fertilizers and chemicals, planting, weeding, harvesting and threshing, shared equally. There are other variations; for example, the whole cost of fertilizers and chemicals in addition to the irrigation fee may be shouldered by the landlords. Leasehold tenancy was limited to a small number of large farmers until the land reform.

The landlord-tenant relation was usually a paternalistic one. No written contracts were exchanged before the land reform. Contract enforcement was mainly based on the sense of reciprocity under a patron-client relation. Although the tenants had no legal claim to land, their tenure position was fairly secure. They were seldom evicted except for significant misconduct. The security of tenure might partly be explained by the history of the settlement of this area. In the process of settlement, landlords gave settlers land parcels gratis and advanced credits for subsistence during the period of land opening, with the understanding that they would enter into a sharecropping arrangement after the gratis period. Therefore, the *de facto* right of tenants to till the land that they or their ancesters opened has been assumed in the village community.

The land tenure relations in this village underwent a major change from 1966 to 1976 (Tables 5–9 and 5–10). Until 1976, about 70% of farms and 60% of rice area were under sharecropping contracts. However, leasehold operation based on the Agricultural Land Reform Code, which began to cover this village in 1968, resulted in a sharp decline in the incidence of share tenancy.

However, despite the law denouncing share tenancy (Republic Act 3844, Section 2), about 30% of the rice area was still under the sharecropping contract in 1976. Share tenants could obtain leasehold titles if they applied to the Regional Office of Agrarian Reform. Why did they not try to change their status? The answer is that their landlords were

Table 5-9.   Distribution of farms by tenure status in the East Laguna Village.

	Number of farmers		Area	
	No.	(%)	Ha	(%)
1956				
Owner/leasehold	2	(7)	10.3	(14)
Leasehold	6	(19)	15.0	(21)
Share/leasehold[a]	2	(7)	8.1	(11)
Share tenancy	21	(68)	38.2	(53)
Total	*31*	*(100)*	*71.5*	*(100)*
1966				
Owner/leasehold	2	(4)	10.3	(10)
Leasehold	7	(15)	18.0	(17)
Share/leasehold	2	(4)	10.1	(10)
Share tenancy[a]	35	(76)	65.9	(63)
Total	*46*	*(100)*	*104.2*	*(100)*
1976				
Owner/leasehold	3	(6)	11.2	(10)
Leasehold[a]	29	(54)	48.5	(46)
Share/leasehold[a]	8	(15)	23.9	(22)
Share tenancy[a]	14	(26)	24.7	(22)
Total	*54*	*(100)*	*108.2*	*(100)*

[a] Includes sub-tenants.

either relatives or friends who had been good to them. In fact, 18 out of 30 plots under share tenancy in 1976 were those whose landlords and tenants were relatives.

It is obvious that significant increases in rice yield per ha widened the income gap between sharecroppers and leaseholders whose rent was fixed by land-reform laws. In fact, even before the land reform programs the rent on leasehold land had been fairly stable, partly because of insufficient information on yield changes and partly because of the time lag involved in contract renegotiation.[3] From 1956 to 1966, the

[3] For example, the *Barrio* Captain (village headman) had been under a leasehold contract, paying rent of 40 cavans (1 cavan = 45 kg) for 2.5 ha until 1969. The landlord had not realized for 10 years that double-cropping had been practiced since the extension of the national irrigation system in 1958. When he found out in 1968, he demanded an additional rent payment of 23 cavans for the dry season crop. However, he was successful in raising the rent only by 9 cavans. In 1975, when a written contract was exchanged as a part of the land reform program, the village headman agreed to increase the rent by another 14 cavans in order to secure the landlord's signature.

Table 5-10.   Distribution of plots by tenure status.

	No. of plots	(%)
1956		
Owned	2	(5)
Leasehold[a]	11	(28)
Sharecrop	25	(64)
Sub-rented	1	(3)
Total	*39*	*(100)*
1966		
Owned	2	(3)
Leasehold[a]	12	(19)
Sharecrop	44	(70)
Sub-rented	5	(8)
Total	*63*	*(100)*
1976		
Owned	3	(3)
Leasehold[a]	44	(47)
Sharecrop	30	(32)
Sub-rented	16	(17)
Total	*93*	*(100)*

[a] Fixed rent in kind.

average rice yield per hectare of paddy field cultivated by leasehold tenants more than doubled, due to the extension of the National Irrigation System that enabled double-cropping. Meanwhile, rent paid in kind increased only by 70%, resulting in a reduction in the average share of rice output received by landlords, from 24% in 1956 to 19% in 1966 (Table 5–11).

Between 1966 and 1976, there was no change in the average share of rent. The average share for the whole leasehold area remained the same, because this calculation included leaseholders who were recently converted from share-tenancy, in which the tenant paid a higher rate of rent than those who had held the leasehold title prior to the Leasehold Operation. However, the share of rent for the old leaseholders continued to decline, from 19% in 1966 to 16% in 1976.

The data show clearly that the economic rent accruing to the service of land equal to its marginal value product and the actual rent paid to landlords widened under the institutional rigidity of the land rental market. Naturally the income position of the leasehold tenants, whose income increased by the amount of the gap between the economic rent and the actual rent, improved relative to that of the share tenants, whose rent payments increased proportionally with yield increases.

Table 5-11.   Changes in average rent and yield per hectare of land under leasehold tenancy (in paddy) in the East Laguna Village.

	Rent (1)	Yield (2)	(1)/(2)
1956		—kg/ha—	
Dry	0	0	—
Wet	599	2,507	0.24
Total	599	2,507	0.24
1966			
Dry	581	2,723	0.21
Wet	414	2,448	0.17
Total	995	5,171	0.19
1976[a]			
Whole area:			
Dry	788	3,852	0.20
Wet	567	3,213	0.18
Total	1,355	7,065	0.19
New leasehold area:			
Dry	842	3,888	0.22
Wet	671	3,213	0.21
Total	1,513	7,101	0.21
Old leasehold area:			
Dry	707	3,785	0.19
Wet	387	3,209	0.12
Total	1,094	6,994	0.16

[a] 1974–76 averages.

Emergence of Sub-Tenancy

This gap between the economic rent and the actual rent provided an economic basis for the emergence of a sub-tenancy arrangement in which the tenant sub-rented a part (or the whole) of his operational holding to landless laborers and extracted from his sub-lessee a surplus of the rent revenue over the payment to his landlord.

Indeed, a remarkable change in the distribution of land plots under various types of tenancy was the increase in the amount of land under sub-tenancy (Table 5–10). The number of plots which tenants sub-rented increased from only 1 in 1956 to 5 in 1966 and further to 16 in 1976, despite the fact that sub-tenancy is illegal in terms of the land reform laws (Republic Act No. 3844, Section 27). Under the laws, if a sub-lessee reports to the District Office of Agrarian Reform and proves that he is the actual cultivator of the land, he can obtain a formal title of leasehold tenancy, and his lessor's title is forfeited.[4] Sub-tenancy

[4] In fact, such cases occurred, one each in 1970 and 1975. The sub-lessees took such action when the sub-lessors tried to take back their land.

contracts are usually made without the formal consent of the land-owners.

Sub-tenancy can be classified into three types. In the first, the sub-lessor and the sub-lessee share output and costs, on a 50–50 basis; this is the most common type. In the second type, the sub-lessor receives a fixed rent from the sub-lessee. This is rather a special type; only two cases belong to this category, in both of which fathers sub-lease their tenanted land to their sons. In the third type, the sub-lessor puts his land in pawn to the sub-lessee; in other words, the sub-lessee advances a credit to the sub-lessor in order to establish a right to cultivate the land until the loan is repaid. All plots under sub-tenancy arrangements are land for which the sub-lessors hold the leasehold titles.

In order to test the hypothesis that the gap between the economic rent and the actual rent provided an opportunity for leasehold tenants to transform themselves into intermediate landlords, the factor shares of rice output were estimated for the 1976 wet season for different tenure types by imputing unpaid factor inputs by market prices.[5] Results show that the share of land was lowest and the operators' surplus highest for the land under leasehold tenancy, in both absolute and relative terms

Table 5-12. Factor payments and factor shares in rice production per hectare in the East Laguna Village, 1976 wet season.

	Factor payments (kg/ha)[a]			Factor shares (%)		
	Leasehold tenancy	Share tenancy	Sub-tenancy	Leasehold tenancy	Share tenancy	Sub-tenancy
Rice output	2889	2749	3447	100.0	100.0	100.0
Factor payments:						
Current inputs	657	697	801	22.7	25.3	23.2
Capital[b]	337	288	346	11.7	10.5	10.1
Labor	918	850	1008	31.8	30.9	29.3
Land	567	698	1305	19.6	25.4	37.8
(Paid to sub-lessor)	(0)	(0)	(801)	(0)	(0)	(23.2)
(Paid to landlord)	(567)	(698)	(504)	(19.6)	(25.4)	(14.6)
Operator's surplus[c]	410	216	−13	14.2	7.9	−0.4

[a] Factor payments converted to paddy equivalents by the factor-output price ratios.
[b] Sum of irrigation fee and paid and/or imputed rentals of carabao, tractor and other machines.
[c] Residual.

[5] Self-supplied current inputs such as seeds were valued at market prices. The costs of family labor and family-owned capital such as carabao and tractors were imputed by applying market wage and rental rates. Land rents to sub-lessors under the pledging arrangement were imputed by applying the interest rate of 40% per crop season, the most common rate in the village.

(Table 5–12).[6] In contrast, the share of land was highest and no surplus was left for farm operators contracting under sub-tenancy. The share of land for sub-tenants was very close to the sum of land share and operators' surplus for other tenure classes. Those observations indicate that a substantial portion of economic rent was captured by leasehold tenants in the form of operators' surplus.

As supporting evidence, the production function for rice was estimated using the same set of data as that used for the calculation of factor shares. The function employed was the unrestricted Cobb-Douglas (linear in logarithms) form, relating the quantity of rice output per farm to the following independent variables:

Land: Area harvested per farm (ha).
Labor: Number of man-days applied per farm.
Capital: Sum of irrigation fee and paid and/or imputed rentals of carabao, tractors and other machines per farm (₱).
Current inputs: Sum of paid and/or imputed costs of current inputs per farm (₱).
Sub-tenancy dummy: Sub-tenancy = 1 and others = 0.
Share-tenancy dummy: Share-tenancy = 1 and others = 0.
Scale dummy: Farms larger than 2 ha = 1 and others = 0.

The results of estimation by the ordinary least-square method are summarized in Table 5–13. All estimates of the production elasticities of inputs have positive signs, as was expected. Although these estimates are not significant at conventional levels of significance except for current inputs, they are at least larger than their standard errors. In contrast, the coefficients of dummy variables are smaller than their standard errors.

Under the assumption of market equilibrium, the production elasticities are equivalent to the functional shares of factors. On the

---

[6] In order to reduce disturbances due to natural calamities such as insects, diseases, rats and floods, the plots for which the rice yields per hectare in the 1976 wet season were below or above 20% of the 1974–76 averages were excluded from the sample. The observations for which the levels of output and inputs per hectare exceeded the range of three standard deviations from their sample means were also excluded, because there is a good chance that such abnormal observations resulted from mistaken recollections of the farmers interviewed. Among those to be excluded according to the first criterion, the observations for which the output and input levels fell within two standard deviations from the mean were retained in the sample. Thus, the sample used for the calculation of factor shares consisted of 46 plots cultivated by 33 farmers (23 plots with 45.8 ha of leasehold-tenancy land, 15 plots with 22.2 ha of share-tenancy land and 8 plots with 6.1 ha of sub-tenancy land).

Table 5-13. Estimation of Cobb-Douglas production function for rice using farm survey data in the East Laguna Village, 1976 wet season.

Regression number	(1)	(2)	(3)	(4)
Coefficients of				
Land	0.343	0.343	0.333	0.352
	(0.203)[a]	(0.207)	(0.206)	(0.215)
Labor	0.299	0.299	0.300	0.292
	(0.200)	(0.204)	(0.203)	(0.210)
Capital	0.135	0.135	0.130	0.139
	(0.099)	(0.101)	(0.101)	(0.104)
Current inputs	0.240	0.241	0.248	0.242
	(0.094)	(0.096)	(0.096)	(0.096)
Sub-tenancy dummy		−0.005		
		(0.147)		
Share-tenancy dummy			−0.058	
			(0.099)	
Scale dummy				−0.019
				(0.129)
Sum of conventional	1.018	1.017	1.011	1.024
coefficients	(0.055)	(0.061)	(0.057)	(0.072)
R^2 (adjusted)	0.931	0.928	0.929	0.928
Standard error	0.248	0.253	0.291	0.253
of estimate				
Intercept	1.019	1.038	0.994	1.041

[a] Standard errors of regression coefficients are enclosed within parentheses.

whole, the estimates of production elasticities in Table 5–13 are similar to the values of relative factor shares in Table 5–12. In particular, the estimates of the production elasticity of land are surprisingly close to the relative share of land for sub-tenants. The results support the hypothesis that sub-tenants have to pay rent at a rate equal to the marginal value product of the land.

On the other hand, leasehold tenants can capture the surplus of the marginal return to the service of land over the actual rate of rent payment to the landowners in the form of operators' surplus by using the land for their own farming operations. Alternatively, they can capture the surplus by sub-renting the land. Thus, population pressure, technological change and the land-reform regulations on the land rental market can be identified as the basic forces underlying the emergence of a multi-stage landlordism.

There is an indication that multi-stage landlordism will progress further. In 1976, two cases were reported where the sub-lessee rented a part of his sub-rented land. In one case, a farmer residing outside the *barrio* received one hectare of land as a pawn from a leaseholder in the *barrio,* and let a landless worker cultivate part of it (0.3 hectare) on a share basis. In another case, a sub-lessee of 0.8 hectare of land pledged 0.4 hectare of the sub-rented land. Thus, if the economic forces that induced the emergence of sub-tenancy increase, the number of layers in multistage landlordism may multiply in the future.

Tenancy Title Transactions

The surplus of the marginal product of land over the actual rent represents a necessary condition for the sub-tenancy system to emerge, but not a sufficient condition. The surplus can be captured by the tenants in the form of operators' surplus. Alternatively, they can capture the surplus by selling the tenancy title at a value equivalent to the capitalized present value of surplus flows. The choice depends on the endowment of managerial resources in their households, as well as on the risk and transaction costs involved therein. It seems reasonable to expect that the same economic forces that led to the emergence of sub-tenancy contracts would have induced the transactions of tenancy titles.

As expected, parallel to the spread of the sub-tenancy system, the number of transactions of tenancy titles has increased sharply since the late 1960s (Table 5–14).[7] It is interesting to observe that the deflated price of a tenancy title tends to increase, while that of a land ownership title tends to decrease. This anomaly arose from the fact that the values of land ownership titles recorded in Table 5–14 are for those with tenants on the land. The buyer of the land had to pay the tenants to move in order to recover his right to the use of "the top of the soil".

Such contrasting trends suggest that the increase in economic rent due to population pressure and productivity increases was captured totally by the tenants. The declining value of land ownership titles should have been affected by the decrease in the expected returns to land purchases, because the share received by landlords was reduced by the conversion of share-tenancy to leasehold-tenancy and also because it became more difficult to raise rent or to evict tenants due to the land reform programs.

It must be cautioned, however, that the data represent rather weak evidence, because land prices are highly variable according to variations in the quality of land. The number of transactions recorded here is too small to nullify the effect of heterogeneity of land quality.

---

[7] By custom, the sale of tenancy titles requires the permission of landlords, whereas the sub-renting of tenanted land does not. The transactions of tenancy titles were not necessarily among tenants. In many cases, landlords paid for tenancy rights by evicting ex-tenants in order to replace them with new ones.

Table 5-14. Transactions of land ownership and tenancy titles in the East Laguna Village.

	Transaction of land ownership title			Transaction of tenancy title			
	No.	Area	Current value	Value deflated by rice price index[a]	No.	Area	Current value	Value deflated by rice price index[a]
		ha		₱/ha		ha		₱/ha
1959	0	0	—	—	1	1.0	150	822
1960	0	0	—	—	1	2.4	125	658
1961	0	0	—	—	0	0	—	—
1962	1	3.0	6,333	28,786	0	0	—	—
1963	1	1.3	7,692	28,489	1	2.0	1,500	5,556
1964	1	3.5	5,429	16,975	0	0	—	—
1965	0	0	—	—	1	3.0	433	1,443
1966	1	1.0	11,000	36,667	0	0	—	—
1967	0	0	—	—	1	1.5	467	1,557
1968	1	1.5	18,000	60,000	3	3.9	611	1,852
1969	1	0.8	14,667	40,742	3	2.5	980	2,722
1970	1	2.0	9,500	27,143	4	6.4	2,100	5,714
1971	1	2.5	10,000	23,256	0	0	—	—
1972	2	1.4	12,143	21,684	4	5.0	1,300	2,321
1973	1	1.0	15,000	17,857	2	3.5	3,086	3,674
1974	0	0	—	—	2	3.1	4,113	4,284
1975	1	0.4	15,600	15,600	4	5.1	4,068	4,068
1976	0	0	—	—	1	1.2	6,667	6,667

[a] The rice price index for the Southern Tagalog area, 1975 = 1.00.

Stratification in Labor Employment Relations

The economic forces that induced changes in the land tenure system had a pervasive impact on labor employment relations. The most significant change was a shift from *hunusan* to *gama* in the harvesting labor contract. As explained in the previous chapter, rice harvesting under the *hunusan* system takes the form of a communal activity in which all villagers can participate and receive a certain share of output. Under the *gama* system participation in harvesting is limited to the workers who helped to weed the field without receiving wages. The traditional output share of harvesters is maintained under the *gama* system, but the implicit wage rate is reduced because the same share is paid for a larger amount of labor which includes weeding work in addition to harvesting work. The process of the shift in the harvesting contract will be explored in detail in this section for the case of the East Laguna Village.

Dependency on Hired Labor

Three categories of labor used for rice production are family labor, exchange or mutual-help labor and hired labor. Table 5–15 shows how total labor inputs for rice production were divided into those of family, exchange and hired labor. As much as 70% of the total labor input was contributed by hired workers. The share of family labor was 27%, of exchange labor only 2%.

Table 5-15. Composition of family, exchange and hired labor used for rice production by task in the East Laguna Village, 1976 wet season.

Task	Man-days per hectare	(%)	Task	Man-days per hectare	(%)
1. Land preparation:			5. Harvesting and threshing:		
Family	4.1	38	Family	3.7	10
Exchange	0.9	9	Exchange	0	0
Hired	5.8	53	Hired	34.1 (27.4)[a]	90 (73)[a]
Total	10.8	100	Total	37.8	100
2. Planting:			6. Seedbed preparation:		
Family	0.2	2	Family	0.9	62
Exchange	0.1	1	Exchange	0.5	37
Hired	8.4	97	Hired	0	1
Total	8.7	100	Total	1.4	100
3. Fertilizer and chemical application:			7. Irrigation control and maintenance:		
Family	4.4	76	Family	6.5	74
Exchange	0.1	2	Exchange	0.2	3
Hired	1.3	22	Hired	2.0	23
Total	5.8	100	Total	8.7	100
4. Weeding:			8. Total		
Family	8.8	28	Family	28.6	27
Exchange	0.2	1	Exchange	2.0	2
Hired	22.5 (16.3)[a]	71 (52)[a]	Hired	74.1 (43.7)[a]	71 (42)[a]
Total	31.5	100	Total	104.7	100

[a] Hired labor under the *gama* system is in parentheses.

The low rate of dependency on family labor can partly be explained by the large seasonal fluctuations in labor demand in rice production. Dependence on hired labor was especially high for planting and harvesting; both are tasks which require precise timing and are difficult to carry out with family labor alone.[8] But why was the dependence on hired labor so high and on exchange labor so low?

[8] Even though planting and harvesting require a high rate of hired labor, the types of labor contract used are entirely different. In transplanting, the organizer of a team

The answer may be sought in a system common in rice-producing regions in the Philippines. Farmers were employed by other farmers— they employed each other in their farm operations. The system developed under output and cost-sharing tenancy in an attempt by tenants to minimize the landlord's share (Takahashi, 1969). In that system, even if the family labor income from rice production on their farm was reduced by the amount paid to neighbors, the reduction would be more than compensated for by the family's wage earnings from the neighbors. This resulted in a higher level of labor income for tenants in the village as a whole.

This system, which may be called "labor exchange with wage payments", is more beneficial for share tenants than *bayanihan* or *suyuan* in which labor is exchanged without payment. Even though a majority of share tenants have recently become leaseholders, this system has not changed, partly because of social inertia and partly because of social compulsion within the community to employ landless members.

From Hunusan to Gama

The *hunusan* contract in which all villagers can participate in harvesting and receive an output share can be considered a typical case of "labor exchange with wage payments". If the village community is homogeneous, consisting of small share tenants, today's employer will be tomorrow's employee. However, as the community became stratified into leasehold tenants and landless laborers because of population pressure and land reform programs, those who employ became different from those who are employed. Insofar as *hunusan* was a system of mutual employment, a high share of output for harvesters was not disadvantageous to employers because they could recover it from neighbors' harvests. However, as the employment relation became one-way rather than mutual, the high share rate became intolerable for farmer employers.

It appears that the process of stratification in the village community was paralleled by the cumulative increase in the gap between the marginal product of labor and the wage rate implicit in the harvesters' share. In earlier years, when labor was scarce and rice yield per hectare was low, the traditional one-sixth share for harvesters would have been close to a market wage rate which could approximate the marginal product of harvesting labor. However, as the yield level increased while

---

of transplanters called *kabisilya* usually contracts with farmers on a per-hectare basis or in terms of the number of workers that he supplies. In any case, the *kabisilya* receives a lump-sum payment from which he/she pays workers a certain daily rate.

the increase in labor supply kept the wage rate from rising, one-sixth of the harvest became substantially larger than the prevailing wage rate.

In such a situation the *gama* system was introduced as an institutional innovation to reduce the gap between the marginal labor productivity and the harvesters' share. Indeed, the *gama* system was introduced to this village shortly after the construction of an irrigation system (1958), and it diffused rapidly during the late 1960s and the early 1970s (Table 5-16).

Table 5-16. Diffusion of *gama* system in the East Laguna Village.

	Employers' side			Employees' side		
	Number of farmers adopting *gama*	Total number of farmers		Number of *gama* worker households	Total number of landless workers	
	(1)	(2)	(1)/(2)	(3)	(4)	(3)/(4)
1959	0	n.a.		1	n.a.	
1960	1	n.a.		1	n.a.	
1962	2	n.a.		5	n.a.	
1964	6	n.a.		11	n.a.	
1966	14	46	0.30	21	20	1.05
1968	15	n.a.		23	n.a.	
1970	24	n.a.		26	n.a.	
1972	33	n.a.		40	n.a.	
1974	43	54	0.80	52	40	1.30
1976	45	54	0.83	66	54	1.22

In order to test the hypothesis that the *gama* system represents an institutional instrument to equate the harvesters' output share with marginal labor productivity, an imputation was made of labor inputs applied to rice production under the *gama* system by using market wage rates; imputed wage costs were compared with the actual shares of *gama* harvesters. The results show a remarkable affinity between the imputed wages and the actual harvesters' shares (Table 5-17). Such results, together with the affinity between the output share of labor (Table 5-12) and the production elasticity of labor (Table 5-13), support the hypothesis of an equality between the actual payment to *gama* workers and the marginal product of labor.

A major question is why *gama* was chosen among alternative methods of reducing the wage rate for harvesters. The wage rate can be reduced by reducing the share rate under the *hunusan* system or by replacing *hunusan* with the labor of daily wage workers (*upahan*). A number of

Table 5-17.   Comparison between the imputed value of harvesters' share and the imputed cost of *gama* labor in the East Laguna Village, 1976 wet season.

	Based on employers' data	Based on employees' data
No. of working days of *gama* labor (days/ha)[a]		
Weeding	20.9	18.3
Harvesting/threshing	33.6	33.6
Imputed cost of *gama* labor (₱/ha)[b]		
Weeding	167.2	146.4
Harvesting/threshing	369.6	369.6
(1) Total	536.8	516.0
Actual share of harvesters:		
In kind (kg/ha)[c]	504.0	549.0
(2) Imputed value (₱/ha)[d]	504.0	549.0
(2) — (1)	−32.8	33.0

[a] Includes labor of family members who worked as *gama* laborers.
[b] Imputation using market wage rates (daily wage = ₱8.0 for weeding; ₱11.0 for harvesting).
[c] One-sixth of output per hectare.
[d] Imputation using market prices (1 kg = ₱1).

advantages can be counted for the *gama* system, as was explained in the previous chapter. To recapitulate, first, it incorporates a mechanism to reduce laborers' shirking, because the incentive for employees to do more conscientious work in weeding is built in in the form of output sharing. Second, even though labor is normally abundant, it can be difficult for an individual farmer to find a sufficient number of daily wage workers at the right time for his harvesting. Under the *gama* system, the availability of labor at harvest time is guaranteed by contract. From the employee's side, *gama* is more secure, involving less risk in finding employment in the narrow labor market.

However, the most critical consideration in the choice of the *gama* system appears to be the fact that *gama* is more congruent with traditional moral principles in village communities, such as mutual help and income-sharing, and thereby involves less social friction. Farmer employers could have lowered the real wage rates of harvesting labor by reducing the output share of harvesters or by employing laborers from the market with a fixed daily wage contract. However, the cost arising from resistance to a change in long-established village custom—such as the one-sixth share of harvesting workers—would not have been small. In the next chapter, we will describe a village where large farmers abandoned the *gama* system and reduced the share of the harvesters from one-sixth to one-seventh. They met with indignation from the villagers, and one crop was destroyed during the night. The basic institutional environment, the customs of the village community, make some contractual innovations less costly to establish than others.[9]

Structure of Peasant Stratification

Let us summarize the pattern of peasant stratification as observed in the case study of the East Laguna Village.

Originally, this village consisted mainly of relatively homogeneous peasant-sharecroppers. Later strong population pressure on land resulted in a sharp increase in the number of landless agricultural laborers, who formed a lower stratum of the village community. Labor demand has been increased by the intensification of rice farming resulting from improvements in the irrigation system and the diffusion of seed-fertilizer technology. However, the wage rate has been held constant by the rightward shift in labor supply due to population growth. As a result, the economic rent or the return to land has increased relative to the wage rate. Partly because of social inertia and partly because of land reform regulations, the actual rent paid to landlords has not risen so much. A major portion of the increase in the economic rent of land has been captured by tenants, especially those who were converted from sharecroppers to leaseholders by the land reform operations. Thus, the income gap between tenant farmers and landless laborers widened.

Despite the growing inequality in this village, no sign of movement towards polarization of the peasant community into large commercial farmers and landless proletariat has been observed. As attested by changes in the farm-size distribution, few of the wealthy tenants have attempted to increase the scale of their operations, even though the buying and selling of tenancy titles has been commonly practiced. Instead, there has been a tendency for them to become intermediate landlords by sub-renting their holdings to landless laborers despite land reform laws which prohibit the sub-tenancy arrangement. Thus, the strata of peasant sub-classes have been multiplied.

Further, labor employment has not moved towards a capitalistic system based on the impersonal labor market. The traditional *hunusan* system in which all villagers can participate in harvesting and receive a

---

[9] The relation between the basic institutional environment and the secondary institutional arrangements observed in this village seems analogous to the historical change in the manorial system in medieval Europe analyzed by North and Thomas (1971).

certain output share has been replaced by the *gama* system in which only those who helped with weeding without receiving wages are employed for harvesting and receive the output share. By means of this institutional innovation the wage rate has been adjusted to a level consistent with the marginal product of labor, while the personalized employment relation of a patron-client type has been maintained or even strengthened. Under the *gama* system, landless laborers have continued to be a peasant sub-class in the sense that they share both work and output in the peasant production process to a limited extent; the alienation of labor from its product in Marx's sense has been avoided.

Why has the growing inequality taken the form of peasant stratification in this village? Stratification has developed through institutional innovations such as sub-tenancy and the *gama* system. In both arrangements, the analytical results are consistent with a basic postulate: changes in institutional arrangements governing the use of production factors will be induced when disequilibria between the marginal returns and the marginal costs of factor inputs emerge as the result of changes in economic variables such as resource endowments and technology, given the institutional rigidity of factor markets; the direction of institutional change will be towards the restoration of equilibria.

But why have arrangements like *gama* which have a tendency to promote peasant stratification been chosen as specific means to restore the factor cost-return equilibrium? In general, output-sharing contracts have advantages in reducing labor enforcement costs and spreading risk. However, the more basic factor appears to be the institutional environment and the high degree of social interaction in this village community.

The basic institutional environment has consisted of the traditional moral principles of mutual help and income-sharing within the village. Because such arrangements as sub-tenancy and *gama* are consistent with the basic institutional environment, they have been considered legitimate by villagers and received social sanction. In a community characterized by a high degree of social interaction, it would have been costly to enforce contracts not considered legitimate by community members. By contrast, legitimate arrangements from the village point of view are enforceable even if they violate the formal laws, as shown by the diffusion of the sub-tenancy arrangement despite the land reform regulations. We hypothesize that, in terms of transaction costs, peasant stratification based on institutional innovations in the guise of mutual help and income-sharing has been the most efficient route to reducing the disequilibria between marginal factor costs and returns in this village community.

Chapter 6

A Village en Route to Polarization[1]

The previous chapter reported the case of a village wherein peasant stratification has been induced by a decline in the economic return to labor relative to the return to land due to strong population pressure on land. However, the same economic force does not necessarily result in peasant stratification. The growing inequality arising from the relative decline in the return to labor may result in polarization of the peasant community into large capitalist farmers and a landless proletariat.

This chapter presents a case study of a village in which polarization has been progressing in a dramatic manner. By comparing this village with the one in the previous chapter, we will try to identify the conditions of two different types of agrarian change that Asian village communities are experiencing.

The survey on which this study is based was conducted in September 1977. Therefore, the data collected were primarily for the 1977 dry season (approximately November 1976–April 1977), but we tried to collect as much as possible on 1967, so that changes in the previous decade could be identified.

Structure of Land Concentration

The *barrio* under study is located on the south coast of the Laguna de Bay—henceforth we call it the "South Laguna Village". Like the East Laguna Village analyzed in the previous chapter, this village is

---

[1] This chapter draws heavily on Kikuchi and Hayami (1980b).

characterized by a complete rice monoculture, with duck and hog raising as sideline enterprises. The two villages are almost identical in terms of farming practices, structure of income sources and degree of commercialization. Yet, in contrast to the East Laguna Village, landholdings are highly concentrated in the South Laguna Village. We will look for the reasons as we compare the two villages.

Hacienda Barrio

Both villages are characterized by pervasive absentee landlordism. Only 3 hectares, or less than 2% of the 208 hectares of rice land in the South Laguna Village, are owned by village residents. However, a major difference exists in the pattern of land ownership distribution (compare Table 6-1 with Table 5-1). In general, the Coastal Region including the East Laguna Village is characterized by scattered landholdings of small to medium landlords. In this respect the South Laguna Village, where the hacienda type of holding has been developed, is atypical of the region.

Table 6-1.   Distribution of landlords owning rice land in the South Laguna Village, 1977.

	Number of landlords	Area owned (ha)
Distribution by residence:		
This *barrio*	1	3.0
The same municipality (except this *barrio*)	0	0
Laguna province (except this municipality)	9	16.4
Batangas province	11	43.2
Quezon province	1	5.5
Manila	9	140.4
Total	*31*	*208.5*
Distribution by ownership size:		
Less than 1 ha	4	2.0
1 to 2.9 ha	15	25.3
3 to 6.9 ha	7	26.9
More than 7 ha	5	154.3
Total	*31*	*208.5*

In terms of size distribution of land ownership, only 13% of the total area was owned by the 19 landlords whose holdings were below 3 ha; more than 70% was owned by only 5 landlords (who lived in Manila). This pattern of land ownership is in sharp contrast with that of East

Laguna Village, in which the majority of the land was owned by relatively small landlords living in the same municipality. The ownership of land in two haciendas in this *barrio* has been subdivided through inheritance. However, if we sum up the paddy fields owned by the 12 families descending from the two original landlords, the area amounts to 160 hectares, as much as 80% of the total paddy area.

The hacienda type of holdings, which is atypical of the Coastal Region, has been developed through a unique process of settlement. This *barrio* belongs to the most recently settled rice area in Laguna. Settlement began late because its highly marshy topography required a large-scale investment in drainage systems before individual settlement became possible.

The area was part of a large land grant by the Spanish Crown, transferred in the form of wild fields to a few native Philippine landlords after the beginning of the nineteenth century. Those landlords opened marshy jungles and installed drainage and irrigation facilities. In this way, a few small haciendas (small compared with those in Inner Central Luzon but large in Laguna) were developed in this area.

The major area of this *barrio* was developed as the haciendas of two landlords. Settlement began in the 1930s and was completed in the 1940s. As the infrastructure was created by the haciendas, marginal areas were settled by smallholders and squatters. The cultivation frontier was closed by the 1950s.

Population Pressure and Technological Change

During the past decade this village experienced major technological advances of the same nature as in the East Laguna Village. In 1967 no farmer had tried modern varieties, whereas in 1977 all the farmers planted modern varieties. The diffusion of modern varieties, since *IR-8* was first tried in 1968, was accompanied by the application of fertilizers and chemicals and by the adoption of improved cultural practices such as intensive weeding and straight-row planting.

As a result, the average paddy yield per hectare increased as follows:

	Wet season	Dry season	Total
		—m.ton/ha—	
1967	2.1	2.8	4.9
1977	2.8	4.0	6.8

Another major technological change was the mechanization of land preparation by hand tractors. In the marshy paddy fields, carabao often became stuck in deep mud. Therefore some of the areas were left uncultivated during the wet season. The introduction of hand tractors with flotation wheels made operations much easier. In 1977 there were 24 tractors cultivating the major area of the *barrio*. Carabao, only 2 head in all, were used for cultivating the edges of paddy fields.

The changes in rice technology were paralleled by high rates of population growth. At the time of our survey in September 1977, the total population was 747 persons in 125 households. According to the 1960 Census, the population that year was 411 persons. Therefore, the population growth rate during the 17-year period was as high as 3.6%. The high rate of population growth is reflected by the triangular age distribution of the population (Figure 6-1).

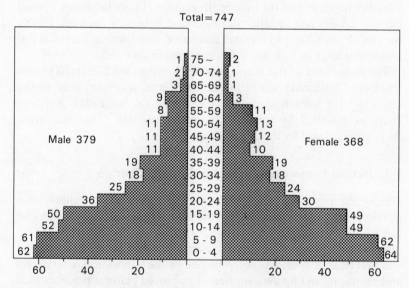

Fig. 6-1. Age distribution of population in the South Laguna Village, 1977.

Population pressure on the limited area for cultivation resulted in an increase in the proportion of landless laborers. Among the total of 125 households, 72 households or 57% belonged to the landless-laborer class. The households were formed either by children becoming independent from parents in the *barrio* or through migration from outside the *barrio*. In both cases the ratios of landless laborers in the newly created households rose over time (Table 6-2); this trend is very similar to that in the East Laguna Village (Table 5-5).

Table 6–2. Formation of households in the South Laguna Village (number of households).

Date of household formation	Farmer households			Landless laborer households			
	Independence (1)	Migration (2)	Total (3) = (1) + (2)	Independence (4)	Migration (5)	Total (6)= (4) + (5)	Total (7) = (3) + (6)
Before 1939	2	6	8	6	0	0	8
	(25)	(75)	(100)	(0)	(0)	(0)	(100)
1940–49	10	8	18	2	1	3	21
	(48)	(38)	(86)	(9)	(5)	(14)	(100)
1950–59	3	13	16	9	6	15	31
	(10)	(42)	(52)	(29)	(19)	(48)	(100)
1960–69	5	3	8	12	9	21	29
	(17)	(10)	(27)	(42)	(31)	(73)	(100)
1970–77	2	1	3	15	18	33	36
	(6)	(3)	(9)	(41)	(50)	(91)	(100)
Total	22	31	53	38	34	72	125
	(18)	(25)	(43)	(30)	(27)	(57)	(100)

[a] Figures inside the parentheses are percentages.
[b] Three landless laborers later became farmers under sub-tanancy arrangements, with the result that the numbers of farmers and landless became 56 and 69, respectively, at the time of our survey.

Polarization in Progress

Population pressure, however, does not necessarily result in an increase in the population of landless workers. Instead, farms can be fragmented unimodally to accomodate the growing labor force in a larger number of smaller-size farms as is the case in the East Laguna Village. Underlying the rapid increase in the landless-laborer population in the South Laguna Village was the concentration of land in the hands of large farmers as well as the population pressure itself.

Farmland is unusually concentrated in this village: there are three large farms, averaging 45 hectares each, while most Philippine villages have no farm larger than 10 hectares. Those three large farms covered 135 hectares or 65% of the total rice area in the *barrio*, whereas the rest of the 53 small farmers, who accounted for 95% of all farms, operated only 35% of the total area (Table 6–3).

Traditionally, this village consisted of two large-scale farms (C and D) under the direct administration of hacienda owners and a large number of small share tenants. Later, two tenant farmers (A and B) gradually accumulated landholdings through direct rental from landlords and purchase of tenancy titles from other tenants (Table 6–4). One may

Table 6-3.   Farm-size distribution in terms of operational holdings in the South Laguna Village, 1967 and 1977.

	1967				1977			
	No. of farms		Rice area		No. of farms		Rice area	
	No.	%	Ha	%	No.	%	Ha	%
Small farms								
Below 1 ha	7	16	4.2	2	22	39	11.2	5
1.0–2.9 ha	27	60	46.4	24	26	47	44.8	22
3.0–9.9 ha	7	15	26.0	14	5	9	17.5	8
Total	*41*	*91*	*76.6*	*40*	*53*	*95*	*73.5*	*35*
Large farms								
A			14.0	7			80.0	38
B			27.0	14			41.0	20
C			14.0	7			14.0	7
D			60.0	32			—	—
Total	*4*	*9*	*115.0*	*60*	*3*	*5*	*135.0*	*65*
Total	*45*	*100*	*191.6*	*100*	*56*	*100*	*208.5*	*100*
Average farm size (ha)								
Small farms			1.9				1.4	
Large farms			28.8				45.0	

Table 6-4.   Accumulation of operational holdings by large tenant operators in the South Laguna Village, 1949–1977.

	Area added	Tenure status[a]	Cumulative total	Method of acquisition
	Ha		Ha	
Operator A				
1949	1	S	1	Rented from landlord
1962	6	L	7	Purchase of tenancy title
1962–67	7	L	14	Rented from landlord
1970	60	L	74	Rented from landlord
1973	3	L	77	Purchase of tenancy title
1975	3	0	80	Purchase of ownership title
1977	—	—	80	
Operator B				
1949	3	S	3	Inherited tenancy title from father
1962–65	14	L	17	Rented from landlord
1967	10	L	27	Rented from landlord
1968	2	L	29	Purchase of tenancy title
1970	6	L	35	Purchase of tenancy title
1972	6	L	41	Purchase of tenancy title
1977	—	—	41	

[a] S = share tenancy area; L = leasehold area; O = owned area.

wonder why land reform programs were not effective in preventing the concentration of operational landholdings.

The Leasehold Operation began to cover the village in 1968, and with the proclamation of Presidential Decrees No. 2 and No. 27 in 1972 under the martial-law regime all the share tenants were converted into leaseholders. Thus, the land-tenure distribution in this village underwent a significant change from 1967 to 1977 (Table 6–5). However, this village was not covered by Operation Land Transfer which aims to transfer land ownership to tenants under the conditions of annual amortization payments in 15 years. The village was not covered by this operation, even though the retention limit of landlords was successively reduced from 75 hectares to 7 hectares under the martial-law regime,

Table 6-5. Distribution of farms by tenure status in the South Laguna Village, 1967 and 1977.

Tenure status	1967		1977	
	No.	(%)	No.	(%)
Owner	2	(4)	1	(2)
Owner/leasehold	0	(0)	1	(2)
Leasehold	8	(18)	42	(75)
Share tenancy	32	(71)	0	(0)
Lease/sub-tenancy	0	(0)	1	(2)
Sub-tenancy	3	(7)	11	(19)
Total	45	(100)	56	(100)

and the two big landlords owned much more than this reduced retention limit. The reason was that the land subject to Operation Land Transfer was limited to "tenanted land", and there was no retention limit for land under the direct administration of landlords. Major areas owned by the two big landlords were officially under their direct administration, and areas under tenancy contracts were subdivided into smaller units below the retention limit under the titles of family members and relatives.

Land reform programs are intended to prevent the concentration of operational landholdings by tenant farmers. Presidential Decree No. 27 stipulated a family-size farm of 3 irrigated hectares or 5 nonirrigated hectares. The Department of Agrarian Reform has tried to keep the tenant farm size below this limit (DAR Memorandum Circular No. 2-A, 19 June, 1973). However, such a regulation could easily be evaded by registering tenancy titles under the names of family members separately.

A major event in the accumulation of operational holdings by the large tenant farmers was the transfer of one of the two large farms under the direct administration of its owner to management by a large tenant operator (D to A) in 1970. Formally, the contract was such that Farmer A was employed as manager of the estate under the direct administration of the landlord. In substance, however, the contract was nothing but a leasehold contract in that Farmer A paid fixed rent to the landlord.

As a result of the accumulation of operational holdings by the two large tenant farmers, the skewness in the farm-size distribution worsened from 1967 to 1977 (Table 6–3). Especially noteworthy is the rapid increase in the number of farms below 1 hectare, which tripled within the 10 years. In contrast, the number of farms in the 1–3-hectare class decreased. The average size of operational holdings by small farms declined from 1.9 hectare in 1967 to 1.4 hectare in 1977, while the average size of large farms increased from 28.8 hectares to 45.0 hectares. Such trends reflect the transfer of land from small and medium family farms to large-scale commercial operations—a typical process of polarization.

The history of land accumulation by Farmers A and B in the South Laguna Village represents a case of polarization of a village community through the rise of a "new power elite". There is also the possibility of polarization by an "old elite". In fact, a case was found in a neighboring *barrio* where a hacienda owner expanded the area under his direct administration by purchasing back the tenancy titles from his tenants. This landlord developed this hacienda himself in the 1930s and 1940s, and he and his family still own about 150 hectares of paddy land. His hacienda had been farmed by sharecroppers until they were converted to leaseholders in 1972. Subsequently, he purchased back the tenancy titles from 34 tenants and, by 1977, had consolidated an area of 73 hectares under his direct administration (Table 6–6).

Thus, in this area where the hacienda type of holding developed

Table 6-6.   Accumulation of operational holdings under the direct administration of a landlord through the purchase of tenancy titles in a village neighboring the South Laguna Village, 1972–1977.

	No. of transactions	Area acquired (ha)	Cumulative total (ha)
1972	4	13.5	13.5
1973	7	16.9	30.4
1974	9	19.3	49.7
1975	8	15.3	65.0
1976	3	4.7	69.7
1977	3	3.7	73.4

as an exceptional case in the Coastal Region, polarization has been carried out by both new and old elites depending on their management abilities.

Are There Economic Advantages for Large Farms?

What is the major factor underlying the polarization process in the South Laguna Village? It is common among radical political economists in the Marxian tradition to assume scale economies in modern agricultural technology as a basic cause of polarization. It is argued that modern technology represented by large machinery is characterized by indivisibility of capital inputs; it can be profitably used only by large farmers; and, thereby, it contributes to the widening of the productivity difference between large and small farmers.[2]

The new seed-fertilizer technology heralded as the "green revolution" has been identified by these economists as a variation of modern technology to promote productivity differences among different farm-size classes. As explained in Chapter 3, it has been argued that modern varieties of rice and wheat tend to be monopolized by large commercial farmers who have better access to new information and better financial capacity to purchase modern inputs such as fertilizers and chemicals; the large profit resulting from the monopolistic adoption of the new technology stimulates the adopters to enlarge their operational holdings by consolidating the farms of small nonadopters through land purchase and tenant eviction; the polarization process is further accelerated by an intrinsic tendency of the large commercial farms to introduce large-scale machineries.

The major question to be investigated in this section is whether large farms have advantages over small farms in production efficiency with the use of new rice technology such that polarization is induced.

Organizational and Technical Efficiency

Figure 6–2 shows the contrasting organizational characteristics of the large and the small farms in the South Laguna Village. In the small farms, it is common for the operators and their family to do seedbed preparation, fertilizer and chemical application, and water control.

---

[2] For the Marxian concept of agricultural production, see Mitrany (1951, Chapter 2). For a strong criticism of the Marxian doctrine, see Schultz (1964, Chapter 8).

Land preparation by farmers who own tractors is carried out by family labor supplemented by labor hired at a fixed wage rate. Farmers who do not possess tractors usually contract their land preparation on a tractor-custom basis for a payment depending on the area prepared (*pakyaw*). Rice planting depends primarily on a crew of fixed-wage laborers organized by a *kabisilya*. The *kabisilya* receives ₱0.50 for each worker mobilized. Harvesting and threshing are done by labor hired on a harvest-share basis (*hunusan* or *gama*). Weeding is partly done by the family and partly by fixed-wage (*upahan*) or *gama* labor. The relations between the small farmers and the laborers are direct, except for transplanting which is contracted through the *kabisilya*.

In contrast, the large farms are characterized by a management hierarchy. Employment contracts and supervision are done through a manager-foreman system. The farmer employs a manager who is responsible for overall coordination and supervision. In the case of one of the farms studied intensively, the manager's wife kept records of farm expenses. Under the manager, there is an overseer to hire and supervise laborers. The overseer employs the laborers through another overseer for land preparation operations; through a *kabisilya* for rice planting, weeding and maintenance of ditches and banks; and through the *hunusan* and *gama* systems for harvesting and threshing. The farm also employs two persons full-time for the control of the irrigation systems

Despite the organizational differences, little difference was observed between large and small farms in farming practices. Both had completely adopted modern varieties and straight-row planting. Weeding was done to more or less the same degree of intensity. The average fertilizer application per hectare by both large and small farmers was 4 bags (50 kg/bag).

There was also not much difference in the degree of mechanization. Two of the large farms owned five and three hand tractors, respectively,

Table 6-7.   Capital assets of large and small farms in the South Laguna Village, 1977.

	2 large farms (A and B)		53 small farms	
	Total	Per 100 ha	Total	Per 100 ha
Farm area (ha)	121	—	74	—
Hand tractors	8	6.6	14	18.9
Carabao	1	0.8	1	1.4
Power thresher	3	2.5	1	1.4
Sprayer	7	5.8	21	28.4
Rotary weeder	25	20.6	73	98.6

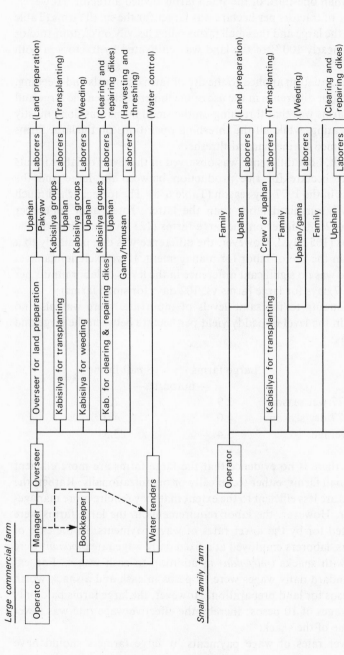

Fig. 6-2. Organizational charts of large and small farms.

while less than one-third of the small farms owned a tractor. However, the number of tractors per hectare was larger for the small farms (Table 6–7). Both the large and the small farms relied heavily on custom-tractor work, and nearly 100% of the land was cultivated by tractors in both cases.

The same situation applied to the use of farm chemicals and weeding. The only major difference in the use of machinery between the large and the small farms was that threshing on the small farms was done mostly by hand beating, while all the threshing operations on the large farms were performed by mechanical threshers.

As a result, little difference was observed in the levels of labor inputs applied per hectare for rice production between the large and the small farms in the 1977 dry season (Table 6–8). The former relied much more heavily on hired labor than the latter. Total labor input per hectare was 20% higher on the large farms (123 days/ha) than on the small farms (105 days). However, the difference was due primarily to a difference in the use of labor for management. If we exclude management, there was no significant difference in the levels of labor inputs per hectare (107 days for large farms vs. 102 days for small farms).

Corresponding to the same levels of input use, there was also no difference in the level of paddy yield per hectare between the large and small farms:

	Large farms	Small farms
	—m.ton/ha—	
1977 wet season	2.9	2.6
1977 dry season	4.0	4.0
Average	3.4	3.3

Overall, there is no evidence that the large farms are more efficient than the small farms, either technically or organizationally. Rather, the large farms are less efficient to the extent that they require more management labor. However, the labor requirements in the large farms were compensated for by the lower rates of wage payments. In the case of small farms, laborers employed at a fixed daily wage rate (*upahan*) were provided with snacks (*mirienda*) in addition to cash wages. For example, standard daily wages were 10 pesos in cash and a snack worth about 2 pesos for land preparation. However, the large farms paid only the cash wages of 10 pesos; thereby the effective wage rate was lower by the value of the snack.

The lower rates of wage payments by large farmers should have

Table 6-8.   Labor inputs for rice production per hectare, large vs. small farms, in the South Laguna Village, 1977 dry season.

	2 large farms (A and B)			Small family farms		
	Man-days/ha		%	Man-days/ha		%
	Total	Hired	Hired labor share	Total	Hired	Hired labor share
	(1)	(2)	(2)/(1)	(3)	(4)	(4)/(3)
Land preparation	12.0	12.0	100	10.5	7.3	70
Transplanting	9.6	9.6	100	9.5	8.9	94
Weeding	34.0	34.0	100	35.1	18.4	5˙
Harvesting & threshing	30.0	30.0	100	34.4	30.8	9ʋ
Seedbed preparation & care	2.0	2.0	100	1.6	0.3	19
Fertilizer & chemical application	3.0	3.0	100	2.8	0.5	18
Clear & repair dikes	16.0	16.0	100	7.9	1.9	24
Management	16.0	14.0	88	3.0	0	0
Total	*122.6*	*120.6*	*98*	*104.8*	*68.1*	*65*

been based on their strong bargaining power which could not be matched by small farmers. However, the revulsion of laborers against such mean treatment as the termination of the traditional custom of serving snacks would have increased the workers' noncompliance or propensity to shirk. Large farmers could cope with this problem because they employed specialized agents for labor management and formed a manager-foreman hierarchy. On the other hand, small farmers would have considered it more efficient to rely on the principle of reciprocity or the patron-client relationship in a barter between more generous treatment and loyal service. In terms of the Becker theory of social interaction, to continue serving snacks can be considered a payment by small farmers to purchase the goodwill of laborers and, thereby, to reduce the cost of labor enforcement (see Chapter 2).

The stronger bargaining position of the large farms is more clearly reflected in the output-sharing rates for harvesting workers. The traditional harvest sharing rates in this *barrio* were one-sixth for the dry season and one-fifth for the wet season. In 1975, the two large tenant farmers reduced the sharing rates to one-eighth and one-seventh, respectively. Their action met substantial resistance from workers. After they announced the reduction of the sharing rates, some of their fields were destroyed during the night. However, they were successful in changing the custom because of their bargaining power.[3]

[3] Unlike most villages in Laguna, the *gama* system was not commonly used in the

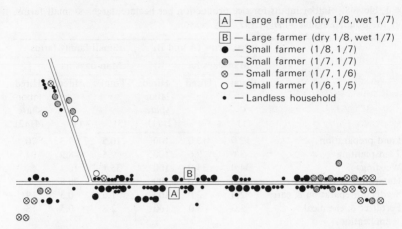

Fig. 6-3.   Locational contribution of households in the South Laguna Village in terms of the share of harvesters in relation to large farmers A and B.

The reduction in harvesters' output-sharing rates was thus initiated by the operators of the large commercial farms, followed by the small farmers with a time lag. This process is reflected in the geographical distribution of the sharing rates: farms located near the two large farms had lower rates, and those far away had higher rates (Figure 6–3).

Cost-Return Calculations

The economic advantages of large vs. small farms can be evaluated by comparing the relations between farm output values and input cost. Table 6–9 makes the comparison by estimating how farm outputs were distributed among various factors used for rice production and how much surplus (net profit) was left to the farm operators.

The cost-return structure measured in terms of the factor shares of rice output per hectare was similar for the large-scale commercial farms and the small family farms operating under leasehold tenancy. As shown in Table 6–8, average labor input per hectare was higher on large farms than on small farms because of a larger labor requirement for management on the former. However, the labor requirements on

South Laguna Village. Only 13% of the rice area was harvested under the *gama* system, 84% under the *hunusan* system and 3% by family labor at the time of our survey. The reason the *gama* system was not commonly adopted was because the strong bargaining power of the large farmers made it possible to reduce the harvesting wage rates by lowering the harvesters' share under the *hunusan* system.

the large farms were compensated for by the lower wage rates based on their stronger bargaining power, resulting in the same level of labor cost as for the small farms.

The capital cost per hectare was slightly higher for the large farms, reflecting a higher capital intensity. The lower capital cost of the small farms was, to a large extent, cancelled by the higher land rent paid to the landlords. There was no significant difference in the levels of operators' surplus between the large farms and the small farms with leasehold titles. Hence, these data fail to support the hypothesis of higher profitability of large-scale rice farms compared with small-scale rice farms.

The cost-return structure of small farms operating under sub-tenancy arrangements is in sharp contrast to those of the small farms under leasehold tenancy. The sub-tenants had to pay a large share of output to intermediate landlords (sub-lessors); therefore no surplus was left for the operators. The findings for this village are very similar to those for the East Laguna Village (refer to Table 5–12).

Contrasting patterns in the cost-return structures between the lease-hold tenants (both large and small) and the sub-tenants show clearly that the large surpluses of the leaseholders consisted mainly of the difference between the actual rent paid to landlords and the economic rent, defined as the return to the service of the land. This difference was

Table 6-9.   The cost-return structure of rice production, large vs. small farms, in the South Laguna Village, 1977 dry season.

	Factor payments (kg/ha)[a]			Factor shares (%)		
	Large	Small farms		Large	Small farms	
	farms	Leasehold	Sub-tenancy[b]	farms	Leasehold	Sub-tenancy
Rice output	3960	3996	3866	100	100	100
Factor payments:						
Current inputs	540	477	544	14	12	14
Capital[c]	531	333	383	13	8	10
Labor	1143	1085	1215	29	27	31
Land	697	873	1742	18	22	45
(Paid to landlord)	(697)	(873)	(662)	(18)	(22)	(17)
(Paid to sub-lessor)	(0)	(0)	(1080)	(0)	(0)	(28)
Operator's surplus	1049	1228	−18	26	31	0

[a] Measured in rice equivalents.
[b] Excluding those sub-tenanted farms in which the two contracting parties are relatives.
[c] Sum of paid or imputed rentals of carabao, tractors and other machines.

generated by the institutional rigidity of land rental rates, fixed by law, in the face of growing population and technological change.

Conditions of Polarization

The results of our study revealed a dramatic trend towards polarization in one atypical village in the Philippines in the presence of rapid diffusion of modern rice technology. Our study shows that, in terms of the levels of farming technology, no significant difference exists between large and small farms. Both adopted modern varieties for 100% of their area. There was no difference in the levels of fertilizer and chemical application and in the methods of seedbed preparation, transplanting and weeding.

There was also no significant difference in the levels of mechanization and labor input applied directly to rice production operations per hectare, although the labor input required for management was larger for larger farms. Correspondingly, rice yields per hectare were the same. Overall, no technological advantage seems to exist for large-scale commercial operations. Rather, they seem less efficient technically to the extent that they require more management inputs and have higher capital costs.

On the other hand, the large farms had an advantage in exercising their strong bargaining power to pay hired workers lower wage rates and to pay landlords lower rents. The advantage in bargaining position and the technological disadvantage from a more complex organization of large farms cancelled each other out, leaving the same level of net profit or operator surplus per hectare. In terms of economic efficiency and profitability, not much incentive seems to exist for the farms to expand their scale of operation.

Nevertheless, large tenant farmers have accumulated landholdings and consolidated them into larger units of operation. The reason is that this is a safer way to capture a part of the economic rent of leased land than sub-renting one's holdings in small parcels. As the comparison of the cost-return structures between sub-tenants and leasehold tenants shows, the large surplus for leasehold operators was really the gap between the economic rent and the actual rent paid to landlords. If so, profits for the large leasehold tenants should be the same irrespective of whether they cultivate land by themselves or sub-rent it, at least in the village studied. However, under the land reform laws, sub-renting is very dangerous for the lessor because his leasehold title may be forfeited if the sub-lessee reports to the Agrarian Reform Office.

Considering such a probability, the transaction costs involved in contract negotiation and enforcement would be prohibitive to making sub-tenancy arrangements beyond a limited circle of relatives and close friends. The cost of managing large-scale farms for large holders would be much less than the expected transaction cost involved in sub-tenancy contracts; this seems to be the basic reason why they prefer to consolidate their holdings into large units. Underlying this process was the increasing gap between the economic rent and the actual rent due to the growing population pressure on land.

A major question may be asked: Why did the factors that promoted polarization in the South Laguna Village not operate in the East Laguna Village? Under the same circumstances, the size distribution of operational holdings has become smaller but more uniform, and the peasant mode of production has continued to dominate in the East Laguna Village with the more common practice of sub-tenancy and *gama* arrangements. The answer should be sought in the differences in the social structures of the two villages.

First, the South Laguna Village was developed as a hacienda *barrio* based on landlords' investment in land infrastructure. Land ownership distribution was highly skewed from the beginning, and the distribution of operational holdings was also skewed because of the existence of large farms under the direct administration of landlords. In contrast, the East Laguna Village was settled by smallholders and squatters in an unorganized way. Ownership and operational farm size distributions were relatively equal. Therefore, compared to the East Laguna Village, people in the South Laguna Village should have been more used to *modus operandi* of large farms, including the exercises of their monopsonistic powers. In the East Laguna Village, there would have been stronger resistance against any members of the community who tried to exercise such powers. Also, the initial existence of landlords' large holdings under direct administration in the South Laguna Village made the expansion of large tenant operations much easier because large areas of the landlords' holdings were commissioned to the tenants' commercial operations in lump sums.

Second, the South Laguna Village was developed more recently, in a shorter period, through organized settlement by large landlords. Therefore, kinship relations in the South Laguna Village are less common than in the East Laguna Village (the ratio of families sharing common names is only 33% in the South Laguna Village as compared with 59% in the East Laguna Village). Migration into and out of the *barrio* has been more frequent in the South Laguna Village. Overall, the solidarity of the *barrio* community based on the mutual-help principle has been much less well developed in the South Laguna Village; this facilitated the direct exercise of hierarchical power against the custom of the village community, such as the abolition of the service of *mirienda* (snacks) to workers and the reduction in the output-sharing rate of harvesters.

In contrast, in the East Laguna Village, even landless workers were guaranteed decent shares of village income through the *gama* system. In such a social environment the cost of contract enforcement involved in a sub-tenancy arrangement would have been much smaller because the benevolent relations among friends and relatives reduced the risk of sub-tenants' taking legal action against sub-lessors.

Comparison of the ways in which the two village communities adjust their institutions in response to population pressure, technological change and the land reform programs sheds light on the process by which the same economic forces can produce different institutions, depending on different social environments created through different ecologies and histories. Most important, it suggests that there is a threshold of inequality in wealth and power beyond which polarization will occur.

Part **III**

Agrarian Change in Indonesian Villages

In Java, stalk-by-stalk rice harvesting using the *ani-ani* knife (above) is being replaced by sickle cutting (below).

Chapter 7

Agricultural Involution or Evolution?

In the previous three chapters we investigated the process of agrarian change in the major rice-producing area of the Philippines. Broad observation over a wide area as well as intensive village case studies seem to indicate that the majority of village communities have been moving towards peasant stratification and that those moving towards polarization represent exceptional cases; it appears that most farmers who became partial proprietors as leaseholders or amortizing owners through land reform programs have preferred to behave as "legitimate patrons" in terms of traditional norms rather than to become commercial entrepreneurs using large machineries and wage laborers; the peasant mode of production has been preserved with institutional innovations such as the *gama* and sub-tenancy arrangements despite major changes in the return to land relative to labor.

A major question is whether the peasant stratification is a transitory phenomenon. Will the growing population pressure continue simply to add strata to peasant sub-classes? Or will a point eventually be reached where those who belong to the lower strata begin to reproduce themselves as wage workers completely alienated from the product of their labor?

In order to shed light on this issue, we attempt to analyze agrarian changes in Java in this and the next two chapters. Java serves as a social observatory uniquely suited for the problem concerned, because it has experienced a high rate of population growth since the nineteenth century and is now characterized by the highest population density in the world. There have been serious concerns that the population pressure, together with other modernization forces such as new technology and commercialization, is destroying traditional village institutions and resulting in the polarization of peasant communities with sharp class conflicts.

In this chapter we develop a historical and geographical perspective on agrarian changes in Java, which will serve as an introduction to an intensive village study in the next chapter.

Population Growth and Agricultural Involution

Java is the most densely populated major area in the world. In 1976 there were 645 inhabitants per square kilometer, far more than in densely populated industrial countries and more than in any other developing country except Bangladesh (Table 7-1). The major population problem in Indonesia is that Java, which accounts for only 7% of the total area of the country, is crowded by more than 60% of its population.

Table 7-1.   Population density per square km, 1976.

Java (and Madura)	645
Indonesia	71
Bangladesh	558
India	189
Philippines	144
Thailand	84
Japan	303
Belgium	316
Netherlands	337
United Kingdom	230

Sources: World Bank, *World Development Report 1978*, Washington, D.C., 1978; and Biro Pusat Statistik, *Statistik Indonesia 1975-76*, Jakarta, 1977.

The high population density in Java has been considered a result of the high population growth rate since the beginning of the nineteenth century. If Sir Thomas Stamford Raffles is correct, the population of Java was stationary during the eighteenth century due to wars, epidemics and oppression by native chiefs reinforced by exploitation by the Dutch East India Company (Raffles, 1830, Vol. 1, pp. 66–73). During the nineteenth century, the population increased from Raffles's census figure of 4.5 million in 1815 to 28.4 million for an average growth rate of 2.2% per year (Table 7-2). The high rate of population growth has traditionally been attributed to such causes as peace under Dutch rule, increased food supply, improved hygiene and public health measures,

Table 7-2.   Population growth in Java (and Madura), 1815–1976.

	Population (million)	Annual growth rate (%)
1815	4.6	
1845	9.5	2.5
1860	12.7	1.8
1880	19.8	2.2
1900	28.7	1.9
1920	35.0	1.0
1930	41.7	1.9
1950	50.5	1.0
1960	61.9	2.0
1970	75.1	1.9
1976	85.3	2.1

Sources: Widjojo Nitisastro, *Population Trends in Indonesia,* Ithaca and London, Cornell University Press, 1970, pp. 5–6; Biro Pusat Statistik, *Statistik Indonesia,* Jakarta, various issues.

and the extension of markets that prevented local crop failures from turning into famines (Geertz, 1970, p. 80). However, this view has recently been criticized on the ground that the apparent population explosion in the nineteenth century was a statistical fiction due to under-reporting in earlier censuses and that the population of Java had already been quite large long before the nineteenth century (Nitisastro, 1970).

In any event, the population of Java has increased rapidly since the beginning of the twentieth century: it has trebled since 1900 and doubled since 1930, when fairly reliable census data became available. A similar increase in population was experienced by Western Europe and Japan during the process of modern economic growth; there industrial development provided sufficient employment opportunities in the urban sector to absorb more than the increments in total population. In Java, however, the population growth was not accompanied by such structural transformation. The majority of the people remained in the rural sector, and the ever-increasing rural population pressed hard on limited land resources. Agricultural land use has long passed the point where further expansion of cultivated land area seriously endangers ecological balance.

The strong population pressure "resulted in an increased parcelling of the land into dwarf holdings, in the accumulation of large holdings wherever land-tenure practices allowed it, in the formation of a class of landless agricultural laborers, in widespread indebtedness, in the growth of tenancy, in the decline of rural incomes, and in poverty, malnutrition, and food shortage" (Pelzer, 1948, p. 165).

However, unlike those in the Philippines, Javanese village communities did not bifurcate into noncultivating landlords and landless tenants. A majority of peasants continued to be dwarf-sized owner operators. Large estates of the hacienda type did not emerge in the subsistence sector, which is based mainly on rice culture. Under the colonial regime, plantations of tropical export crops developed dramatically, but they did not destroy traditional village communities. The plantation sector was "superimposed" on the indigenous peasant economy to create "dual societies" (Boeke, 1953). On the surface, at least, Javanese villages maintained their posture as a relatively homogeneous peasant society bounded by traditional norms. The unique pattern of agrarian organization in Java seems to be explained largely by Dutch colonial policy.

Colonial Heritage[1]

Dutch rule in Java dates from 1619 when the Dutch East India Company occupied Batavia (Jakarta) and the surrounding territory. Dutch colonialism was characterized by "indirect rule". As a mercantile country, the Netherlands' interest lay in the procurement of tropical agricultural products for export at the minimum administrative cost. To this end the Dutch recognized the rule of native chieftains insofar as they supplied them with the commodities that they wanted. To the extent possible, the Dutch abstained from interference with native life.

Under the Dutch East India Company, the local rulers (Regents) were responsible for securing the delivery of produce that native cultivators were compelled to grow and sell to the Company at a set price —so-called "forced deliveries". In addition, commodities for export were collected by "contingencies", a form of tax payable in kind from areas under the direct control of the Company. The Company flourished on the basis of this produce collected essentially as tribute. However, in the course of time its prosperity was undermined by breaches in the Company's trade monopoly by smuggling and the corruption of the Company's servants. At the end of the eighteenth century, the Company went bankrupt due to war with England and to the French Revolution, and its possessions were taken over by the state.

During the 1811–16 British occupation of Java during the Napoleonic Wars, Lieutenant Governor Raffles reoriented colonial policy in a liberal direction based on economic freedom and equal law. The English, like the Dutch, wanted tropical produce. But whereas the Dutch had to obtain it as tribute because they had no goods to sell, the

---

[1] This section draws heavily on Furnival (1944; 1948).

English wanted to sell Western goods like the cheap textiles of Manchester which, after the industrial revolution, could be sold in Asia at lower rates than native manufactures. For the English, trade was more profitable than tribute. Following the British model in India, Raffles tried to establish "direct rule" by substituting European magistrates and judges for the native Regents and by replacing tribute in kind with money taxes.

When the Dutch recovered their possessions, they found that "under a system of economic freedom the English monopolized the trade of Java, while the Dutch had to bear the cost of government" (Furnival, 1948, p.220). The Dutch had to revive the traditional methods used by the East India Company. A new plan, known as the Culture System, was devised by Van den Bosch in 1830. This system provided that each village set one-fifth of its cultivated land aside for the production of export crops, which had to be delivered to the government in lieu of land tax; or, alternatively, villagers had to work for 66 days a year on government-owned estates or other projects.

The Culture System was astoundingly successful for the promotion of export crop production and for increasing government revenue. Under this system, despite enormous expansion in cash crop production, the solidarity of traditional village communities was not weakened but strengthened. The system was implemented through native administrative channels running from the Regents to the village headmen; the village was utilized as a unit of communal production and labor mobilization. The penetration of the market economy was kept minimal because the cash crop yield was collected through a non-market channel. In order to preserve the basis of the Culture System, the government tried to prevent the alienation of village land under cultivation to foreign merchants and moneylenders.

The profits of the Culture System not only enriched the Dutch Treasury but also revived Dutch commerce and industry which had been destroyed by the Napoleonic Wars. Private enterprises soon began to demand a liberal policy under which they would have greater freedom to engage in profit-seeking activities in the colony. Thus, because of the very success of the Culture System, it was replaced by the Liberal System which dominated colonial policies for the last three decades of the nineteenth century.

The Agrarian Law of 1870 provided for the gradual abolition of the Culture System and opened the doors to private plantation development in Indonesia. However, the long-established principle of Dutch rule that native land should not be alienated to foreigners was maintained. The government feared that if the people were allowed to dispose of their land to foreigners, large areas would be transferred to European planters and Chinese moneylenders and that social unrest would result.[2] Accordingly it resisted the demand by liberals to apply Western concepts of property rights in land.

Under the Agrarian Law, foreign planters could only acquire land on lease—either government-owned wasteland on long lease or native villagers' land on short lease. In general, plantations based on long-term leases of wasteland grew perennial crops such as coffee, tea and pepper, and those based on short-term leases grew annual crops such as sugar and tobacco. Thus, the plantation production of sugar and tobacco was interlocked with the peasant production of subsistence crops; in particular, sugar and rice were integrated into a uniquely interdependent relationship based on the use of paddy fields.

In Java, sugar planters rented rice land on lease contracts extending from 3.5 years to 21.5 years. The lessee was allowed to occupy only one-third of the village land at any one time (16 months); the other two-thirds had to be left for rice cultivation by villagers. The land planted in sugar had to be exchanged for another third after each harvest. This rotation was designed to prevent planters from gaining a permanent hold on village lands. Under this system, the intrusion of plantation activities did not destroy the communal organization of traditional villages but reinforced it: "Contracts were usually closed with the village heads rather than with individual peasants, thus strengthening traditional tendencies toward communal landholding; in the periodic reapportionment of plots to individual cultivators, the village heads assigned each claimant a parcel in each of the three sections into which the village *sawah* area had been divided in order to make possible rotational leasing by an estate" (Pelzer, 1971, p.146). The communal organization of the village saved the sugar planters transaction costs because they could negotiate land leases with only one *lurah* (village head) rather than with a large number of villagers.

A unique aspect of the Dutch colonial rule was that, unlike other colonial powers, the Netherlands did not try to impose Western institutions such as private property rights in land. Traditional village institutions were maintained and utilized as a lever to extract tropical agricultural products from the colony at the minimum administrative cost. The effort to preserve the village community continued in the Ethical

---

[2] Raffles in the British regime and Daendels in the preceding French regime sold about 1.5 million ha of state land to private persons to raise money for treasury. These private estates became the source of social unrest and disruption because estate owners' treatment of natives was often harsh and oppressive. In 1911, the Dutch colonial government began to purchase back such lands.

Policy which followed the Liberal System. Ethical reformers, holding that the Liberal policy weakened village solidarity and resulted in peasant hardships, aimed to strengthen the village and to use it as a lever to enhance the social welfare of the natives. Their view found expression in the Village Act of 1906 which endowed the village with the power to administer village affairs, property and land under the general council of villagers. Other efforts to promote social welfare by means of education, agricultural extension and irrigation improvement were also attempted, though the results of such efforts often ended up disappointing the reformers.[3]

The doctrine of Ethical Policy drew on a humanistic concern over "the diminishing welfare of the people of Java" as evidenced by the falling per-capita income of the native population despite the growth of plantations and the swelling volume of exports. However, it can also be viewed as a policy to prevent an increase in the cost of colonial administration, which was expected to rise due to social unrest. Preservation of traditional village communities had been instrumental in the Dutch extraction of export crops from the colony ever since the foundation of the East India Company. It appears that the Ethical Policy implicitly aimed to strengthen the village as a shelter against modernization forces, a place where a reserve army of meek labor for export crop production could be reproduced.

With the purposive effort of Dutch colonialism, the traditional institutions of Javanese villages were maintained or even strengthened. Land tenure was subject to strong communal regulation. In a form of tenure called "communal possession", a villager has the right to use a share of communal land of the village, usually subject to a periodic rotation, which he has no freedom to dispose of except for his own cultivation. In a tenure called "heritable individual possession", an individual occupies a plot perpetually and can dispose of it subject to certain communal restrictions; often its sale is prohibited or limited to those living in the same village. According to a large-scale survey conducted in 1868–69 by Dutch colonial authorities covering 808 villages throughout Java, communal possession was found in as many as 60% of the villages (Kano, 1977). Although comparable data are not available for later

---

[3] The disillusionment of Ethical reformers trying to improve the native economy is reflected in Boeke's theory of sociological dualism (1953). Boeke argued that the native Indonesian economy operates under principles entirely different from those of Western capitalistic economies to which neoclassical marginalism can be applied. He believed it futile to attempt to introduce Western technology and institutions into the native economy; the only effect of efforts to introduce modern technology and inputs would be an acceleration in the rate of population growth. For a critical evaluation of the Boeke thesis, see Higgins (1955–56).

dates, it seems reasonable to assume that such communal regulations on landholding were preserved to a large extent until the end of the Dutch regime.

With the independence of Indonesia, colonial land laws were replaced by a series of new laws enacted in 1960. Among them, the Basic Agrarian Law (Law No.5) put an end to the dualistic property rights which had attempted to accommodate the interests of Dutch capital within the social framework of indigenous village communities. "The new legislation substituted a single code based on Indonesian traditional (*adat*) law purified from 'feudal' and 'capitalistic' elements. The new legislation qualified indigenous law in various ways, although in vague terms . . . . These limitations gave the new law more of a western than eastern tenor" (Utrecht, 1969). In fact, the basic right on land recognized by the law was the individual hereditary right of ownership (*hak milik*) which is similar to the Western concept of private property rights, although it is not absolute but subject to government regulations on the use of land for administering natural resources in the national interest. The *hak milik* right was given only to "autochthonous" Indonesian citizens.

The agrarian legislation of 1960 did not intend to open the door to private accumulation of landholdings. On the contrary, it had the aim of redistributing land in order to foster independent peasants. For this purpose, absentee ownership was forbidden, and maximum limits for individual holdings were set as follows according to population density (Law No. 56, Article 1 and Supplement):

Population/square km	Paddy field (ha)	Upland field (ha)
Less than 50	15.0	20
51–250	10.0	12
251–400	7.5	9
Over 400	5.0	6

Land in excess of these maximums was supposed to be taken over by the state for distribution among the landless population. Furthermore, a minimum limit of 2 hectares for subdivision was set in order to prevent excess fragmentation of landholdings.

Both the upper and lower limits of landholding set by the Law were very high for Java, where the average holding per peasant was less than half a hectare. Almost no land held by peasants fell in the category subject to expropriation. For this reason the land redistribution program could have little impact outside the plantation sector. Further, land reform programs under this Law and the Sharecropping Law (Law

No.2) designed to regulate tenancy contracts have become a dead letter, especially since the suppression of communists in 1965. Despite its intentions, the Basic Agrarian Law has contributed to private land accumulation and the development of landlordism (Soentoro *et al.*, 1980).

Involution or Evolution?

The preservation of traditional village organization and institutions under Dutch rule did not mean that the village remained a homogeneous peasant community. Instead, due to strong population pressure on land, Javanese villages had been stratified into a number of layers based on landownership (including claims to communal land). At the top of the social strata was a group of villagers, known as *gogols,* who owned both paddy fields (*sawah*) and gardens (*pekarangan*); they had all the rights that village community members had and also shared all the burdens. The second group, who were called *setengah gogols,* owned garden land and houses but no fields. The third group, called *menumpangs,* owned houses only. The lowest rank, called *kumplans* or *nuspus,* consisted of those who possessed neither land nor houses but lived as boarders in other persons' houses.[4] All evidence indicates that the proportion of landless and near-landless community members increased over time (Pelzer, 1948, pp. 167–168; Pelzer, 1971, p.137).

However, Clifford Geertz, based on his observation of post-independence Java, argued that the class differentiation based on landownership does not necessarily reflect income inequality in the village community. He assumed an income-sharing mechanism which would maintain a comparatively high degree of social and economic homogeneity by dividing the economic pie into a steadily increasing number of small pieces, a situation he referred to as "shared poverty" (Geertz, 1970, p.97). He identified village institutions in the form of work- and output-sharing arrangements as the basis of shared poverty:

The productive system of the post-traditional village developed, therefore, into a dense web of finely spun work rights and work responsibilities spread, like the reticulate veins of the hand, throughout the whole body of the village lands. A man will let out part of his one hectare to a tenant—or to two or three—while at the same time seeking tenancies on the lands of other men, thus balancing his obligations to give work (to his relatives, to his dependents, or even to his close friends and neighbors) against his own subsistence requirements. A

---

[4] The class hierarchy with *gogols* on the top has been undermined since the proclamation of the 1960 Basic Agrarian Law (Kano, 1979, pp. 182–186).

man will rent or pawn his land to another for a money payment and then serve as a tenant on that land himself, perhaps in turn letting subtenancies out to others. A man may agree, or be granted the opportunity, to perform the planting and weeding tasks for one-fifth of the harvest and job the actual work in turn to someone else, who may, in *his* turn, employ wage laborers or enter into an exchange relationship with neighbors to obtain the necessary labor. The structure of land ownership is thus only an indifferent guide to the social pattern of agricultural exploitation, the specific form of which emerges only in the intricate institutional fretwork through which land and labor are actually brought together. In share tenancy and associated practices the ever-driven wet-rice village found the means by which to divide its growing economic pie into a greater number of traditionally fixed pieces and so to hold an enormous population on the land at a comparatively very homogeneous, if grim, level of living. What elsewhere has been sought through land reform—the minimization of socioeconomic contrasts based on differential control of agricultural resources—the Javanese peasant, whose farms were minute to start with, achieved through that more ancient weapon of the poor: work spreading (Geertz, 1970, pp. 99–100).

Geertz identified the technological basis of work sharing or spreading as the great labor-absorption capacity of wet rice culture that allowed successive intensifications of labor application per unit of land without resulting in a major decline in the marginal productivity of labor:

Wet-rice cultivation, with its extraordinary ability to maintain levels of marginal labor productivity by always managing to work one more man in without a serious fall in per-capita income, soaked up almost the whole of the additional population that Western intrusion created, at least indirectly. It is this ultimately self-defeating process that I have proposed to call "agricultural involution" (Geertz, 1970, p. 80).

Through ever-increasing intensification of rice cultivation, such as multiple cropping, more careful weeding and irrigation control, coupled with meticulous work-sharing arrangements, Javanese agriculture became involuted with a constant productivity of labor, and village people continued to share their poverty. Despite the high population pressure and the increased commercialization, polarization of peasant communities into large commercial farmers and landless wage workers did not occur.

Geertz's view has recently been challenged by, among others, William Collier.[5] Collier maintains that Geertz built his theory on village observation in East Java during 1952–54. These were the years when the economy was still subject to the aftereffects of World War II and the revolution. Commercial activities were depressed, and the village was relatively static and self-contained as a result. Collier argues that the situation in rural Java changed so radically in the 1960s and 1970s that a theory built on observations of the 1950s can hardly be applicable; increasing commercialization and government modernization programs have given large farmers opportunities to seek profits by introducing new technology and neglecting traditional obligations of work and income sharing; because the new technology relies more on modern purchased inputs than on labor, its adoption has resulted in an increase in output per unit of labor input; on the other hand, labor employment opportunities for poor villagers have decreased.

The whole process, Collier argues, should be termed "evolution" rather than "involution". Collier's concept of evolution seems to be largely equivalent to the Marx-Lenin concept of polarization since it involves a process in which the traditional peasant community is decomposed into large commercial farmers and a landless proletariat under the reckless forces of commercialization and modern technology —a view shared by radical political economists.[6]

Collier's argument has a strong intuitive appeal. It is often observed that the traditional *ani-ani* (hand knife) for cutting rice stalks has been replaced by labor-saving sickles. Some farmers stop observing the traditional practices of work and income-sharing, such as the *bawon* system in which everyone can participate in harvesting and receive a certain share of output. It is not uncommon to find cases in which large landholdings have been concentrated in the hands of a few since the promulgation of the 1960 Basic Agrarian Law, even though "large" landholders in the Java context are still very small by world standards. How pervasive is the evolution or polarization process in Java? Are the traditional arrangements of work and income-sharing soon to disappear? Has the Geertz concept of shared poverty entirely lost its relevance?

Changes in Rice Harvesting Systems[7]

Collier considers that recent changes in rice harvesting systems in Java

---

[5] Among his many writings, see Collier (1977) and Collier *et al*. (1974). For a review of Collier's arguments vis-à-vis the Geertz thesis, see Kano (1980).
[6] See the references in footnote 5 of Chapter 3, p. 52.
[7] This section draws on Hayami and Hafid (1979).

represent the most dramatic evidence in support of his "evolution" thesis. The traditional *bawon* system that allowed wide sharing of output has been replaced by the new *tebasan* system that limits participation in harvesting work and reduces the share due to harvesters. The change has been attributed mainly to population pressure and new technology. The shift from *bawon* to *tebasan* has been documented by Collier so persuasively that it has virtually come to be accepted as an established paradigm of the nature of agrarian change in Java.

In this section we attempt to examine the paradigm on the basis of a broad survey of Java.

From Bawon to Tebasan : A Paradigm

First, let us summarize the logical context of the paradigm of the changes in rice harvesting systems that has been established by Collier and others (Collier *et al.,* 1973 and 1974; Husken, 1979; Sinaga and Collier, 1975; Utami and Ihalauw, 1973).

In the traditional *bawon* system, rice harvesting is a community activity in which all or most community members can participate and receive a certain share of output. When the crop is ripe, a horde of harvesters enter the field and harvest the paddy using the *ani-ani* to cut the stalks at the neck of the panicles. The harvested stalks are bundled and brought to the farmer's house, where the harvesters receive a certain share (*bawon*) such as one sheaf out of eight. Typically, harvesting is open to anybody. By tradition, the farmer cannot limit the number of harvesters who participate.

Since around 1970, it is said, this system has rapidly been replaced by a new system called *tebasan.*[8] In the *tebasan* system, farmers sell their standing crops to middlemen called *penebas* a few days before the harvest. Because the middlemen in their role as *penebas* are free from the traditional obligations of the village community, they close the harvest to the majority of villagers and employ a smaller number of regular workers to harvest their purchased crops. Typically, they pay cash wages to the laborers and supply sickles for higher efficiency. In these ways the cost of harvesting is reduced.

A major factor underlying the shift from *bawon* to *tebasan* is said to be population pressure. As population growth presses on the limited area of land under cultivation, the number of landless workers and farmers with holdings too small for subsistence increases. To secure a minumum subsistence income, they swarm into harvesting fields not

---

[8] *Tebasan* itself is an old system. However, until recently it was used primarily for cash crops such as sugar cane and fruit but not for rice.

only in their own villages but also outside as seasonal migrant workers. As the number of harvesters rises above a certain point, significant losses occur from physical damage (e.g. trampled crops) and from cheating and stealing. The *tebasan* system is an institutional innovation enabling farmers to establish and maintain control over the harvesting of their crops.[9]

Another major factor said to have facilitated the development of the *tebasan* system is the new rice technology in the form of modern semi-dwarf varieties (MV). Modern varieties permit the use of the sickle, thus reducing the number of workers needed for rice harvesting. It had been believed that the goddess of rice was offended if rice was cut by sickles. However, MV came from abroad (Philippines) and so were considered unrelated to the native goddess. More important, the technical superiority of the sickle over the *ani-ani* is greater with MV than with traditional varieties. First, MV paddy is short-stalked, which makes it more difficult to cut the panicles. Second, MV paddy is more susceptible to shattering, thus making it preferable to thresh after the crop is harvested by sickles. The introduction of sickles, in turn, by reducing the number of workers employed, encourages reliance on *penebas* and their hired labor force.

The welfare implication of the *tebasan* system in the Collier *et al.* paradigm is that both farmers and *penebas* gain at the expense of laborers, especially those who are not patronized by the *penebas*. The sociopolitical condition that made such a change feasible is identified as a relative decline in the bargaining position of the landless class, partly due to the increasing scarcity of land relative to labor and partly due to the major changes in the political environment in Indonesia after the suppression of communists in 1965.[10]

Survey Procedure

To throw further light on the empirical evidence for the Collier *et al.*

---

[9] Sturgess and Wijaya (1979) argue that *tebasan* can also be considered a credit institution similar to *ijon*, in which a farmer sells a green crop to a middleman several months before the harvest. However, the role of *tebasan* as a credit institution seems minor if it exists at all, according to observations in our survey, since standing crop is usually sold less than 10 days before the harvest. The use of credit for such a short time will not be of much use. Moreover, *penebas* pay farmers only a fraction (most commonly one-fourth) of the total payment at the time of contract. Often, a *penebas* pays the rest several days after the harvested crops are sold; meanwhile, he uses the retained cash as a revolving fund to purchase other farmers' crops. In this case, farmers are the lenders of credit. No respondent in our survey identified need for credit as a reason for adopting the *tebasan* system.

[10] For the impact of political changes on the relations between rural elites and the poor, see Husken (1979) and White (1976).

paradigm, we undertook two extensive survey trips in August and December 1978. Collier *et al.*, and also Utami and Ihalauw, based their postulates on observations at a relatively small number of locations. Our strategy was to cover a large number of locations over a wide area, in order to identify a broad general trend with which the observations of Collier and others could be compared.

For this purpose, we travelled widely around West and Central Java and stopped at random on the way for data collection. Thus, our data can be regarded as derived from "random-walk sampling". We covered 48 villages (*desa*) in 28 districts (*kabupaten*). In each *desa* we interviewed a group of farmers on the basis of a brief questionnaire. We tried to collect information of "common" practices of rice harvesting arrangements in their villages, even though we recognize that arrangements can vary even within a *desa*. To the extent possible, we tried to check the data obtained from the farmers by interviewing workers, *penebas* and *desa* officials. Thus, our survey unit should be thought of as the *desa*.

We tried to cover as wide an area as possible. Time and other constraints, however, limited the coverage of our survey mainly to areas along the highways from the Jakarta-Bogor line to the border between Central and East Java. Obviously, the data collected from such quick-trip surveys are very crude and can be significant only in a rough order of magnitude. The analysis here presented is designed not to draw conclusions but to raise questions for further investigation.

Geographical Distribution

Figure 7-1 gives the geographical distribution of various types of rice harvesting systems based on the results of our survey.

It is important to recognize that the traditional "purely open" *bawon* in the sense that everyone can participate in harvesting is a rather exceptional practice today and has been so for the past ten years. In most cases *bawon* harvesting was already restricted in 1968. The system nearest to the traditional concept of *bawon* harvesting as a communal activity was that in which harvesting was open only to people in the same village, and to outsiders only so long as the number of participants did not exceed a certain limit. A second system did not limit participants to villagers, but set a limit to the total number. Those who arrived at the harvesting site after that number was reached were rejected.[11] The

---

[11] In many cases harvesters regulate the intake among themselves, and those who come late and find the maximum reached go home before the harvest begins.

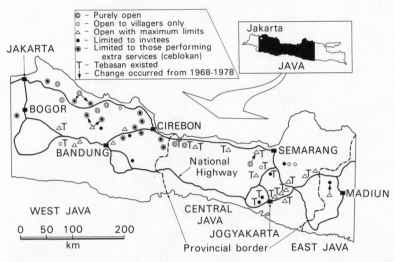

Fig. 7-1. Geographical distribution of harvesting systems in Java, Indonesia, 1978.

third situation involved a more severe restriction: participants were limited to those who received specific invitations from farmers (mostly relatives and neighbors).[12] A fourth system limited the harvesters to those who performed without pay such tasks as transplanting and weeding; this system is called *ceblokan* (also *kedokan* and *ngepak-ngedok*).[13]

Tebasan was practiced in 18 out of our 48 sample villages. In all these villages, the *tebasan* system was practiced side by side with the *bawon* system. If, for brevity, we refer to them as "*tebasan* villages", it must be understood that they are mixed *tebasan-bawon* villages. Figure 7–1 and Table 7–3 show that there is a strong concentration of the *tebasan* system in the Central Java sample, 16 out of the 18 *tebasan* sample villages being located in Central Java. In West Java we observed only two *tebasan* villages, both in *kabupaten* Cianjur, although some of our respondents in *kabupaten* Karawang stated that *tebasan* was practiced elsewhere

[12] A special case classified in this category was a new institution called *gebyokan* in which male workers formed a number of groups and contracted with farmers to harvest on an output-sharing basis. In the *gebyokan* system, the workers cut crops with sickles and threshed the cut crop by hand beating on a big sheet. This case was observed in a *desa* in Ngawi.

[13] *Ceblokan* is an old system in Java, as recorded by van der Kolff (1936). *Ceblokan* contracts vary widely in terms of the services required to establish the right to harvesting. The most common practice we observed required transplanting and weeding without wages but with meals. In some cases only transplanting was required. In others hoeing was required in combination with transplanting or weeding or both. There were also cases where meals were not provided.

Table 7-3.   Distribution of sample villages in Java by type of harvesting system, 1978.

	West Java				Central Java[a]				Total			
	Total	Tebasan villages		Total	Total	Tebasan villages		Total	Total	Tebasan villages		
	No. (1)	No. (2)	% (2)/(1)	No. (3)	No. (3)	No. (4)	% (4)/(3)	No. (5)	No. (5)	No. (6)	% (6)/(5)	
Purely open	4	0	(0)	2	2	2	(100)	6	6	2	(33)	
Open to villagers only	2	1	(50)	3	3	1	(33)	5	5	2	(40)	
Open to all with maximum limits	5	1	(20)	11	11	10	(91)	16	16	11	(69)	
Limited to invitees	3	0	(0)	5	5	3	(60)	8	8	3	(38)	
Limited to those performing extra services (ceblokan)	13	0	(0)	0	0	0	(—)	13	13	0	(0)	
Total	27	2	(7)	21	21	16	(76)	48	48	18	(38)	

[a] Including one village in East Java.

within the *kabupaten*.[14] Except for those two *kabupaten*, all respondents in West Java replied that *tebasan* has never been practiced for rice harvesting in their areas.[15]

It appears that the distribution of *tebasan* is inversely correlated with the distribution of *ceblokan*. In our sample all the *ceblokan* cases were located in West Java; in none of those villages was *tebasan* reported. According to our observation, *ceblokan* was most pervasive on the eastern border of West Java. Respondents in *kabupaten* Majalengka and southern Cirebon stated that all farmers in their areas have been using this system for as long as they could remember. It seems that the *ceblokan* system has been spreading from this area east and north. But we were most surprised to find that as soon as we crossed the provincial border from Cirebon (West Java) to Berebes (Central Java), the system changed from *ceblokan* to open *bawon* coexisting with *tebasan*.[16]

The *bawon* system most commonly coexisting with *tebasan* was the type "open to all with maximum limits". In Central Java more than 90% of *tebasan* villages practiced this type of *bawon* harvesting.[17] We gathered that in those villages the "purely open" system had been traditional; farmers developed the practice of rejecting harvesters above certain numbers as growing population pressure resulted in demands for participation from too many harvesters.

Empirical Tests

Let us now try to examine the postulates of the Collier *et al.* paradigm in the light of our survey data.

Is strengthening control the motive for tebasan adoption? One of the

---

[14] This is consistent with the report of Collier *et al.* (1974), who include Karawang in the *tebasan* area.

[15] Even in these areas the *tebasan* system was practiced pervasively for cash crops, especially for fruits. In his study of rural institutions in West Java, Wiradi (1978) implied that *tebasan* was commonly used in rice harvesting in the Cimanuk Basin (Cirebon, Indramayu, Majalengka, Sumedang and Garut). But his original data did not identify the crops to which *tebasan* was applied. He simply assumed that *tebasan* villages in rice-monoculture areas with more than 90% *sawah* double-cropped for rice used *tebasan* for rice. However, according to our survey, even in the purely rice-monoculture villages *tebasan* applied only to garden crops.

[16] Soentoro (1973) has reported that the *ceblokan* system was practiced in the southwest corner of Central Java (*kabupaten* Kabumen and Banyumas). He has also reported the practice of *ceblokan* in East Java (*kabupaten* Sidoarjo and Jember). Also see Soentoro *et al.* (1980).

[17] In Central Java, a tendency seems to exist for the systems with stricter controls as well as the "open to villagers only" system to be more common in mountain-locked, relatively isolated villages, while the system of "open to all with maximum limits" appears more common in major rice-producing areas located in open, flat plains.

basic postulates of Collier *et al.* was that the primary purpose of farmers in adopting the *tebasan* system was to strengthen their control over the number of harvesters. The geographical distribution of harvesting systems observed in the previous section has an important implication with respect to this postulate. In most cases, it seems, farmers already had some form of control over the number of harvesters 10 years ago. Admittedly, their control may not have been sufficiently strong, and the *tebasan* system could have been instrumental in increasing the degree of control to an optimum level.

This hypothesis is consistent with the fact that the *tebasan* system operated most commonly in the villages where the "open with maximum limits" *bawon* system was practiced. In those villages, farmers' control was less than optimum. We gathered from our farmer respondents that their "maximum limits" are 20 to 30% larger than the numbers they consider optimum. In such a situation it is not unreasonable to assume that farmers adopt the *tebasan* system in order to increase their control over harvesters. Likewise, our observation that *tebasan* has not penetrated into the *ceblokan* areas where the participants in harvesting are strictly limited to those performing extra services seems to reflect the fact that farmers in these areas have had no need to strengthen their control.

In fact, as Table 7–4 shows, the average number of harvesters employed per hectare was much smaller for the types of *bawon* characterized by stronger control, such as "limited to invitees" and "limited to those performing extra services", than for those with looser control. Such a difference provides support for our conjecture that *tebasan* has been adopted in areas where stricter control had not already been established as a village tradition, so that farmers needed to tighten control over harvesting.

Table 7-4.   Average numbers of harvesters employed per hectare under various types of *bawon* system in sample villages of Java.

(persons/ha)

	Bawon villages	Mixed *bawon-tebasan* villages	Total
Purely open	200	120	173
Open to the villagers only	67	190	116
Open to all with maximum limits	130	93	104
Limited to invitees	43	80	59
Limited to those performing extra services (*ceblokan*)	67	—	67
Total	*93*	*104*	*97*

Overall, our data are consistent with the postulate of Collier *et al.* about the motivation of farmers for adopting the *tebasan* system, although the evidence is somewhat indirect.

Have MV facilitated the adoption of the sickle? The postulate that modern varieties have facilitated the adoption of the sickle is strongly supported by our data. A majority of respondents reported that they adopted the sickle within three years after the introduction of MV and that none of them had used the sickle before the introduction of MV (Table 7–5).

Table 7-5. Relation between the years of adoption of MV and sickle in sample villages of Java.

	Year of sickle adoption									
	Before 1970	1970–72	1973	1974	1975	1976	1977	1978	Non-adoption	Total
Year of MV adoption										
Before 1970	2				2	4				7
1970–1972		1			3	3	1		4	12
1973			2		1	1	1		1	6
1974				1	1				1	3
1975					1	1	1			3
1976						6	3		1	10
1977							1		1	2
1978										0
Non-adoption									5	5
Total	2	1	2	1	7	15	7	1	13	48

Has the new technology facilitated the development of tebasan? On the other hand, there is insufficient evidence from our sample to support the hypothesis that the use of the sickle facilitated the spread of *tebasan*. Our respondents in *tebasan* areas reported almost unanimously that *tebasan* was already common in the late 1960s before the introduction of modern varieties and the sickle.[18] This is consistent with the findings of Sairin (1976) for the Yogyakarta area. In his study, 20 out of the 26 villages in which the *tebasan* system was observed had introduced it before 1970.

The fact that the sickle is not a precondition for *tebasan* operation is clearly shown by the data in Table 7-6. There was little difference in the pattern of use of the *ani-ani* and the sickle between *bawon* and *tebasan*

[18] Most of them answered that the *tebasan* system had existed for a long time but became common during the 1960s. This suggests that the major change in the political environment in Indonesia in the mid-1960s may have been a factor in the diffusion of *tebasan*.

Table 7-6. Distribution of sample villages in Java by type of harvesting tools used, 1978.

	Bawon villages		Mixed bawon-tebasan villages			
			Under bawon		Under tebasan	
	No.	(%)	No.	(%)	No.	(%)
Ani-ani	6	(20)	10	(56)	7	(39)
Sickle	4	(13)	2	(1)	3	(17)
Both	20	(67)	6	(33)	8	(44)
Total	30	(100)	18	(100)	18	(100)

users within *tebasan* villages and between *tebasan* and non-*tebasan* villages.

Where the sickle was introduced, *penebas* usually gave their harvesters a free choice between *ani-ani* and sickle. There were even cases where the *penebas* forbade the use of sickles because they were thought to increase shattering loss. There were also cases where farmers prohibited the use of sickles for the same reason.

Does tebasan use cash wages? The shift from *bawon* to *tebasan* is said to be usually accompanied by a change in the form of wage payment from output shares to cash wages. Our data, however, show that there was not much difference in the form of wage payment between the *bawon* and the *tebasan* systems. In 1978, about 80% of *tebasan* cases still used the output-sharing contract (Table 7-7).

Table 7-7. Distribution of sample villages in Java by form of wage payment, 1978.

	Bawon villages	Mixed bawon-tebasan villages			
		Under bawon		Under tebasan	
	No.	No.	(%)	No.	(%)
Output sharing	30	16	(89)	14	(78)
Cash proportional to harvest	0	2	(11)	3	(17)
Fixed cash per day	0	0	(0)	1	(5)
Total	30	18	(100)	18	(100)

It is especially noteworthy that only one out of the 18 *tebasan* villages used the system of a fixed cash wage per day. This has an important implication for employment. So long as wages are paid in proportion to output, whether in kind (output share) or in cash, a reduction of labor input per hectare or per output unit does not reduce costs to employers.

It is only with fixed rates of daily (or hourly) cash wages that an increase in labor efficiency and a resulting reduction in labor employed per hectare become profitable to the *penebas*.

Unless the *penebas* adopts the system of fixed cash wages per day, he has no incentive to increase efficiency and reduce labor input by introducing sickles. Thus, the fact that there was no significant difference in the use of harvesting tools between *bawon* and *tebasan* is quite consistent with the observation that the use of daily cash-wage payment is a very rare exception under the *tebasan* system.

Does tebasan reduce labor employment? The role of *tebasan* in limiting the number of participants in harvesting is reflected by the difference in the number of harvesters employed per hectare between *bawon* and *tebasan* users within the *tebasan* (*i.e.,* mixed *bawon-tebasan*) villages (Table 7-8). The number was smaller under the *tebasan* system irrespective of the choice of harvesting tools. However, on average the difference was only 12%, which was not quite as dramatic as suggested in the earlier studies (Collier *et al.,* 1974, pp. 178-182; and Utami and Ihalauw, 1973, p. 55).

Table 7-8. Average numbers of harvesters and work-hours employed per hectare under the *bawon* and the *tebasan* systems in mixed *bawon-tebasan* villages in Java.

	Under *bawon* (1)	Under *tebasan* (2)	$\frac{(2) - (1)}{(1)}$
			%
Number of harvesters/ha			
Ani-ani	107	103	− 4
Sickle	75	45	−40
Both	110	99	−10
Average	*104*	*91*	*−12*
Number of hours/ha			
Ani-ani	544	529	− 3
Sickle	400	340	−15
Both	497	453	− 9
Average	*512*	*463*	*−10*

Labor employment in terms of hours of work was also 10% smaller under *tebasan* than under *bawon*. These data were estimated by asking a group of farmers in each village about how many hours are commonly required to harvest one hectare with the number of harvesters commonly employed. Considering the difficulty of assessing the time involved in harvesting operations. our data on hours of work do not seem accurate enough to judge whether the 10% difference is significant.

A priori, there does not seem to be any reason to expect a significant reduction in labor requirement with the shift to *tebasan,* since, as we have seen, there are no significant differences in the use of harvesting tools and method of wage payment between *bawon* and *tebasan.* Cases were observed where a *penebas* employed a smaller number of regular workers on his harvesting crew. In such cases, however, the *tebasan* laborers usually worked longer per hectare to finish harvesting than under the *bawon* system.

If the use of labor in terms of hours of work is not greatly reduced, the shift from *bawon* to *tebasan* does not necessarily have adverse effects on the incomes of workers. Even if each *penebas* employs only a limited number of workers on a regular contract basis, total employment in terms of hours worked may remain substantially unchanged, depending on the number of *penebas* and the number of workers each employs. Whether or not this is really the case needs intensive investigation.

Does tebasan reduce the harvesters' share? A clear tendency can be observed from our data for harvesters to receive smaller shares of output under the *tebasan* system (Table 7–9). In the mixed *bawon-tebasan* villages, the harvesters' share was smaller under the *tebasan* system.

Table 7-9.　Distribution of harvesters' shares under the *bawon* and *tebasan* systems in sample villages of Java, 1978.

Harvesters' share[a]	Bawon village		Mixed bawon-tebasan villages			
			Under bawon		Under tebasan	
	No.	(%)	No.	(%)	No.	(%)
1/5 and above	7	(23)	0	(0)	0	(0)
1/6 to 1/8	9	(30)	5	(28)	0	(0)
1/9 to 1/11	12	(40)	8	(44)	6	(35)
1/12 to 1/14	1	(3)	2	(11)	5	(29)
1/15 to 1/17	0	(0)	3	(17)	5	(29)
1/18 and below	1	(3)	0	(0)	1	(6)
Total	30	(100)	18	(100)	17[b]	(100)
Average share (%)	13.6		10.0		8.2	

[a] Cash payments proportional to the amount of harvest were converted into shares, assuming Rp. 50/kg of rough rice.
[b] The case of fixed cash wage per day is excluded.

This conclusion from cross-section comparison can also be confirmed by the changes in harvesters' shares over time. Table 7–10 compares changes in the average shares of harvesters from 1968 to 1978 under the

Table 7-10.   Changes in average shares of harvesters in sample villages of Java, 1968 to 1978.[a]   (%)

	1968 (1)	1978 (2)	(1)–(2)
Mixed *bawon-tebasan* villages:			
Under *bawon*[b]	11.2	10.0	1.2
Bawon to *tebasan*[c]	11.2	8.2	3.0
Bawon villages:			
Ceblokan	18.2	16.3	1.9
Non-*ceblokan*	13.3	11.8	1.5
Average	*15.4*	*13.6*	*1.7*

[a] Share rates adjusted by assuming that harvesters' shares are 10% higher under the system of *ani-ani* cutting and share payment in bundles.
[b] Assuming all farmers stayed with the *bawon* system.
[c] Assuming all farmers shifted from *bawon* to *tebasan* in mixed *bawon-tebasan* villages during 1968–78.

bawon system with the changes that would have occurred if all farmers in the mixed *bawon-tebasan* villages had shifted from the *bawon* to the *tebasan* system. The comparison demonstrates the significant effect of *tebasan* in reducing the harvesters share, although the assumptions are such that the figures may be regarded as the upper-bound estimates of the impact of the introduction of the *tebasan* system.

It is noteworthy that the output shares of harvesters remained much higher in the *bawon* villages, especially those with the *ceblokan* system, than in the *tebasan* villages. This does not mean that wage rates were higher under the *ceblokan* system, but that *ceblokan* workers received larger wage payments in kind for the larger amount of work they did, including both harvesting and other obligatory work such as transplanting and weeding. However, if the opportunity cost of their labor is zero (or close to zero), the *ceblokan* system, by providing more employment opportunities, is more beneficial for workers, even though the wage rates might be the same.

Did harvesters' incomes decline? A major unsettled issue is the impact of *tebasan* on the welfare of workers. It has been observed that the harvesters' share was reduced with the shift from the *bawon* to the *tebasan* system. According to the calculations in Table 7–10, the share of *tebasan* harvesters would have been 10% instead of 8.2% had their employers not adopted the *tebasan* system.

However, such a decline in the harvesters' share due to institutional change does not necessarily mean that the harvesters' total income declined or that the income position of harvesting workers deteriorated relative to that of farmer-employers. During the period under comparison, there was a dramatic diffusion of new rice technology. The diffusion of MV has been accompanied by a significant increase in the application of current inputs such as fertilizers and pesticides. If the spread of seed-fertilizer technology resulted in a gain in output, it is quite possible that, despite the decline in the harvesters' share of output, their absolute income level rose and that even their income position relative to farmer-employers did not deteriorate much.

Such a possibility is illustrated by the calculations in Table 7–11. Let us assume, to be consistent with the case of the *tebasan* villages in Table 7–10, that owing to the adoption of the *tebasan* system the output share for harvesters declined from 10% in the period before the introduction of new rice technology to 8% after the introduction. Using the modal figures in our sample observations, let us assume that average paddy yield per hectare increased from 3 to 4 metric tons, corresponding to an increase in the application of current inputs from a level equivalent to 120 kg to 500 kg of paddy.[19] In this case, harvesters' relative share of income (value added) declined slightly from 10 to 9%, but the absolute wage income of harvesters rose from 300 kg to 320 kg of paddy.

Thus, even if the *tebasan* system facilitated the reduction of harves-

Table 7-11. Illustrative calculation of the impact of technological and institutional changes on the earnings of harvesters.

	Total output (1)	Current input (2)	Value added		
			Total (1)–(2)	Farmers' share	Harvesters' share
Before new technology					
Physical quantity (kg/ha)	3000	120[a]	2880	2580	300
Output share (%)	100	4	96	86	10
Income share (%)			100	90	10
With new technology					
Physical quantity (kg/ha)	4000	470[b]	3530	3210	320
Output share (%)	100	12	88	80	8
Income share (%)			100	91	9

[a] Includes 30 kg of seeds, 50 kg of fertilizer (equivalent to 80 kg of paddy) and 10% of fertilizer cost for chemical and other inputs.
[b] Includes 30 kg of seeds, 250 kg of fertilizer (equivalent to 400 kg of paddy) and 10% of fertilizer cost for chemical and other inputs.

[19] The yield increase assumed here is fairly consistent with the increase in the Java/Madura average from 3.2 tons in 1968 to 4.2 tons in 1976 (*Statistik Indonesia 1975–76*).

ters' output share in the way illustrated in the above calculations, not only farmers' but also harvesting workers' incomes could have increased. It needs to be borne in mind also that without such a reduction in the harvesters' share, the farmers' profit margin, and thus their incentive to adopt the new rice technology, would have been less. In that case harvesters' earnings would not have risen as much as in the illustrative examples given in Table 7–11.

Of course, whether profit incentives were as effective in reality is an empirical question to be resolved by more intensive study.

Research Agenda

The examination of the Collier *et al.* paradigm on the *tebasan* system in the light of our survey data has raised more questions than it has answered.

A tendency was observed for the *tebasan* system to be more common in areas where relatively open *bawon* systems had been practiced and where, therefore, stronger control might have been desired. This is consistent with the hypothesis that the *tebasan* system was introduced by farmers in order to strengthen their power to limit the number of harvesters.

There is clear evidence that the new rice technology was the major factor underlying the introduction of sickles. But the postulate that the sickle facilitated the emergence of the *tebasan* system is in conflict with the time sequences observed. The postulate is also logically inconsistent with the fact that fixed cash wage payments per day were rarely made.

The number of harvesters employed per hectare under the *tebasan* system does seem somewhat smaller than under the *bawon* system. Our data are too crude to allow us to assess whether there is a difference in the use of labor measured in terms of hours worked. However, there is no logical reason for expecting such a difference. If every worker in a village has a patron-client relationship with one *penebas, tebasan* need have no adverse effect on employment for anybody. To determine whether or not this has been the case requires a major study.

The output share for harvesters was significantly lower for *tebasan* than for *bawon,* indicating that the *tebasan* system was instrumental in reducing the harvesters' share. However, the lowered output share does not necessarily mean a lower income for harvesters or proportionately greater inequality between workers and employers. In the process of the introduction of seed-fertilizer technology, harvesters' incomes may well have increased even if their share was reduced. Again, whether or not this was the case remains a major question.

We do not deny the possibility that the *tebasan* system promotes polarization in rural communities, resulting in greater misery for the poor.[20] However, there is also a possibility that the *tebasan* system results in a net gain to harvesters as well as to farmers. This is an empirical question which should be resolved through solid empirical research.

It is dangerous to conclude from broad but crude data such as ours that the *tebasan* system has benefited the rural poor. However, it is no less dangerous to conclude from casual observation that the *tebasan* system is an exploiting institution promoting polarization. Such a hasty conclusion is as dangerous as the stereotyped view that middlemen are monopolistic exploiters, an assumption that has often resulted in policies calculated to destroy relatively efficient marketing systems in developing countries.

[20] In fact, we found that the *tebasan* operations in *kabupaten* Kendall, where one of Collier's study sites is located, were almost exactly what are described by Collier *et al.* (1973; 1974). There must be a number of other villages where *tebasan* is of the Collier type, c.f. Husken (1979). However, they would seem to be rather exceptional according to our observations over a wide area.

Chapter 8

A Technologically Stagnant Village

The previous chapter reviewed major controversies over agrarian change in Java. A critical issue was whether modern agricultural technology (such as modern semi-dwarf varieties of rice) is a factor in promoting polarization in rural communities and results in greater misery for the poor. A broad survey on changes in rice harvesting systems in Java raised more questions than answers.

In this chapter and the next we attempt to analyze the effects of modern technology on rural community institutions and income distribution through intensive village case studies. The methodology used is similar to that applied to two Philippine villages in Chapters 5 and 6. We chose two villages of different characteristics within the same geographic district—one characterized by the stagnation of technology and another characterized by significant progress in technology. By comparing the two cases, we try to isolate the effects of technological change.

As a first step, a village with stagnant technology is analyzed in this chapter. The study site was one of six hamlets (*kampung*) in a village (*desa*) in the Regency (*kabupaten*) of Subang, located about 120 km east of Jakarta and about 40 km northeast of Bandung (Figure 8–1). We conducted a survey in January 1979. The stock data collected are those for January 1979. The flow data such as those for rice output, costs and returns are for the 1978 dry season. Our survey was based on interviews with the heads of all the households in the hamlet and their wives.

This *desa* was one of the villages covered by the Rice Intensification Survey (*Intensifikasi Padi Sawah*—hereafter referred to as the IPS Sur-

---

[1] This chapter draws heavily on Kikuchi, Saleh, Hartoyo and Hayami (1980a; 1980b).

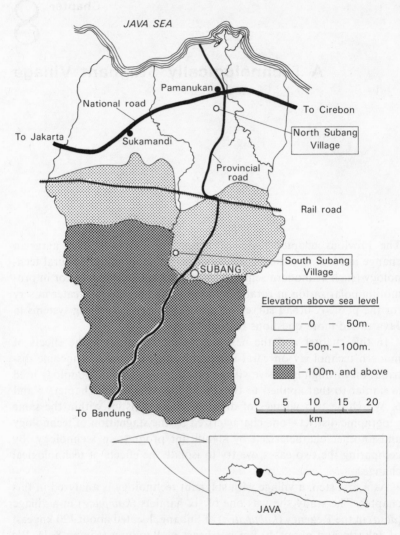

Fig. 8.1.   Map of the Regency of Subang, West Java, Indonesia.

vey) conducted by the Agro-Economic Survey of Indonesia for 1968–72. The data collected from the IPS Survey provide the benchmark information with which historical changes can be ascertained. In the following analysis, the averages of the IPS data for 1968–71 will be used for comparison with our survey data. However, the years for which data were not recorded or were subject to obvious errors were deleted.

Population Pressure and Class Differentiation

Village Profile

The village under study is located at the foot of the mountains on the southern border of the Subang Regency—henceforth we call it the South Subang Village. It was connected to the City of Subang by an unpaved road of about 5 km. A major area in the village consisted of rice terraces waving in gradual undulation, among which houses were clustered in *kampung* groups under groves of palms and bananas.

The *kampung* for which our survey was conducted had 29 hectares of land, of which 26 hectares were *sawah* (wet paddy field) and 3 were home gardens and fish ponds. About 90% of the *sawah* was double-cropped to rice. The area was irrigated by a national irrigation system called the Leuwinangka System.

The history of settlement is not very clear. However, from what we gather, the *kampung* was settled by migrants from other *kampungs* in the same *desa* and the neighboring *desas* in the middle of the nineteenth century. The villagers say that for the past several decades there has been virtually no expansion in *sawah* area and no significant improvement in the irrigation system.

The income sources of the villagers were as shown in Table 8–1. Average incomes per household and per capita were US$247 (Rp 148,214) and US$65 (Rp 38,911).[2] Rice production was the major source of income, and it took three forms: income from own rice farming, wage earnings from farm work, and receipt of land rent, which amounted, in total, to 44% of the average income of all households. Non-farm enterprises including a variety of activities, such as rice milling, trades, handicrafts, and pedicab (*becak*) driving, were the second most important source, with an income share of 34%. Non-farm wage earnings with a share of 12% were primarily from construction work. Non-rice farming such as livestock raising and fruit growing was a relatively minor income source.

The income level of large farmers was distinctly higher than that of other farmers: the average household income of large farmers was nearly four times higher and their per-capita income about three times higher than those of small farmers and landless workers. For both large and small farmers, rice farming was an equally important income source in terms of its share in total household income. However, while large farmers earned a large share of income from non-farm enterprises, small

---

[2] The exchange rate during the survey period was about 1 U.S. dollar to 600 rupiah.

Table 8-1.   Average household income by source in the South Subang Village, 1978.

	All households (No. = 110)		Large farmers (26)[b]		Small farmers (60)[c]		Landless workers (24)[d]	
	US $[a]	(%)	US $	(%)	US $	(%)	US $	(%)
Farming:								
Rice	68.9	(28)	177.4	(32)	49.5	(34)	0	(0)
Others	18.3	(8)	57.1	(10)	3.4	(2)	13.5	(12)
Total	87.2	(36)	234.5	(42)	52.9	(36)	13.5	(12)
Non-farm enterprise	84.9	(34)	278.6	(50)	18.8	(13)	40.3	(26)
Wage earning:								
Farm	37.7	(15)	9.1	(1)	44.5	(30)	51.5	(32)
Non-farm	28.8	(12)	21.6	(4)	30.3	(20)	33.0	(21)
Total	66.5	(27)	30.7	(5)	74.8	(50)	84.5	(53)
Others:								
Land rent	3.9	(1)	12.7	(2)	1.7	(1)	0	(0)
Interest, grant, etc.	4.6	(2)	5.2	(1)	0.4	(0)	14.5	(9)
Total	8.5	(3)	17.9	(3)	2.1	(1)	14.5	(9)
Total	247.1	(100)	561.7	(100)	148.6	(100)	152.8	(100)
Per-capita income	64.9		131.5		40.2		42.7	

[a] Based on the exchange rate of 1 U.S. dollar to 600 rupiah.
[b] Households with operational landholdings of 0.3 ha and above. Includes a non-cultivating landowner who owns 0.68 ha. Average family size is 4.27 persons.
[c] Households with operational landholdings below 0.3 ha. Includes two non-cultivating landowners who own 0.14 ha each. Average family size is 3.70 persons.
[d] Average family size is 3.58 persons.

farmers' major income source was wage earnings from outside employment. A few wealthy large farmers operated commercial enterprises, such as a small store, a rice mill and a mini-bus. In contrast, almost one-third of the small farmers (19 households) may be called "near-landless" in the sense that their first income source was not farming but wage employment on other farms.

It may be surprising to see that the income level of the landless was slightly higher than that of small farmers. The difference resulted primarily from a large pension received by one retired military officer. However, it is true that a majority of near-landless farmers who had very small holdings or who were farming under a sharecropping arrangement were as poor as landless workers.

Population Pressure

At the time of our survey, this *kampung* consisted of 110 households in which 419 persons were living.[3] Data are not available to estimate population growth rates directly. However, judging from the population pyramid in Figure 8-2, it appears that a significant deceleration in the population growth rate occurred over the past three to four decades. It was found that the average number of children per mother declined dramatically (Table 8-2). If we assume that the average reproductive period of women is 30 years (15 years to 45 years old), it can be estimated as shown in Table 8-2 that the natural rate of population growth declined

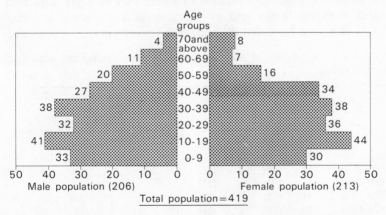

Fig. 8-2. Age distribution of population in the South Subang Village, 1979.

[3] In fact, a total of 113 households existed. However, three were excluded from our analysis because we had difficulty collecting data due to the old age and mental disorder of the household heads.

Table 8-2. Average number of surviving children per mother by mother's age and estimates of the natural rates of population growth in the South Subang Village.

Mother's age	Number of mothers	Children per mother (n) No.	Population growth rate[a] (r) %/year
80 years old and above	24	4.80	3.0
60–79	14	3.93	2.3
50–59	33	3.49	1.9
40–49	17	2.71	1.0
(36–45)	(21)	(2.48)	(0.7)
30–39	43	1.95	—
20–29	32	0.84	—
Below 20	12	0.50	—

[a] Calculated by the formula: $n = 2 (1 + r)^{30}$.

from 3% per year to less than 1% during the past 40-year period.

Such deceleration in the population growth rate might be typical of this area, because, according to data from the Office of Subang, the population growth rate in the Regency declined from 2.1% per year for 1961–70 to 0.7% for 1970–76.

It was 1975 when the government birth control program was introduced in this village. However, the birth rate began to decline much earlier. It is said that many wives had practiced abortion using indigenous methods which were often harmful to health. Such information suggests that by the 1950s the population density had become so high and the income-earning opportunities so scarce that villagers were compelled to reduce family sizes even before the introduction of formal family planning. Note that the population density in this village was as

Table 8-3. Acquisition of *sawah* land plots by present cultivators in the South Subang Village.

	Inherited		Purchase of ownership title		Rented-in		Pawned in ownership title		Total	
	No.	(%)	No.	(%)	No.	(%)	No.	(%)	No.	(%)
Before 1949	18	(90)	2	(10)					20	(100)
1950–1959	18	(95)	1	(5)					19	(100)
1960–1969	16	(73)	6	(27)					22	(100)
1970–1974	17	(65)	7	(27)	1	(4)	1	(4)	26	(100)
1975–1979	10	(30)	8[a]	(25)	10[b]	(30)	5	(15)	33	(100)
Total	79	(66)	24	(20)	11	(9)	6	(5)	120	(100)

[a] Includes one case in which a servant of a large farmer was given 0.14 ha by the master as a grant.
[b] Includes two sub-renting cases.

high as 16 persons per hectare of paddy field, as compared with 6 and 4 persons per hectare, respectively, in the East and the South Laguna Villages in the Philippines which we analyzed in Chapters 5 and 6.

Although the population growth rate seems to have decelerated for the past few decades, the labor force should have continued to increase rather rapidly because of the continued increase in the size of the economically active age group. It appears, however, that the growth of the labor force, too, recently began to decelerate.

The fact that there has been no expansion in cultivated land area is clearly shown by the data in Table 8–3, which show no case of land acquisition by present cultivators through opening new land. Before 1970, all the *sawah* plots were acquired by the farmers in this village either through inheritance or purchase; in earlier years inheritance had been the dominant source of land acquisition, and purchase became a significant source after 1960. Land acquisition through rental or pawning arrangements began to be reported after 1970.

Agrarian Structure

In this village, as in most villages in Java, owner farming was the dominant form of land tenure. At the time of our survey, as much as 83% of *sawah* plots and 89% of *sawah* area were cultivated by the owners themselves (Table 8–5); 81% of farmers were owner-operators, and pure tenants who owned no land were only 2% (Table 8–4). However, as the data in Table 8–3 show, landlordism has been developing rather rapidly in recent years. It appears reasonable to hypothesize that the population pressure on limited land area and the corresponding decrease in the return to labor relative to the return to land has reached a stage where stratification of the hitherto homogeneous peasant com-

Table 8-4.   Distribution of farms by tenure status in the South Subang Village, 1979.

	Number of farms		Area	
	No.	(%)	ha.	(%)
Owner operator	67	(81)	19.00	(77)
Owner/share[a]	9	(11)	2.98	(12)
Owner/lease	1	(1)	1.00	(4)
Owner/pawn	3	(4)	1.13	(5)
Share tenant	1	(1)	0.29	(1)
Pawn in	2	(2)	0.33	(1)
Total	83	(100)	24·73	(100)

[a] Includes two cases of sub-renting under share arrangement.

Table 8-5. Distribution of *sawah* land plots by tenure status in the South Subang Village, 1979.

	No. of plots	(%)
Owned	80	(83.3)
Rented:		
Share tenancy	8	(8.3)
Leasehold tenancy	1	(1.1)
Pawned	5	(5.2)
Sub-rented	2	(2.1)
Total	96	(100.0)

munity into landlord and tenant classes has begun to be significant.

Class differentiation in terms of *sawah* land ownership has already progressed to a high degree. Out of 110 households interviewed, 25 owned no land and 21 owned less than 0.1 hectare (Table 8–6). Class differentiation has also been pronounced in terms of operational land holdings. Forty-four households had operational landholdings of less than 0.1 hectare and earned their livelihood primarily from hired farm work. The size distributions of land ownership and operational landholdings were highly skewed even though the size of the largest holding

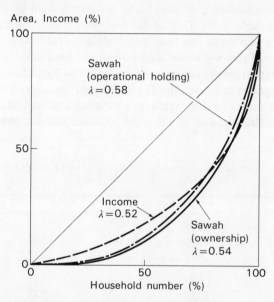

Fig. 8-3. Lorenz curves for the distribution of income and landholdings in the South Subang Village (λ = Gini coefficient).

Table 8–6.   Size distribution of *sawah* land ownership and operational landholdings in the South Subang Village, 1979.

	Ownership holdings				Operational holdings			
	Number of owners		Area		Number of households		Area	
	No.	(%)	ha.	(%)	No.	(%)	ha.	(%)
1.00 ha and above	5	(4)	6.21	(25)	4	(4)	4.72	(19)
0.60 ha–0.99 ha	4	(4)	3.23	(13)	4	(4)	3.30	(13)
0.30 ha-0.59 ha	14	(13)	6.23	(25)	17	(15)	7.44	(30)
0.10 ha–0.29 ha	41	(37)	7.85	(32)	41	(37)	8.17	(33)
0.01 ha–0.10 ha	21	(19)	1.34	(5)	17	(15)	1.10	(5)
0	25	(23)	0	(0)	27	(25)	0	(0)
Total	*110*	*(100)*	*24.86*	*(100)*	*110*	*(100)*	*24.73*	*(100)*
Average area per household (ha)		0.23				0.22		
		(0.29)[a]				(0.30)[b]		

[a] Average area per owner household
[b] Average area per farmer household.

was as small as 1.5 hectare. The size distribution of income was equally skewed as judged from the comparisons in Lorenz curves and Gini coefficients (λ) in Figure 8–3.

We were unable to collect data to ascertain directly how the size distributions of income and landholdings have changed over time. It is our basic hypothesis that the income and asset distributions have become more unequal due to growing population pressure on land. This hypothesis is subjected to empirical test in the analysis in the following sections.

Changes in Rice Farming

The concurrence of increasing population pressure and growing inequality, even if supported by the data, does not represent evidence for a causal relationship. It may be argued that new technology such as modern varieties of rice is the major factor promoting polarization of rural communities and greater hardship for the poor. It is critical for our hypothesis testing to identify what changes have occurred in rice farming technology during the period of analysis.

Varieties and Fertilizers

Rice production in this village is characterized by a high level of yield corresponding to the high application of fertilizers and chemicals.

Average paddy yield for the 1978 dry season was almost 3 tons per hectare, in dry *gabah* (paddy). The level of fertilizer application was very high—the average nitrogen input was as high as 90 kilograms per hectare. No significant difference was found in fertilizer input and rice yield per hectare between farm-size classes.[4]

Despite the large-scale fertilizer application, modern semi-dwarf varieties such as *IR*-varieties and *Pelita* have not been commonly used in this village. The modern varieties (MV) have been introduced since the late 1960s under the *Bimas* Program—a nationwide program of rice production intensification based on a package of modern inputs, credit and extension. However, because they were highly susceptible to insects and pests in the environment of this area, many farmers who tried them have shifted back to traditional varieties. At the time of our survey, only 14% of the farmers were still using MV; the rest used traditional varieties such as *Gembar* and *Sagon*, although as many as 83% of the farmers had once tried MV.

Meanwhile, fertilizer (urea and TSP) application has increased from about 190 kg in 1968–71 to 230 kg in 1978 (Table 8-7). It appears that this increase was induced by the decline in the fertilizer/paddy price

Table 8-7.   Changes in rice yield and rice production inputs per ha of crop area in the South Subang Village, 1968–71 to 1978.

	1968–71[a]	1978[b]	% Change from 1968–71 to 1978
Multiple cropping ratio	1.9	1.9	0
Rice yield (kg/ha)	2,600	2,944	13
Fertilizer input (kg/ha)[c]	191[d]	229	20
Labor input (hours/ha):			
Land preparation	420	494	18
Other preharvest operations	316	434	37
Harvest & threshing	n.a.	324	—
Total (preharvest)	*736*	*928*	*26*
Carabao and cattle use for land preparation (days/ha)	16.4	9.2	−44

[a] Based on the IPS Survey for Phase I to V. Averages for wet and dry seasons.
[b] Based on our survey. Data for dry season.
[c] Urea and TSP.
[d] Average for 1968 and 1970.

[4] Average paddy yields per ha in the 1978 dry season were 3.0 tons for large farmers whose operational holdings were above 0.3 ha and 2.8 tons for small farmers whose holdings were below 0.3 ha. Average fertilizer inputs per ha were 197 kg of urea and 37 kg of TSP for large farmers and 99 kg of urea and 20 kg of TSP for small farmers.

Table 8-8.   Changes in input prices for rice production in the South Subang Village, 1968-71 to 1978.

	1968-71[a]	1978[b]	% Change from 1968-71 to 1978
Paddy price (Rp/kg)	19.4	65.0	235
Nominal input price:			
Fertilizer price (Rp/kg)[c]	29.0[f]	69.0	138
Labor wage rate (Rp/day)[d]	184	550	199
Carabao rental rate (Rp/day)	120	620	417
Real input price[e]:			
Fertilizer price (kg/ha)	1.5	1.1	−27
Labor wage rate (kg/day)	9.5	8.5	−11
Carabao rental rate (kg/day)	6.2	9.5	53

[a] Based on the IPS Survey for Phase I to V. Averages for wet and dry seasons.
[b] Based on our Survey. Data for dry season.
[c] Urea and TSP.
[d] Wage for land preparation assuming 8 hours' work per day. Includes meals.
[e] Nominal price divided by paddy price.
[f] Average for 1968 and 1970.

ratio (Table 8-8). The decline in the price ratio was, to a large extent, a result of the government subsidy on fertilizer under the *Bimas* Program.

The average paddy yield for 1968-71 estimated from IPS data was about 2,600 kg/ha, whereas the average yield for the 1978 dry season from our survey was 2,944 kg/ha. The relatively modest increase in rice yield corresponds to the absence of modern varieties specifically suited to the environmental conditions in this area. It is difficult to ascertain from our data how significant the yield increase was, since the yields were subject to weather fluctuations. However, if we assume that our yield data reflect a real yield increase, it must have been due mainly to the increase in fertilizer application accompanying government fertilizer subsidies rather than to an upward shift in the rice production function.

Labor Input

The average labor requirement per hectare in the 1978 dry season was 1,252 hours or 156 days assuming 8 hours' work for one man-day. Land preparation used the largest share of labor, followed by harvesting, weeding and transplanting, in that order (Table 8-9). These four tasks require large shares of labor input for rice production and are characterized by high dependence on hired labor. There were large differences in the composition of total labor used by large and small farmers. On the average, large farmers depended on hired labor for nearly 80% of the total labor they used for their rice production, whereas only 40% of the labor used for small farmers' production was supplied by hired workers (Table 8–9). It is easy to infer that land preparation, transplanting, weeding and harvesting for large farmers represent major employment opportunities for landless workers and small farmers.

It was estimated that average labor input for preharvest operations in rice production per hectare increased by 26% from 1968–71 to 1978 (Table 8–7).[5] The increase was especially large for weeding, reflecting the intensification of crop care. The increase in labor used for land preparation reflects the substitution of hand hoeing for animal plowing and harrowing due to the decline in the manual wage rate relative to the rental rate of draft animals (carabao and cattle). The real wage rate of manual labor for land preparation declined by about 10%, whereas the real rental rate of draft animals increased by about 50% (Table 8–8). Correspondingly, the human labor used for land preparation increased by 18%, while the input of animal power declined by 44% (Table 8–7).

Changes in Rice Harvesting Systems

Growth in the labor force and the resulting decline in the real wage rate had a pervasive impact on employment relations among villagers. Changes in labor contracts and their effects on income distribution have been expressed most dramatically in the changes in rice harvesting systems. As was observed in the previous chapter, the traditional *bawon* system in Java that allowed wide sharing of output among community members has been replaced by systems such as *tebasan* and *ceblokan* that limit participation in harvesting and reduce the harvesters' share.

From Bawon to Ceblokan

In this village, as well as in neighboring villages, the *tebasan* system was not introduced. However, the traditional *bawon* system was replaced by the *ceblokan* system. In the *ceblokan* system, like the *gama* system in the Philippines, workers who are employed for harvesting are limited to those who performed without pay such extra tasks as transplanting and weeding. The adoption of the *ceblokan* system has the effect of re-

---

[5] Labor requirements for harvesting should have remained about the same because there was no appreciable increase in yield per ha and the traditional harvesting method using *ani-ani* knives continued.

Table 8-9.   Labor inputs for rice production per ha of crop area by task in the South Subang Village, 1978 dry season.[a]

	Large farmer		Small farmer		Average	
	hours/ha	(%)	hours/ha	(%)	hours/ha	(%)
Land preparation:						
Family	111	(22)	309	(67)	179	(36)
Hired	398 [4]	(78)	153	(33)	315 [3]	(64)
Total	509	(100)	462	(100)	494	(100)
Transplanting:						
Family	23	(16)	55	(36)	34	(23)
Hired	121 [119]	(84)	96 [90]	(64)	112 [109]	(77)
Total	144	(100)	151	(100)	146	(100)
Weeding:						
Family	67	(33)	202	(80)	113	(52)
Hired	133 [81]	(67)	50 [21]	(20)	105 [61]	(48)
Total	200	(100)	252	(100)	218	(100)
Harvesting:						
Family	10	(3)	74	(24)	31	(10)
Hired	327 [327]	(97)	233 [225]	(76)	293 [292]	(90)
Total	337	(100)	307	(100)	324	(100)
Others:						
Family	53	(88)	88	(99)	65	(93)
Hired	7	(12)	1	(1)	5	(7)
Total	60	(100)	89	(100)	70	(100)
Total:						
Family	264	(21)	728	(58)	422	(34)
Hired	986 [531]	(79)	533 [336]	(42)	830 [465]	(66)
Total	1250	(100)	1261	(100)	1252	(100)

[a] Figures in brackets are labor hours applied under the *ceblokan* contract.

ducing the real wage rate of harvesters because the same share of output is paid for a larger amount of work.

Although *ceblokan* has been introduced into the Subang area rather recently, it is an old system which has long been practiced in the northeast corner of West Java in such places as the Regencies of Cirebon and Majalenka (for the regional distribution of *ceblokan,* see Figure 7–1).

In this village, the *ceblokan* system was first adopted in 1964 by seven farmers. It replaced the *bawon* system very rapidly, and by 1978 the farmers adopting *ceblokan* exceeded 95% of the total. However, even before the introduction of *ceblokan,* not all the farmers had practiced "purely open" *bawon* in the sense that everyone is allowed to participate in harvesting. The system nearest to the traditional "purely open" (PO) *bawon* harvesting as a communal activity was that in which harvesting was open only to villagers in the same village (OV). Another system placed a further limit on the maximum number allowed to participate

Table 8–10.   Changes in rice harvesting system in the South Subang Village (% of farmer adoptors).

	Bawon^a				Ceblokan^b					Total
	PO	OV	OM	LI	1/6(T)	1/7(T)	1/7(T+W)	1/7(H+T)	1/7(H+T+W)	
1950s	35	29	18	18						100
1960–61	29	31	21	19						100
1962–63	16	34	33	17						100
1964–65	9	16	16	32	27					100
1966–67	3	10	8	27	52					100
1968–69	1	4	6	19	44	24	2			100
1970–71			2	10	33	51	4			100
1972–73				8	17	67	8			100
1974–75				7	15	67	10	1		100
1976–77				4	7	67	18	2	2	100
1978				4		72	19	1	4	100

^a Bawon system: PO—purely open, OV—open for villagers only, OM—open with maximum limit, LI—limited to invitees.
^b Ceblokan system: 1/6, 1/7—harvesters' share; T, W, H—obligatory work to establish the harvesting right (T—transplanting, W—weeding, H—harrowing).

(OM). A more severe restriction was involved in the system where participants were limited to those who received specific invitations from farmers (LI). As can be clearly seen in Table 8-10, farmers had gradually shifted from more open *bawon* to more restricted *bawon* until *ceblokan* was introduced.

Likewise, the *ceblokan* system itself includes a spectrum of arrangements in terms of harvesters' shares and obligatory work. Originally, *ceblokan* harvesters received a traditional share of one-sixth for the additional service of rice transplanting without pay (usually meals were served even though cash wages were not paid). Later, their share was reduced to one-seventh, and weeding and harrowing were added to the list of obligatory work required to establish the harvesting right. Changes in harvesting systems in this village show successive shifts from more open and more generous arrangements to more restrictive and less gen-

Table 8-11. Average hired labor time and wage earnings per household employed in rice production in the South Subang Village, 1978 dry season.[a]

	Hours employed		Wage earned[b]	
	Hours	(%)	US $[d]	(%)
Land preparation:				
Fixed wage[c]	89.3	(35)	10.9	(44)
Ceblokan	2.9	(1)	0.2	(1)
Total	*92.2*	*(36)*	*11.1*	*(45)*
Transplanting:				
Ceblokan	31.7	(13)	1.1	(4)
Weeding:				
Fixed wage	12.7	(5)	1.1	(4)
Ceblokan	23.1	(9)	0.9	(4)
Total	*35.8*	*(14)*	*2.0*	*(8)*
Harvesting:				
Ceblokan	89.2	(35)	10.4	(42)
Bawon	1.5	(1)	0.1	(0)
Total	*90.7*	*(36)*	*10.5*	*(42)*
Others:				
Fixed wage	2.6	(1)	0.2	(1)
Total:				
Fixed wage	104.6	(41)	12.2	(49)
Ceblokan	146.9	(58)	12.6	(51)
Bawon	1.5	(1)	0.1	(0)
Total	*253.0*	*(100)*	*24.9*	*(100)*

Note: [a] Average for 54 small farmer households and 23 landless worker households.
[b] Includes meals.
[c] Includes wage payments according to area-rate contracts.
[d] Based on the exchange rate of 1 U.S. dollar to 600 rupiah.

erous arrangements (Table 8–10). Underlying this process was the decline in the return to labor relative to the return to land and capital due to the growth of the labor force against limited land resources.

By 1978 the shift from *bawon* to *ceblokan* was almost completed. The amounts of labor employed and wages earned under the *ceblokan* system became dominant in total hired employment and in the wage income of laborers. On the average for all households whose family members were hired for rice production during the 1978 dry season, labor employed under the *ceblokan* system was about 60% of total hired-labor time and income from the *ceblokan* work was about 50% of total wage earnings (Table 8–11).

Employer-Employee Relations

In the shifts from more open and more generous arrangements to less open and less generous ones, large farmers usually took the lead and small farmers followed. As a result, the larger the farmers were, the less

Table 8-12. Distribution of employers and employees in rice harvesting by type of contract and by size of operational holding in the South Subang Village, 1978 dry season.[a]

| Farm-size class (ha) | Family only | Bawon (1/7) | Ceblokan | | | Total |
			1/7 (T)	1/7 (T + W) or (T + H)	1/7 (T+W+H)	
Employer						
Below 0.1 (no.)	6		11			17
(%)	(35)		(65)			(100)
0.1 to 0.29 (no.)	1	2	34	4		41
(%)	(2)	(5)	(83)	(10)		(100)
0.3 to 0.59 (no.)			10	6	1	17
(%)			(59)	(35)	(6)	(100)
0.6 & above (no.)			1	6	1	8
(%)			(13)	(74)	(13)	(100)
Employee						
0 (no.)			7	18		25
(%)			(28)	(72)		(100)
0.01 to 0.1 (no.)			6	10	1	17
(%)			(35)	(59)	(6)	(100)
0.1 to 0.29 (no.)		1	22	9	4	36
(%)		(3)	(61)	(25)	(11)	(100)
0.3 to 0.59 (no.)			10	1		11
(%)			(91)	(9)		(100)

[a] 1/7—harvesters' share; and T, W, H—obligatory work to establish the harvesting right (T—transplanting, W—weeding, and H—harrowing).

Table 8-13.   Matrix of employer-employee relations in rice harvesting in terms of paddy area contracted (ha) in the South Subang Village, 1978 dry season.[a]

Employee Employer	0 ha (landless)	0.01 to 0.1 ha	0.1 to 0.29 ha	0.30 to 0.59 ha	Outside *kampung*
Below 0.1 ha	0.13	0.71	0.24	0.02	0
	(2)	(14)	(3)	(1)	(0)
0.1 to 0.29 ha	1.31	1.41	3.26	0.62	0.35
	(20)	(28)	(37)	(31)	(23)
0.3 to 0.59 ha	1.56	1.18	2.50	0.88	0.72
	(24)	(24)	(29)	(43)	(46)
0.6 ha & above	2.96	1.54	2.15	0.36	0.48
	(46)	(31)	(25)	(18)	(31)
Outside *kampung*	0.52	0.13	0.52	0.14	—
	(8)	(3)	(6)	(7)	
Total	6.48	4.97	8.67	2.02	1.55
	(100)	(100)	(100)	(100)	(100)

[a] Percentages are in parentheses.

generous their arrangements in the employment of harvesters tended to be (the upper half of Table 8-12), and the less generous were the arrangements under which landless workers and near-landless farmers (below 0.1 hectare) were employed (the lower half of Table 8-12).

These data suggest that the rich (large farmers) employed the poor (landless workers and near-landless farmers), whereas the middle-class (medium-scale farmers) employed one another. Such relations are confirmed by the matrix that relates employers to employees for different farm-size classes (Table 8-13). The data show that, while landless workers and near-landless farmers with landholdings below 0.1 hectare depended most heavily on large farms with 0.6 hectare and above for their employment opportunities, medium-scale farmers in the size brackets of 0.1–0.29 hectare and 0.3–0.59 hectare found the largest employment opportunities on the farms of their own size class. Therefore, the employment relations among medium-scale farmers were, by nature, equivalent to labor exchange. In contrast, the patron-client relation characterized the employment of landless workers by large farmers.

The Role of Ceblokan

The *ceblokan* system, like *gama* in the Philippines, can be considered an institutional innovation used by employer farmers to reduce the wage rate for harvesting to a level equal to the market wage rate. In earlier days, when labor was scarcer and the rice yield was lower, the one-sixth share of output under the traditional *bawon* system might have been equivalent to the market wage rate, close to the marginal product of harvesters' labor. However, as the labor supply became more abundant and the rice yield increased, one-sixth of the output would have become substantially larger than the market wage rate. In this particular village the disequilibrium was created mainly through decreases in the marginal productivity of labor due to population pressure instead of to increases in yield per hectare.

In such a situation, farmers could increase their income by replacing the *bawon* system with the labor of daily wage workers. However, the cost of resistance to change in long-established custom in the village community would have been quite large. Another possibility was to reduce harvesters' share in the *bawon* system; this would have been easier and was, in fact, done. However, the reduction of the share rate was not quite so consistent with basic village moral principles such as mutual help and income-sharing. In terms of patron-client relationships in a village community characterized by multi-stranded ties, it would have involved less social friction to add some additional obligations while maintaining the same share rate.

Thus, we hypothesize that the *ceblokan* system was an institutional innovation that entailed the least cost for reducing the harvesters' share of output in line with the market wage rate. As a test, an imputation was made of the wage rates for alternative harvesting arrangements. In the calculation, meals served to laborers doing obligatory work such as transplanting and weeding were valued as one-half of the wage rate per day (meals were not served for harvesting work). The results summarized in Table 8-14 indicate that the harvesters' share under the *bawon* system with the one-seventh share was 40% higher than the mar-

Table 8-14.   Imputation of wage rates for harvesting work in the South Subang Village.

Number of working hours of *ceblokan* labor (hours/ha):		
(1) Harvesting		324
(2) Transplanting		111
(3) Weeding		147
Actual share of *ceblokan* harvester:		
Quantity of paddy (kg/ha)		421
(4) Imputed value of paddy (Rp/ha)[a]		27,365
Imputed wage rate (Rp/hour):		
(A) *Bawon* 1/7	(4)/(1)	84
(B) *Ceblokan* 1/7 (T)	(4)/[(1) + 0.5(2)][b]	72
(C) *Ceblokan* 1/7 (T + W)	(4)/[(1)+0.5(2)+0.5(3)][b]	60
Market wage rate (Rp/hour)		60

[a] Figures use Rp 65/kg for the market price of paddy.
[b] Assumes that the cost of meals served for transplanting and weeding was one-half of the wage rate for those tasks.

ket wage rate; a shift to the *ceblokan* system with the obligation of transplanting alone reduced the gap between the harvesters' share and the market wage rate to 12%; with the further addition of weeding to the obligation, the harvesters' share was equalized to the market wage rate. Such results are highly consistent with our hypothesis.

An important advantage of *ceblokan* for employers could be the work incentive built into this system in the form of output-sharing, which reduces the cost of monitoring laborers' performance. The *ceblokan* system might also be preferred because it helps strengthen the patron-client relation between employers and employees by giving the exclusive right of harvesting to specific laborers. With the tightening of the patron-client bond, the patron farmers could further economize on the labor-enforcement cost of supervising the performance of laborers. From the employee's side, *ceblokan* might also be preferred because of the stronger patron-client bond which reduces the risk of finding employment.

The shift from *bawon* to *ceblokan* represents a shift from mutual help and income-sharing within a whole village community to the patron-client and reciprocity relationships in smaller groups. However, this shift does not mean that some members of the community were excluded from employment opportunities. All members were inlaid into the employment matrix in the community, although employer-employee relations distinctly differed among classes—the labor-exchange type among medium-class farmers and the patron-client type between large farmers and landless/near-landless people.

Even the disadvantaged villagers were not excluded. For example, it was two large farmers who adopted the least generous arrangements of *ceblokan* with the obligation of transplanting, weeding and harrowing. However, they exempted widowed households from harrowing work because land preparation was considered a male's task. This example suggests that the community moral principles of mutual help and income-sharing have not entirely lost their power and that it entails cost to behave in contradiction with the principles.

Ceblokan did not contribute to the development of labor-saving technology. It was up to the harvesters whether to use *ani-ani* or sickles. In the harvest of the 1978 dry season, almost all the fields were harvested by *ani-ani*.

Thus, employment in this village did not move towards a capitalistic system based on an impersonal market. With the development of the *ceblokan* system the rate of return to harvesting labor was adjusted to a level equivalent to the market wage rate which had been reduced by strong population pressure. However, under the *ceblokan* system, landless/near-landless people continued to share both work and output in the peasant production process, even to a limited extent. The direction of social change in this village was towards peasant stratification instead of polarization.

Changes in Income Distribution

A dismal picture has been drawn in previous sections of the economy of the South Subang Village; income and asset distributions are highly skewed even though average income and the average size of landholdings are very small; population pressure had long ago reached its limit and population growth decelerated, but the labor force has continued to grow; technology has been stagnant because modern varieties suited to the environmental conditions of this specific location have not been available; fertilizer application has increased not because of new technology but because of low fertilizer prices under the *Bimas* Program. Gains in rice yields have not been so significant; the increase in labor force against limited land resources under stagnant technology resulted in a decrease in the economic return to labor; the real wage rate for land preparation has declined, inducing the substitution of hand hoeing for animal plowing; and a reduction in the real wage rate for harvesting work has been brought about through institutional change in the form of the shift from the *bawon* to the *ceblokan* system.

The whole process suggests that income distribution has become more skewed. Data are not available to identify over-time changes in the size distributions of income. Therefore, we will try to make inferences based on changes in the shares of income from rice production.

Factor Shares of Rice Output

Changes in the average factor shares of rice output per hectare from 1968–71 to 1978 were estimated (Table 8–15). During the period the average yield per hectare increased by a little more than 10%. Both payments to hired labor and the imputed cost of family labor increased very slightly, less than 5%. Operators' surplus (residual) recorded a major increase in the case of owner-farmers. In the case of tenant farmers, operators' surplus was almost zero and land rent paid to landlords was equivalent to owner-farmers' surplus. Such results show clearly that the operators' surplus of owner-farmers consisted mainly of the return to their land. Thus, the major gain in owner-farmers' surplus implies an increase in the economic rent of land. Altogether, the relative share of labor declined and the relative share of land increased. What do such estimates imply about the income distribution between farmers and landless laborers? Table 8–16 attempts to show how the income (value added) from rice production per hectare was distributed between farmers and hired laborers. Farmers' income consists of operators' surplus and the returns to family labor and capital. Farmers' total income in paddy terms increased from 1968–71 to 1978 by 25% whereas laborers' income increased by only 4%. The wage earnings of laborers from preharvest activities increased, mainly because of larger employment opportunities in land preparation due to the substitution of hand hoeing for animal plowing. But the increase was compensated for, to a large extent, by the decline in earnings from harvest and postharvest employment, primarily due to declines in the harvesters' share rate. On the other hand, farmers' income increased significantly, primarily due to the increase in the return to land captured in the form of operators' surplus. As a result, farmers' income share increased and laborers' share declined. The data clearly imply that income distribution became more skewed.

It is most probable that the size distribution of income between far-

Table 8-15. Changes in factor payments and factor shares in rice production per ha of crop area in the South Subang Village, 1968–71 to 1978.

	Factor payment (kg/ha)			Factor share (%)		
	1968–71[a]	1978[b]		1968–71	1978	
	Owner	Owner[c]	Tenant[d]	Owner	Owner	Tenant
Paddy output	2,600	2,942	3,080	100.0	100.0	100.0
Factor payment[e]:						
Current input[f]	345	293	321	13.3	10.0	10.4
Capital[g]	136	125	76	5.2	4.2	2.5
Labor	1,257	1,301	1,341	48.3	44.2	43.5
(Family)	(427)[h]	(438)	(476)	(16.4)	(14.9)	(15.4)
(Hired)	(830)[h]	(863)	(865)	(31.9)	(29.3)	(28.1)
Land	0	0	1,262	0	0	41.0
Operator's						
surplus	862	1,223	80	33.2	41.6	2.6

[a] Based on the IPS Survey for Phase I to V. Averages for wet and dry seasons.
[b] Based on our survey. Data for dry season.
[c] Averages of 74 owner-farmers cultivating 20.4 ha.
[d] Averages of 9 tenant operators cultivating 1.8 ha.
[e] Factor payments converted to paddy equivalents by the factor-output price ratios.
[f] Seeds, fertilizers and chemicals.
[g] Animal rental for land preparation and irrigation fee.
[h] Assumes the same composition of family and hired labor as for 1978.

mers and laborers became more skewed than the data in Table 8–16 show. From 1968–71 to 1978 the number of landless and near-landless households increased faster than the number of farmers. Therefore, the share of income per landless household should have declined by a greater extent than the share of income per hectare. It is highly likely that per-household or per-capita income from rice production for landless and near-landless households has declined in absolute terms, even though the rice income per hectare has increased slightly.

The Economic Basis of Greater Inequity

The dismal history of growing poverty and inequity in the South Subang Village approximates the world predicted by classical economists like David Ricardo. As the growing population presses hard on limited land resources under constant technology, cultivation frontiers are expanded to more marginal land and greater amounts of labor are applied per unit of cultivated land; the cost of food production increases and food prices rise; in the long run, laborers' incomes will be lowered to a subsistence minimum barely sufficient to maintain a stationary population, and all the surpluses will be captured by landlords in the form of increased land rent. This is exactly what has occurred in this village.

It is obvious that labor input per hectare of wet rice field has, long before, moved out of the range of constant return assumed in Geertz's thesis of "agricultural involution". His concept of "shared poverty" based on work-sharing still seems valid, as exemplified by the pattern

Table 8-16. Changes in shares of income from rice production per ha of crop area in the South Subang Village, 1968–71 to 1978.[a]

	Income in paddy (kg/ha)		Income share (%)	
	1968–71	1978	1968–71	1978
Value added[b]	2,255	2,649	100.0	100.0
Farmer:				
Family labor	427	438	19.0	16.5
Capital	136	125	6.0	4.7
Operator's surplus	862	1,223	38.2	46.2
Total	1,425	1,786	63.2	67.4
Hired laborer:				
Preharvest work	397	443	17.6	16.7
Harvest & postharvest				
work	433	420	19.2	15.9
Total	830	863	36.8	32.6

[a] Data rearranged from Table 8-15 for owner-operated farms.
[b] Output value minus current input cost.

of labor employment relations in rice harvesting. However, it is valid to a very limited extent because the income equalizing effect of work-sharing is grossly insufficient to compensate for the negative effect of decreasing returns to labor relative to land and to prevent widening differentials in income and asset-holding among peasant subclasses.

If the basic underlying economic factor is the decreasing return to labor relative to land, it would be difficult to stop the Ricardian process in the absence of effective policies to raise the relative productivity of labor by improving the land infrastructure and developing land-saving and labor-using technology. Modern semi-dwarf varieties were tried in this village but not accepted because they did not adequately suit the environment of this area in the absence of adequate adaptive research and development. Both the data and the economic logic suggest that, contrary to the pervasive presumption, growing inequity has resulted, not because of the introduction of modern technology but because of stagnation in technology.

Chapter 9

A Technologically Progressive Village[1]

The previous chapter reported the case of a village wherein population pressure under a stagnant technology resulted in a Ricardian process of growing poverty and inequality. If a basic factor underlying this process was, in fact, the stagnation of technology, the opposite should have been the case if major advances in technology were realized.

This chapter presents a case study of a village where significant increases in rice yield per hectare have been recorded for the past decade as the result of improvements in irrigation systems and rice-growing technology. By comparing this village with the case in the previous chapter, we will try to identify the impact of technological progress on income distribution in the village community.

Choice of Village and Data Collection

For the sake of comparison with the South Subang Village studied in the previous chapter, we tried to choose a village for this study among those located within the Regency of Subang which had previously been covered by the IPS (*Intensificasi Padi Sawah*) Survey, one which belongs to a rice monoculture area but which, unlike the South Village, has experienced major advances in rice production technology for the past decade. A village that satisfied such conditions was found in the rice-producing area along the coast of the Java Sea, about 20 kilometers north of the South Subang Village (see Figure 8–1). This village is henceforth referred to as the "North Subang Village".

Unlike the South Subang Village, which has an undulating top-

[1] This chapter draws heavily on Kikuchi, Yusuf, Hafid and Hayami (1980).

195

ography surrounded by mountains, the North Subang Village is on a completely flat coastal plain. This area was recently covered by the Jatiluhur Irrigation System, the biggest irrigation system in Java. Before 1968, when the Jatiluhur System was extended, paddy fields in this village had been served by a local irrigation system called the Macan System. This system irrigated the fields only during the wet season, and its water supply had been unreliable; rice yields had been low and unstable. Since the Jatiluhur System was extended, double-cropping of rice has been commonly practiced and modern varieties diffused widely, with the result being significant increases in yield per hectare. The dynamic change in rice production technology in the North Subang Village is, thus, in sharp contrast with the stagnation in the South Subang Village.

We tried to apply to data collection in the North Subang Village the same methodology as that applied to the South Subang Village (and to the two Philippine villages analyzed in Chapters 5 and 6). Unfortunately, however, in none of four hamlets (*kampung*) in this village (*desa*) was the number of households sufficiently small to allow us to apply the complete enumeration survey intensively under the constraints of given time and resources. Therefore, we were forced to adopt a sample survey, except for basic statistics such as land area, population and the number of households. We chose the smallest *kampung* in this *desa* as the study site and selected 60% of farmer households and 40% of non-farmer households for the sample survey (Table 9–1). The survey was conducted in November and December 1979.

Because the complete enumeration survey was not applied, we were unable to obtain detailed information on inter-class relations in the village community, such as landlord-tenant and employer-employee

Table 9-1. Total and sample compositions of households in the North Subang Village, 1979.

	Village total		Sample size	Sample
	No. (1)	(%)	No. (2)	ratio (2)/(1)
Farmer				
Large (1.0 ha and above)	30	(16)	19	0.63
Small (less than 1.0 ha)	45	(23)	28	0.62
Total	*75*	*(39)*	*47*	*0.63*
Non-farmer				
Landless worker	111	(58)	44	0.40
Non-cultivating landowner	5	(3)	2	0.40
Total	*116*	*(61)*	*46*	*0.40*
Total	191	(100)	93	0.49

relations. Furthermore, we had difficulty obtaining data from the biggest landlord, who owned nearly one-third of the *sawah* (wet paddy field) in the village and who was understandably unwilling to disclose information on sensitive issues such as the process by which he accumulated his land. As a result, the data pertaining to the agrarian structure of this village are less complete and reliable than those for the other villages we studied. On the other hand, there is not much difference in the quality of data on rice production costs and returns.

In light of these data problems, analysis in this chapter is focused on changes in rice production technology and their income distribution implications.

Demographic Pattern and Agrarian Structure

Recognizing the data limitations, we will try to outline the demographic pattern and the agrarian structure of this village as background information for the analysis in the next section.

Compared with the South Subang Village, where all evidence suggests that population density reached a saturation point, the man-land ratio in the North Subang Village was not quite so high. Total population in 1979 was 774 persons (375 males and 399 females) for 65 hectares of wet paddy field (*sawah*); the man-land ratio of 12 persons per hectare of rice land in this village was favorable compared with that of 17 persons in the South Village.

The information on demographic trends that we were able to obtain was very limited. The only information of any significance was the data on the number of children per mother by mother's age, as shown in Table 9–2 in comparison with those of the South Subang Village. Those data for the North Subang Village are subject to underestimation, because the time and resource constraints made it difficult to trace grown children who had moved out of their parents' households, as was done carefully for the case of the South Subang Village. Since the problem of underestimation is considered especially serious for mothers in the old age brackets, the data for mothers above 49 years old were deleted from analysis.

Recognizing the data limitations, the comparison in Table 9–2 shows clearly that the natural rate of population growth for recent years was much higher in the North Village than in the South Village. Moreover, a large number of migrants flowed into this village. If we trust the memory of old villagers, the number of households in the North Subang Village in 1940 (just before World War II) was about

Table 9-2. Average number of surviving children per mother by mother's age and estimates of the natural rates of population growth in the South and the North Subang Villages.

| Mother's age | North Village | | South Village | |
	Children per mother (n) No.	Population growth rate[a] (r) %/year	Children per mother (n) No.	Population growth rate[a] (r) %/year
40–49	3.25	1.6	2.71	1.0
(36–45)	(3.16)	(1.5)	(2.48)	(0.7)
30–39	2.57	—	1.95	—
20–29	1.80	—	0.84	—

[a] Calculated by the formula: $n = 2(1 + r)^{30}$.

40, which had increased to 191 at the time of our survey. Assuming no change in average family size, the rate of population growth over the past four decades has been about 4% per year. Such a high rate of population increase reflects a rapid inflow of migrants to this village.

A relatively favorable man-land ratio and the rapid population growth involving a large inflow of migrants seem to be explained by the recent origin of this village. Unlike the South Subang Village, which was settled in the distant past beyond the reach of present settlers' memories, the settlement of the North Village began in the 1920s. Settlement was late because it was more difficult to build an irrigation system at the local level on this flat coastal plain than in the undulating mountain-locked areas such as that of the South Subang Village.

Initial settlers in the North Subang village opened a no-man's land and practiced very extensive farming under rainfed conditions. Because the rice yield under rainfed conditions was only about 1.5 tons per hectare, an operational holding of about 2 hectares was required for a family's subsistence. Thus, relatively large-scale holdings by Javanese standards had been established. Rice yields in this village were raised significantly after the local Macan System began to irrigate the village fields during the wet season.

Corresponding to the intensification of rice farming due to irrigation development, labor demand increased and a large number of migrants flowed into this village. These new migrants settled in this village as sharecroppers to the old settlers or as landless laborers. The same process was repeated after the extension of the Jatiluhur System made irrigation possible in both wet and dry seasons. Class differentiation in the forms of skewed distribution of landholdings (Table 9–3) and high incidence of tenancy (Tables 9–4 and 9–5) was thus developed through the waves of migration.

Table 9-3.   Size distributions of *sawah* land ownership and operational landholdings in the North Subang Village, 1979.

	Ownership holdings				Operational holdings			
	Number of households		Area		Number of households		Area	
	No.	(%)	Ha	(%)	No.	(%)	Ha	(%)
3.00 ha and above	2	(1)	27.97	(43)	2	(1)	7.81	(12)
2.00–3.00 ha	5	(3)	10.13	(16)	5	(3)	10.84	(17)
1.00–2.00 ha	10	(5)	12.83	(20)	23	(12)	26.54	(40)
0.50–1.00 ha	13	(7)	8.01	(12)	23	(12)	14.99	(23)
Below 0.50 ha	23	(12)	5.45	(9)	22	(11)	5.38	(8)
0	138	(72)	0	(0)	116	(61)	0	(0)
Total	*191*	*(100)*	*64.39*	*(100)*	*191*	*(100)*	*65.56*	*(100)*
Average area per household (ha)		0.34				0.34		
		(1.21)[a]				(0.87)[b]		

[a] Average area per owner household.
[b] Average area per farmer household.

Table 9-4.   Distribution of farms by tenure status in the North Subang Village, 1979.

	Number of farms		Area	
	No.	(%)	Ha	(%)
Owner operator	36	(48)	29.07	(44)
Owner/share	8	(11)	9.83	(15)
Owner/pawn	1	(1)	2.84	(4)
Owner/share/pawn	2	(3)	4.92	(8)
Share tenant	23	(30)	15.47	(24)
Pawn	5	(7)	3.43	(5)
Total	*75*	*(100)*	*65.56*	*(100)*

Table 9-5.   Distribution of *sawah* land plots by tenure status in the North Subang Village, 1979.

	No.	(%)
Owned	47	(53)
Rented:		
Share tenancy	33	(38)
Pawned	8	(9)
Total	*88*	*(100)*

At the same time, stratification progressed among the old settlers. Some of them acquired land from others through money-lending operations. It was common for farmers in need of cash to pawn their land to their well-to-do neighbors. If they defaulted at the end of the loan period, they lost ownership of the land. A typical case was the process of land accumulation by the biggest landlord. He was the son of an original settler who opened up a wild field. Through money lending, he accumulated more than 20 hectares in this village and some more in other villages—he refused to give us detailed information on this process.

Such land transfer has been especially common in this village because the systems of mutual help and insurance within the village community have not been well developed. All the loan cases that we encountered in the North Subang Village, without exception, stipulated interest payments at a rate of 50% per crop season; this represents a sharp contrast to the South Subang Village where interest-free loans were frequently found among relatives and friends. Paddy savings-and-loan associations formed by neighboring households (*lumbung rukun tetanga* or *koporasi*), which were common in the South Subang Village, were also absent in the North Subang Village. It appears that the community in the North Subang Village has not yet been sufficiently solidified to establish such mutual help and insurance systems because of its recent settlement and large inflow of migrants. Early settlers were mainly Sundanese who moved to this village from the surrounding districts. Many recent migrants were the Javanese from the eastern edges of West Java or even from Central Java. The village's ethnic heterogeneity seems to be one of the reasons why the community has been loosely structured.

As the result of land accumulation by a few land owners, tenant farming became more common in this village than in the South Subang Village (compare Tables 9–4 and 9–5 with Tables 8–4 and 8–5). In the South Subang Village, less than 20% of sawah land was cultivated by tenants, whereas the ratio was nearly 50% in the North Subang Village. The percentage of tenants (mostly sharecroppers) of the total number of farmers was correspondingly higher for the North Subang Village.

Changes in Rice Farming

The most important change in the village economy in the past two decades was the extension of the Jatiluhur Irrigation System to this village. Major laterals had been built by 1968 but it was not until 1972 that secondary and tertiary laterals were completed and the whole area in the village became amenable to rice double-cropping. According to the IPS Survey, double-cropping was practiced in about one-half of the *sawah* area in 1968–71. In 1979, when our survey was conducted, the whole area was double-cropped.

Introduction of the double-cropping system was facilitated by the diffusion of modern semi-dwarf varieties (MV) which mature early and are nonphotosensitive. According to the IPS Survey, 7% of farmers planted in MV in 1968–71. The ratio went up to 100% in 1978/79. The MVs commonly used were *IR 26, IR 36, IR 38,* and *Asahan* developed by the Central Agricultural Experiment Station at Sukamandi near the North Subang Village. *Ani-ani* knives were replaced by sickles for harvesting MV rice.

With the diffusion of MV accompanied by increased application of fertilizers, average rice yield per hectare of crop area increased from 2.5 tons in 1969–71 to 3.9 tons in 1978/79 for the wet season and from 2.1 tons to 2.9 tons for the dry season (Table 9–6). Considering the increase in the multiple-cropping ratio from 1.5 to 2.0, the average rice output per hectare of *sawah* land per year increased more than 80% during the past decade.

Dramatic improvements in irrigation and technology resulted in a major change in labor demand for rice production. As shown in Table 9–6, labor input per hectare of rice crop area did not increase so much for either wet or dry seasons. Although data are not available to assess changes in labor requirements for harvesting and threshing, it appears reasonable to assume that total labor input per hectare of crop area increased by only about 10% during the past decade. A major

Table 9-6. Changes in rice yield and rice production inputs per ha of crop area in the North Subang Village, 1968–71 to 1978/79.[a]

	1968–71[b]	1978/79[c]	% change from 1968–71 to 1978/79[g]	
Multiple-cropping ratio[d]	1.5	2.0	33	
Rice yield (kg/ha)	2,411	3,368	40	(86)
Fertilizer input (kg/ha)[e]	75	209	179	(179)
Labor input (hours/ha):				
Land preparation	219	233	6	(42)
Other preharvest operations	419	468	12	(49)
Harvesting & threshing	n.a.	254	—	
Total (preharvest)	638	701	18	(46)
Carabao use for land preparations (day/ha)[f]	9.6	13.2	38	(83)

[a] Averages for wet and dry seasons. [b] Based on the IPS Survey for Phase I to V.

[c] Based on our survey. Averages for 1978/79 wet season and 1979 dry season.

[d] Total crop area divided by total *sawah* land area.

[e] Urea and TSP. [f] Data for wet season.

[g] Figures in this column are rates of increase per hectare of crop area (gross sown area). Those in parentheses are the rates per hectare of paddy field (net sown area).

increase in labor demand was brought about by the introduction of the double-cropping system.

Because the wet crop season in this village extends from October to April and the dry season from April to October, land-preparation operations for one season overlap with harvesting and threshing for another. A labor bottleneck was thus created for the overlapping periods. The use of carabao in land preparation increased in order to avoid the bottleneck (Table 9–6). As a result of substitution of animal power for human labor in land preparation, the average labor input per hectare of crop area per season for rice production in the North Subang Village was only 955 hours, nearly 300 hours shorter than in the South Subang Village (compare Table 9–7 with Table 8–9).[2]

Table 9-7.   Labor inputs for rice production per ha of crop area by task in the North Subang Village (averages for 1978/79 wet season and 1979 dry season).

	Large farmer		Small farmer		Average	
	hours	(%)	hours	(%)	hours	(%)
Land preparation:						
Family	55	(25)	103	(40)	69	(30)
Hired	167	(75)	155	(60)	164	(70)
Total	222	(100)	258	(100)	233	(100)
Transplanting:						
Family	7	(4)	22	(13)	11	(7)
Hired	158	(96)	151	(87)	156	(93)
Total	165	(100)	173	(100)	167	(100)
Weeding:						
Family	22	(12)	106	(53)	46	(24)
Hired	168	(88)	94	(47)	146	(76)
Total	190	(100)	200	(100)	192	(100)
Harvesting and threshing:						
Family	8	(3)	14	(5)	10	(4)
Hired	241	(97)	251	(95)	244	(96)
Total	249	(100)	265	(100)	254	(100)
Others:						
Family	73	(63)	78	(85)	75	(69)
Hired	43	(37)	14	(15)	34	(31)
Total	116	(100)	92	(100)	109	(100)
Total:						
Family	165	(18)	323	(33)	211	(22)
Hired	777	(82)	665	(67)	744	(78)
Total	942	(100)	988	(100)	955	(100)

[2] Unlike in the South Subang Village, where cultivation practices are not so different between wet and dry seasons, there is a clear difference in the practice of land preparation in the North Subang Village. Land prepration in the wet season depends on animal plowing and harrowing supplemented by manual hoeing and harrowing,

Despite the effort to save labor, the increase in labor demand due to the diffusion of double-cropping exceeded that of supply as manifested by the rise in real wage rates (Table 9-8). Such a situation in the North Subang Village represents a sharp contrast to the case of the South Subang Village, in which population pressure under a stagnant technology resulted in a decline in real wage rates that induced the substitution of human labor for animal power.

Table 9-8. Changes in input prices for rice production in the North Subang Village, 1968–71 to 1978/79.[a]

	1968–71[b]	1978/79[c]	% Change from 1968–71 to 1978/79
Paddy price (Rp/kg)	19.3	67.5	250
Nominal input price:			
Fertilizer price (Rp/kg)[d]	28.0	70.0	150
Labor wage rate (Rp/day)[e]	153	775	407
Carabao rental rate (Rp/day)[f]	170	950	459
Real input price[g]:			
Fertilizer price (kg/ha)	1.5	1.0	−33
Labor wage rate (kg/day)	7.9	11.5	46
Carabao rental rate (kg/day)	8.8	14.1	60

[a] Averages for wet and dry seasons.
[b] Based on the IPS Survey for Phase I to V. Averages for wet and dry seasons.
[c] Based on our survey. Averages for 1978/79 wet season and 1979 dry season.
[d] Urea and TSP.
[e] Wage for land preparation assuming 8 hours' work per day. Includes meals.
[f] Data for wet season.
[g] Nominal price divided by paddy price.

Consequences of Technological Progress

As observed in the previous section, significant progress in technology—broadly defined as an upward shift in the production function—was realized in the North Subang Village as the result of development in irrigation systems and the introduction of modern varieties. Let us now try to analyze the impact of this technological progress on institutional arrangements and income distribution in the village community.

Changes in Rice Harvesting Systems

As in the South Subang Village, the traditional from of rice harvesting

whereas dry season land preparation mainly consists of cutting straw (*babat jerami*). In terms of labor requirement per hectare, however, there is no significant difference in land preparation between wet and dry seasons (241 hours vs. 225 hours). Labor requirements for other tasks are also fairly similar.

contract in the North Subang Village was a purely open *bawon* system in which everyone can participate in harvesting and receive an output share. However, unlike the South Subang Village, the harvesting system in this village did not change in the direction of limiting participation. Farmers continued to use the purely open *bawon* system, although they reduced the share rate for harvesting workers (Table 9-9). It is interesting to observe that some of the farmers tried to introduce the *ceblokan* system in the 1960s, at about the same time that it was initially introduced to the South Subang Village. However, they soon shifted back to the *bawon* system.

One of the reasons why the system of more strict control did not develop seems to be the loose community structure of this village. Because this village was settled recently and has many new migrants of different ethnic groups, the identity of villagers as members of an organic community has not been established so strongly. As we discussed previously, loose community ties in this village are reflected in the absence of mutual help and insurance schemes among small neighborhood groups. Such a social climate would not have been conducive to development of harvesting arrangements that limit participation to villagers only or to a specific group of villagers under the guise of patron-client relations.[3]

Another basic factor underlying the continuation of the open *bawon* system seems to be the shortage of labor in the months of harvest that coincide with those of land preparation for the next crop in the double-cropping system. Needless to say, there is little incentive to limit participation under conditions of labor shortage.

While the open *bawon* system was sustained, the output share for harvesters declined successively from one-fifth to one-tenth (Table 9-9). However, the decline in the share rate did not mean a decline in the wage rate of harvesters under conditions of rising yields per hectare. The imputed wage rates for *bawon* harvesting and threshing were found to be roughly in equilibrium with the market wage rates for land prep-

[3] In earlier periods when population pressure was not so great and harvesters were primarily limited to villagers without resorting to formal restrictions, the open *bawon* system would have worked adequately as a system of sharing income widely among villagers. However, as the number of seasonal migrant workers has increased due to increased population pressure, the open *bawon* system has become less adequate as a mechanism to share work and income within the village community. It appears that the open *bawon* system, which was once a symbol of mutual help and income-sharing in the village, has now been working to loosen the community tie. Today, the traditional role of the open *bawon* system in strengthening the community seems to be played by patron-client relations such as *ceblokan*, although the latter can contribute to strengthening personal ties within a smaller group than the village community as a whole.

Table 9-9. Changes in the rice harvesting system in the North Subang Village (% of farmer adoptors).

| | Bawon (purely open) | | | | | | Ceblokan[a] | |
	1/5	1/6	1/7	1/8	1/9	1/10	1/5(T)	Total
1940's	100							100
1950's	77	23						100
1960–64	57	30					13	100
1965–68	56	34	6	4				100
1969–70		53	23	17	7			100
1971–72		35	23	21	12	9		100
1973–74		23	23	27	11	16		100
1975–76		2	18	36	11	33		100
1977–78			16	32	9	43		100
1979			11	28	7	54		100

[a] Ceblokan system with 1/5 bawon share and with transplanting and pulling seedlings as obligatory work.

aration for the overlapping periods (Table 9–10). Such results seem to suggest that the bawon share rate was reduced in response to rising yields so as to equate the implicit wage rate for harvesting with the marginal productivity of labor for both harvesting and land preparation. It seems reasonable to assume that the harvesting wage rate implicit in the bawon share increased in line with the rise in wage rates for land preparation in the course of technological progress.

The same equilibrium between marginal labor cost and return could have been achieved by an alternative method, such as ceblokan in which additional obligatory work is required for harvesting workers to be employed for the same output-share rate. Why was the reduction of the bawon share rate used in this village to restore equilibrium,

Table 9-10. Imputed wage rate for bawon harvesting and threshing in the North Subang Village, 1978/79.

	Wet season (1/10)[a]	Dry season (1/10)[a]
Yield (kg/ha)[b]	4,177	3,396
Bawon share (kg/ha)	418	340
(1) Imputed value (Rp/ha)	27,588	23,460
Labor input for harvesting and threshing		
(2) (hours/ha)	257	266
Imputed wage rate (1)/(2); (Rp/hour)	107	88
Market wage rate (Rp/hour)	100[c]	94[d]

[a] Output share rate for bawon harvesters.
[b] Average yield per ha for the fields for which the share rate of 1/10 was applied.
[c] Wage rate of land preparation for dry season.
[d] Wage rate of land preparation for wet season.

instead of the *ceblokan* system as in the South Subang Village? The answer should be sought in the differences in community structure, as we have discussed previously.

Changes in Income Distribution

In both the North and South Subang Villages, the labor used for rice production increased. However, the increased application of labor in the South Village was accompanied by a decline in the labor wage rate relative to the rental rate for draft animals, which implied a substitution of labor for capital along a fixed production function. In the North Village, the increased labor input was accompanied by a rise in the real wage rate, which should have been the result of a shift in the production function. How was such a difference reflected in changes in income distribution?

Changes in the average factor shares of rice output per hectare in the North Subang Village from 1968–71 to 1978/79 were estimated (Table 9–11). During this period the average yield per hectare for wet and dry seasons increased by 40%. Despite such a rapid increase in

Table 9-11.   Changes in factor payments and factor shares in rice production per ha of crop area in the North Subang Village, 1968–71 to 1978/79.[a]

	Factor payment (kg/ha)			Factor share (%)		
	1968–71[b]	1978/79[c]		1968–71[b]	1978/79	
	Owner	Owner	Tenant[d]	Owner	Owner	Tenant[d]
Paddy output	2,342	3,203	3,272	100.0	100.0	100.0
Factor payment[e]:						
Current input[f]	152	300	280	6.5	9.4	8.5
Capital[g]	47	154	154	2.0	4.8	4.7
Labor	947	1,322	1,295	40.4	41.3	39.6
(Family)	(117)	(252)	(357)	(5.0)	(7.9)	(10.9)
(Hired)	(830)	(1,070)	(938)	(35.4)	(33.4)	(28.7)
Land	0	0	1,495	0	0	45.7
Operator's surplus	1,196	1,427	48	51.1	44.5	1.5

[a] Averages for wet and dry seasons.
[b] Based on the IPS Survey for Phase I to V.
[c] Based on our survey.
[d] Data for share tenants.
[e] Factor payments converted to paddy equivalents by the factor-product price ratios.
[f] Seeds, fertilizers, and chemicals.
[g] Animal and machine rental and irrigation fee.

output, the relative share of labor remained almost constant. Meanwhile, the shares of both current inputs and capital increased. As a result, the share of operators' surplus declined in the case of owner-farmers.

In the case of tenant farmers, operators' surplus was almost zero and rent paid to landlords was equivalent to owner-farmers' surplus, implying that the operators' surplus of owner-farmers consisted mainly of the return to their land. Thus, the results in Table 9–11 are consistent with the hypothesis that technological progress in this village was biased in a land-saving and capital-using direction and was more or less neutral with respect to the use of labor. Such results for the North Village represent a sharp contrast to the case of the South Village where the share of land increased sharply at the expense of the share of labor (Table 8–15).

The data in Table 9–11 are rearranged in Table 9–12 to show how the income (value added) from rice production per hectare was distributed between farmers and hired laborers. Farmers' income consists of operators' surplus and returns to family labor and capital. Laborers' income consists of wage earnings from hired farm work. Both farmers and laborers recorded significant gains in absolute income, while their relative shares remained largely unchanged. Again, such results contrast with the case of the South Village where the income of laborers did not show a significant increase and their relative income share declined (Table 8–16).

Table 9-12.   Changes in shares of income from rice production per ha of crop area in the North Subang Village, from 1968–71 to 1978/79.[a]

	Income in paddy (kg/ha)		Income share (%)	
	1968–71	1978/79	1968–71	1978/79
Value added[b]	2,191	2,903	100.0	100.0
Farmer:				
Family labor	117	252	5.3	8.7
Capital	47	154	2.2	5.2
Operator's surplus	1,197	1,427	54.6	49.2
Total	*1,361*	*1,833*	*62.1*	*63.1*
Hired laborer:				
Preharvest work	467	686	21.3	23.7
Harvest & postharvest work	363	384	16.6	13.2
Total	*730*	*1,070*	*37.9*	*36.9*

[a] Data rearranged from Table 9–11 for owner-operated farms.
[b] Output value minus current input cost.

The Two Villages in Simple Economics

The contrasts between the North and South Subang Villages can best be understood in terms of the simple economics developed in Chapter 3.

The South Village almost exactly fits Case I in Figure 3-2. Both the production function (f) and the labor demand function (D) remained constant, reflecting technological stagnation, while the labor supply function (S) shifted to the right due to population growth. Corresponding to a change in the market equilibrium point from A to B, the wage rate declined and the land rental rate rose. Both the absolute income and the relative income share of labor declined.

The North Village is largely equivalent to Case II in Figure 3-2. The production function shifted upward and the labor demand curve shifted to the right. Although, unlike the model, population growth in the North Village resulted in a rapid shift in the labor supply curve to the right, the demand shift due to technological progress outpaced the supply shift. As a result, both the labor input and the wage rate increased. Though the shift in the production function was not sufficient to increase the relative income share of labor, workers' absolute income increased significantly.

The comparative analysis of two villages has shown clearly that, as the simple economic model predicts, greater poverty and inequality are the inexorable fate of Asian village economies if efforts to generate technological progress remain insufficient to overcome the decreasing return to labor due to the growing population pressure on land.

Part **IV**

Agrarian Change in Perspective

Weeding (above) is required as obligatory work in order to be employed for harvesting under the *gama* system in the Philippines. Both weeding and transplanting (below) are often required under the *ceblokan* system in Indonesia.

Chapter 10

A Prospect from Village Studies

In this concluding chapter we summarize the major findings from our village studies in order to make some inferences on the course of agrarian change in Asia.

Structure of Agrarian Change

In this section we try to outline the pattern of agrarian change as we observed it in studies of specific villages, with reference to the perspective developed in Chapter 3.

Population Pressure, Technological Change and Income Distribution

In Chapter 3 we postulated that the basic force for change in the agrarian structure of developing countries in Asia today is the strong population pressure on land. The population growth rate in the Third World has continued to accelerate since the 1920s and 1930s, due to the propagation of modern public health measures and also due to the market expansion that reduced the incidence of famine. The increase in nonagricultural employment has been grossly insufficient to absorb the increments to the labor force, resulting in rapid increases in rural labor population pressing hard on limited agricultural land.

If population continues to grow under constant technology, the outcome will approximate the world of classical economists like Ricardo: cultivation frontiers are expanded to more marginal areas and greater amounts of labor are applied per unit of cultivated land;

211

the marginal return to additional labor input declines and the cost of food production rises; the real wage rate measured in food grain declines and the land rent increases; land's share of agricultural income rises relative to labor's share, resulting in more unequal income distribution. In the real world, of course, technology has not stayed constant. Significant efforts have been made to develop irrigation systems and seed-fertilizer technology that have had the effect of counteracting the decreasing return to labor. In many areas, however, such efforts have failed to overcome the negative effect of strong population pressure, with the result being widening income differentials among the rural population.

The hypothesis summarized above represents a sharp contrast to that advanced by radical political economists. They argue that new technology such as modern varieties (MV) of rice and wheat is the major factor in promoting inequality and class differentiation: the new technology tends to be monopolized by large farmers who have better access to new information and financial sources; adoption of MV is difficult for subsistence-level farmers who have little financial capacity to purchase modern inputs such as fertilizers and chemicals; the large profit resulting from the exclusive adoption of the new technology stimulates large farmers to enlarge their operational holdings by evicting tenants or by purchasing small farmers' plots; further, the large commercial farms with their economies of scale have an intrinsic tendency to introduce large machineries that reduce employment opportunities and wage rates for laborers; polarization of peasant communities into large commercial farmers and a landless proletariat is thus promoted.

Indeed, growing inequality and class differentiation were concurrent with increasing population pressure and the development of modern technology in the villages that we studied. Both the high rates of population growth and the rapid diffusion of MV technology were associated with sharp increases in the population of landless laborers. The increase in the landless population occurred not simply because the land area was limited; it often also reflected a polarization process in that large landholders accumulated more land at the expense of small holdings (examples are the South Laguna Village in Chapter 5 and the North Subang Village in Chapter 9). The major question is whether the MV technology was responsible for this process.

Findings from our village studies are clearly inconsistent with placing blame on the new technology. The four village cases invariably show that farm size was not a factor in adoption of MV. In the three villages with environmental conditions suitable for MV (the East and the South Laguna Villages in Chapters 5 and 6, and the North Subang Village in Chapter 9), both large and small farmers planted MV in nearly 100% of their paddy areas. On the other hand, both large and small farmers rejected MV when they found the MV to be unsuited to their environment (the South Subang Village in Chapter 8). In neither case was a significant difference observed in the levels of either yield or application of modern inputs such as fertilizers.

Further, detailed comparison of rice production costs and returns between large commercial farmers and small peasants in the South Laguna Village has clearly shown that large farmers were no more efficient technologically but rather were less efficient than small farmers to the extent that the large operations required more resources for management and supervision; the advantage of the large farmers in using their bargaining position to command lower prices for land and labor could barely compensate for their technological inefficiency (Chapter 6).

Thus, our data failed to support the radical hypothesis that the MV technology is heavily biased towards a larger scale for technological or other reasons and, therefore, benefits the large farmers exclusively. One may argue, in turn, that even if the new technology benefits both large and small farmers equally, it does not benefit landless laborers at all and hence widens the income gap between farm operators and hired laborers. Such a view is refuted by our comparative analysis of two villages in West Java (Chapters 8 and 9). In the South Subang Village, technology was stagnant because the MV suitable for its environment were not available. In response to the growth in the labor force, the real wage rate was bid down and the relative income share of hired labor declined; the absolute income of hired labor was kept barely constant despite the increase in labor use due to a regressive shift from carabao plowing to hand hoeing. In contrast, in the North Subang Village, where significant yield increases were recorded as a result of irrigation improvement and MV diffusion, the real wage rate rose despite rapid increases in both labor force and animal power. The real income of hired laborers increased absolutely even though their relative income share remained constant. The comparison clearly supports the hypothesis that population pressure is the basic cause for growing inequality and that the inequality can be reduced by investments in irrigation and technology in order to save or augment land.

There was no evidence for complementarity between MV and farm mechanization. In the East and the South Laguna Village, carabaos were replaced by power tillers (Chapters 5 and 6). However, this process preceded the introduction of MV, and there was no indication that MV promoted mechanization further. On the contrary, in many villages in Inner Central Luzon the diffusion of early maturing and nonphotosensitive MV's worked as an incentive to substitute hand threshing for threshing by big machines (Chapter 4). No evidence was found that the MV technology reduced farm employment and wage rates by promoting farm mechanization.

These findings are largely consistent with those from many other case studies reviewed in Chapter 3.

Polarization and Peasant Stratification

Although efforts to improve technology and land infrastructure have been intensified in Asia in recent years, they have been insufficient in many areas to overcome the strong population pressure on land. As a result, the return to labor has declined relative to the return to land, and income distribution has become more skewed in rural communities. Changes in agrarian structure corresponding to the growing inequality may take two different forms. One is the polarization of the peasant community into large commerical farmers and a landless proletariat, as predicted by Marx and Lenin. Another is peasant stratification—a multiplication of peasant subclasses in a continuous spectrum ranging from landless laborers to non-cultivating landlords within the social mode of the peasant community in which villagers are tied to one another in multi-stranded personalized relations in contrast to the impersonal market relations which accompany polarization.

The results of intensive village studies as well as of extensive trip surveys over rice-producing areas of Java and Luzon show that polarization cases were rather exceptional. It was more common to observe small farms becoming smaller and the landless population increasing. In the rice areas we seldom found large commercial farms dependent on hired labor from the market.

Typical cases were the East Laguna Village (Chapter 5) and the South Subang Village (Chapter 8). In both villages the landless population increased in recent years. However, this was not the result of land accumulation by large farmers; rather, operational holdings became uni-modally smaller for all farm-size classes. Yet income and asset distributions in the communities became more unequal, and the income gap between farmers and landless laborers widened, because the return to labor declined relative to the return to land. These villages developed a meticulous network of work-sharing and output-sharing arrangements. In the South Subang Village small owner-farmers began to rent out parts of their holdings to the landless in a crop-sharing arrangement. In the East Laguna Village tenant farmers, who became leaseholders under land reform, developed subtenancy contracts.

Traditional employment contracts, such as the *bawon* system in Subang and the *hunusan* system in Laguna, that allowed village-wide participation in harvesting were replaced by new systems called *ceblokan* or *gama*, that limited participation to laborers who contributed their unpaid services for such tasks as weeding and transplanting. Under these new systems the work-sharing and output-sharing arrangements were not weakened but strengthened, although participants were limited to smaller groups. The shifts from *bawon* to *ceblokan* in Java and from *hunusan* to *gama* in Luzon imply a shift from a village-wide mutual-help relationship in a relatively equal peasant community to a patron-client relationship between relatively better-off farmers and worse-off landless or near-landless people in a more stratified community. Unlike the polarization case, laborers continued to have some claims to output from the land they worked.

The pattern of agrarian change in the two villages summarized above can most appropriately be called peasant stratification in our terms. According to our observations over wide areas of Luzon and Java (Chapters 4 and 7), such a pattern seems dominant. However, we also found examples of polarization. A typical example was the South Laguna Village (Chapter 6). This village was developed as a hacienda *barrio*, and its farm-size distribution had originally been skewed. In recent years two tenant farmers greatly expanded the scale of their operations, mainly through the purchase of tenancy titles from other tenants. The community was bifurcated into large commercial farmers and the landless and near-landless population. However, we found that the large commercial operations were no more efficient than the small peasant operations. Large operators' surpluses for the large farmers were found to be nothing but the gap between the marginal product of land and the actual rent that they had to pay to landlords under the rent control of land reform programs. They could have earned the same income from rent revenue if they had sub-rented their holdings to landless laborers in small parcels. However, they preferred to enlarge their operations because it was dangerous to expand subrenting arrangements beyond a circle of relatives or close friends under the land reform laws which prohibit such arrangements.

Comparison of the East and South Laguna Villages shows clearly that the same economic forces resulting in a decline in the return to labor relative to the return to land can induce very different patterns of agrarian change—peasant stratification in the former and polarization in the latter—under different social environments. This point will be discussed in more detail in the next section.

Process of Institutional Adjustment

We have identified the basic force inducing agrarian change in Asia as the decline in the return to labor relative to the return to land resulting from the strong population pressure that tends to outpace efforts to augment land by means of improvements in agricultural technology and land infrastructure. In this section we try to summarize our observations on the process of institutional adjustment in village communities in terms of the theories advanced in Chapter 2.

Inducements to Institutional Change

Institutions, defined as rules sanctioned by community members, are the framework within which scarce economic resources are allocated. It is our basic hypothesis that institutional change will be induced when the resulting gain is expected to exceed the cost. A situation of net gain from institutional change implies disequilibria or sub-optimal resource allocation under the old institutions. The disequilibria emerge when the market is inactive or inflexible in reallocating resources in response to changes in relative resource scarcities corresponding to changes in factor endowments and technology. Adjustments in institutional arrangements can thus be considered a substitute for market-pricing mechanisms of the Walrasian type in equating marginal factor costs to marginal factor returns.

The hypothesis summarized above was confirmed by the results of analysis of several institutional adjustments at the village level. In the Philippine villages the increased application of labor per hectare due to population pressure resulted in an increase in the marginal product of land, whereas land rent was fixed by the land reform laws; the gap induced the development of sub-tenancy contracts; through this institutional innovation the land rent including payments to both original and intermediate landlords was equated to the marginal product of land, as confirmed by the production function analysis (Chapter 5).

Similarly, in many villages in both Java and Luzon the population pressure resulted in a decline in the marginal product of labor, whereas the wage rates were slow to adjust, especially for harvesting labor, because of the institutional rigidity of the harvesters' output share rate; the gap induced the shifts from traditional harvesting arrangements such as *bawon* and *hunusan* to *ceblokan* and *gama*; by adding extra obligatory services to harvesters' work the implicit wage rates for harvesting labor were equated to the market wage rates (Chapters 4,5 and 8).

Our findings shed light on the famous controversy between the classical and neoclassical schools over wage determination in the rural (traditional) sector of developing countries—the former school assumes an institutionally determined wage rate higher than the marginal value product of labor (Lewis, 1954; Ranis and Fei, 1961), and the latter assumes a wage rate equal to labor's marginal value product (Jorgenson, 1961; Schultz, 1964). The results of our quantitative analysis are consistent with the neoclassical proposition that in equilibrium labor is paid equal to its marginal product. However, the wage adjustment process towards equilibrium seems to involve a mechanism very different from the market mechanism assumed in neoclassical economics. The fact that labor's share in the traditional output-sharing contract, such as one-sixth of the harvest, is institutionally fixed implies that wage rates cannot adjust directly to changes in labor's marginal productivity. Adjustments in wage rates are allowed only through modification of institutional arrangements themselves, such as a shift from *hunusan* to *gama*. In other words, "institutional wages" based on a system of community-wide work- and income-sharing similar to the classical concept can adjust to the neoclassical equilibrium through institutional innovations.

Choice of Institutional Arrangements

A major question is why a specific form of institutional adjustment was chosen over the others. The gap between the harvesters' output share and the market wage rate could have been closed by institutional adjustments other than *ceblokan* or *gama*—for example, by reducing harvesters' share rates while maintaining the traditional crop-sharing contract or by replacing the crop-sharing contract with a time-rate wage contract.

By now it has been generally agreed that a specific form of institutional arrangement will be chosen in terms of risk and transaction cost. We hypothesized that, in a village economy based on biological production processes in which production activities are difficult to standardize and are subject to a high degree of uncertainty, a multi-stranded personalized relationship of the patron-client type is preferred because it reduces risk and saves transaction costs. The choice of institutional adjustments in the form of *ceblokan* or *gama* is consistent with our hypothesis. In these new arrangements, extra obligatory work such as transplanting and weeding was added to the harvesting work itself in exchange for a share of output; transactions became more multi-faceted, and the personal tie between employer and employee was strengthened. The employer was assured of a timely labor supply for harvesting, and the employee was secure in finding employment. Laborers' dishonesty or shirking was reduced partly because better work would be rewarded by a share of output to be increased, and partly because the discovery of shirking in one operation (*e.g.* weeding) would endanger the whole set of transactions.

The transaction costs involved in a specific arrangement or contract depend, to a large extent, on the basic institutional environment in the Davis-North sense. In village communities the basic institutional environment consists mainly of traditional customs and moral principles. An arrangement that violates the traditional customs and morals would be considered illegitimate by community members. Such an arrangement would be difficult to enforce. The fact that *ceblokan* and *gama* were congruent with the traditional *bawon* and *hunusan* systems and that they were consistent with moral principles such as mutual help and income sharing would have made them less difficult to accept for the village communities.

The legitimacy of a new institutional arrangement in terms of the basic institutional environment could have a more critical implication than mere enforcement of the particular arrangement itself. If a farmer employer imposed a contract inconsistent with village customs and morals, such as replacement of the traditional crop-sharing contract with a time-rate wage contract of the market-economy type, he would have lost his legitimacy as a patron. Then, not only would he face the problem of enforcing the contract against laborers' resistance but he might even encounter the difficulty of protecting his property and maintaining his influence in the community. Such an example was found in the South Laguna Village where, when a large farmer tried to reduce the harvesters' share rate, his crop was destroyed during the night.

Thus, in the village community a strong motivation exists to preserve or strengthen the multi-faceted and enduring relationships involving highly personalized transactions among various resource contributors. In such a community, market prices are usually not flexible enough to adjust to rapid changes in relative resource scarcities corresponding to changes in factor endowments and technology. As a result, disequilibria between factor prices and marginal factor productivities will be created, which will call for institutional adjustments. One possible direction of adjustment would be a shift away from personalized transactions to market transactions. However, such a shift is usually a less efficient way to close the disequilibria in the socioeconomic environment of village communities. Rather, it is often advantageous for reducing risk and transaction costs to strengthen the personalized relationship of the patron-client type, as exemplified by a shift from *bawon* to *ceblokan* or from *hunusan* to *gama*. This seems to be the basic reason why the dominant trend in agrarian change in Southeast Asia has been toward peasant stratification rather than polarization.

Social Structure and Social Interactions

To maintain and strengthen the multi-faceted and enduring relationship of the patron-client type involves social interactions in Becker's sense. Village elites tend to simulate benevolent patrons insofar as they expect gratitude and loyal service from the poorer members of the community or fear their resentment, shirking and cheating. In return, the poor villagers will simulate loyal clients if they expect patrons' goodwill and benevolent treatment in the form of stable employment opportunities on a long-term basis.

The institutional arrangements or contracts implicitly involved in such a patron-client relationship can be more easily enforced if the community is more tightly structured in the sense that people are expected to conform to social norms such as reciprocal rights and duties which are defined clearly by tradition. We hypothesize that village social structure will become tighter as the scarcity of non-labor resources relative to labor increases over a long time period involving several generations.

The hypothesis is consistent with our observations on the differences in social structure between the East and the South Laguna Villages (Chapters 5 and 6) and between the South and the North Subang Villages (Chapters 8 and 9). In particular, the tight social structure of the South Subang Village, in which the population pressure on land had reached a near-saturation situation already two or three decades ago, represented a clear contrast with the loose community structure of the North Subang Village, in which settlement was more recent and population density per unit of paddy field area is lower. A similar contrast, though less marked, can be seen between the East and the South Laguna Villages.

In both the North Subang Village and the South Laguna Village, which was settled more recently, a large inflow of new migrants (many of them belonging to different ethnic groups in the North Subang Village) made it more difficult to develop social cohesion in the village communities. In those two villages institutional adjustments which tended to strengthen the patron-client relationship, such as *ceblokan* and *gama*, were developed or adopted to a much lesser extent than in the other two villages which were settled earlier. Rather, as was more typical in the South Laguna Village, institutional adjustments tended to shift away from the personalized relations of the patron-client type to a market relationship, with the result that agrarian change moved towards polarization. The polarization process was also enhanced by the originally skewed land-asset distribution in this village, which was developed as a hacienda *barrio*. It appears that there is a threshold of inequality in wealth and power distribution beyond which polarization will begin.

Thus, the historically developed social structure of a village community is a key factor in determining the type of institutional adjustment and the direction of agrarian change in that village.

The Prospects for Agrarian Change

Asian village economy is now at a crossroads in a dual sense. In one dimension, a critical question is whether the poor majority in village communities will become further impoverished with smaller shares of income and assets. In another dimension, if inequality increases, will the village community structure move toward polarization or toward peasant stratification?

The answer to the first question hinges critically on whether the strong population pressure on limited land resources can be counteracted effectively, so that the trend of decreasing returns to labor relative to land can be reversed. Policy efforts to this end should be pushed on various fronts such as population control, the opening of new land for cultivation, and the creation of off-farm employment opportunities. However, whatever efforts may be made on these fronts, it is unlikely that the land-labor ratio in the rural sector of developing countries will cease to decline for some years to come. Thus, it is imperative to accelerate the development of land-saving and labor-using technology in order to counteract the decreasing return to the ever-larger amount of labor applied per unit of cultivated land.

If these efforts are insufficient, the income of the poor who have no resources but their own labor will inevitably decline. The distribution of land assets will also become more skewed. In general, the higher rate of return to land provides a strong incentive to accumulate more land, especially where there is an underdeveloped capital market in that alternative investment opportunities, such as corporate stocks and securities, are not easily available. The concentration of landholdings induced by the higher rate of land rental makes income distribution more skewed, which promotes the further concentration of land.

It is not easy to stop this process simply through land reform laws and regulations, given the present power structure of rural communities. In some cases, these laws and regulations can have the effect of promoting the polarization process in the absence of adequate design and will to implement. A number of cases have been reported in which land reform regulations such as rent control or planned land confiscation and redistribution resulted in the large-scale eviction of tenants in order to establish landlords' direct cultivation by use of agricultural laborers. In the case of the South Laguna Village, the reform laws and regulations were not effective in preventing the accumulation of land in the hands of a few large farmers at the expense of small peasants' holdings; the law prohibiting sub-tenancy arrangements induced the large tenant farmers to cultivate their accumulated land under their own management instead of sub-renting it to landless laborers in small parcels. It is easy to point out loopholes in the laws and regulations. But the real problem is the economic and social conditions in developing countries that make the loopholes common in the practice of land reform. We do not disagree with the idea that land reform, if properly designed and implemented, can be a strong basis for both economic growth and equity. Unfortunately, however, we find ourselves compelled to agree with the despair of an ardent advocate of land reform: "The radical land reform we so strongly argued for . . . becomes almost an impossibility within the existing socio-economic set-up" (Dasgupta, 1977).

It is common to refer to the success of drastic redistributive land reforms in Japan and Taiwan in the post-World War II years as a model for developing countries in Asia. However, major differences in socio-economic conditions severely limit the likelihood of reproducing the East Asian experience in South and Southeast Asia today. It should be recalled that Japan's reform was executed under the authority of U.S. occupation forces and Taiwan's executed by the Nationalist Government which was exiled from the continent and,therefore, alienated from the landed interests of the island. Equally important was the huge backlog of data and administrative experience with landownership and tenure systems accumulated in this area since long before World War II. In addition, various measures for controlling tenure relations that had developed during the war had weakened the position of the landlords considerably (Hayami and associates, 1975, pp. 64–70). However, the critical difference that should be recognized is the economic conditions specific to East Asia that have preserved the results of the land reforms. In both Japan and Taiwan, rapid expansion of nonagricultural employment has resulted in reduced population pressure on land; the agricultural labor force has declined absolutely and real wage rates have risen (Tables 3–6 and 3–9 in Chapter 3). If Japan and Taiwan had continued to be subject to population pressure on land similar to that being experienced in South and Southeast Asia today, the results of the land reforms would have been seriously undermined by such developments as sub-tenancy arrangements similar to those we observed in Philippine villages.

No doubt, to achieve the intended goal of more equitable distribution of assets and income, land reform programs must be supported by stronger political will and more effective implementation. At the same time, if the real economic force underlying polarization is the decline in the return to labor relative to the return to land, land reform programs have little chance of success in achieving their income-equalizing objectives unless the programs are supported by efforts to reverse this unfavorable economic trend.

The popular argument which labels new technology as a cause of growing inequality and land reform as its cure is clearly counterproductive for the income-equalizing objective alone. Instead, both poverty and inequality will be the inexorable fate of Asian village communities unless the efforts to develop new technology and irrigation and to achieve equitable distribution of land assets can be strengthened in such a way as to maximize their basic complementarity.

Resource requirements for the development of agricultural technology and land infrastructure on a scale sufficient to counteract the strong population pressure on land will be extremely large. Part may be supplied from external sources through bilateral and multilateral arrangements, but the major part must come from within developing countries themselves. A major potential source is the land tax. Land taxation is not only effective for extracting necessary funds from the rural sector but is also highly effective in reducing the income gap between the landed and landless classes by taxing out the increased share of agricultural income attributable to land. Although land taxation and land reform may be equally subject to resistance from the landed class, the former is administratively easier and more feasible than the latter. It is an anomaly that land taxation has attracted less attention from development planners than land reform.

Another major potential source of indigenous resources is the mobilization of local resources with low opportunity costs, especially rural labor during idle seasons, for the construction and improvement of land infrastructure systems such as irrigation. Success in mobilizing such local resources depends on the "social technology" to design and implement effective community work programs that can best utilize village-community organizations and institutions. The state of the art in such social technology today is grossly insufficient relative to its need.

If, despite all efforts, the trend of decreasing return to labor relative to land can not be counteracted effectively, will the village communities move toward polarization or toward peasant stratification? Which way the Asian village economy will go depends, to a large extent, on the power structure in village communities, but it also depends on the comparative advantage in risk and transaction costs between the impersonal market of the urban type and the personalized "market" (or pseudo-market) of the village type in achieving efficient resource allocation under changing resource endowments and technology. The impersonal market system should be more efficient in transmitting information on demand and supply quickly in the form of changing prices: the wage rate will be bid down if labor supply exceeds demand, and resource allocations will be adjusted accordingly. The personalized market in villages bound by community obligations could be less efficient in this regard: in these villages a new institutional arrangement such as the *gama* system needs to be invented before the wage rate can be reduced, for example. On the other hand, both risk and transaction costs can be lower for the personalized market in the village environment where production is subject to weather uncertainty and its tasks are difficult to monitor under infinite variations in ecological conditions. The village organization can also be more effective in coordinating the use of public or semi-public goods such as irrigation water for which the impersonal market fails to achieve efficient resource allocation.

The advantage of the personalized village system would not be great for loosely structured communities where reciprocal rights and duties are not clearly defined and social interactions are not effective in enforcing contracts implicit in the personalized relationship. Therefore, villages that are characterized by loose community structures for historical and/or environmental reasons would seem to have a good chance of moving toward polarization.

The penetration of the urban market economy may enhance the trend towards polarization. More stable demand and supply of labor in an enlarged market, for example, will make it less attractive for both employers and employees to maintain labor-tying arrangements within a patron-client relationship. Increased access to urban credit and insurance markets may have the same effect, although it is inconceivable that in most villages in the developing countries of Asia such markets will be developed to the extent that they reduce the need for the risk-reducing function of the patron-client relationship for years to come.

Technology is a critical determinant of transaction costs, especially the cost of labor enforcement. In general, machineries have an inherent tendency to standardize tasks and to reduce the cost of monitoring labor. One tractor driver is much easier to supervise than dozens of manual workers and bullock teams. Therefore, the introduction of larger and more efficient machinery will have the effect of making the impersonal market system more efficient and, thereby, of inducing polarization. On the other hand, the introduction of more complex cropping systems which need greater personal judgment and care will induce a shift from large-scale farm operations based on market-wage contract labor to small tenant operations.

Government intervention in land and labor markets can have critical implications for the choice of agrarian system. For example, ceteris paribus, minimum wage laws might stimulate a shift from an operation based on market-wage labor to tenant operations. The opposite will be the case for government regulation of land rent and tenure forms. Similarly, government intervention in the capital market can have critical influences. Because small farmers owning few assets usable for collateral are usually subject to capital rationing, special programs to allocate institutional credits to smallholders are theoretically justified on both efficiency and equity grounds. In reality, however, it is common to observe that large farmers and landlords preempt scarce institutional credit through their pull with government agencies and cooperatives. The same applies to input-subsidy programs. Thus, programs designed to assist small farmers often promote inequality and polarization because of the social organization and power structures of rural communities.

Irrespective of which route is followed, income and asset distributions will become more skewed, insofar as the increase in the supply of labor will outpace the increase in labor demand. However, if small peasant holdings are consolidated into large commercial farms, the transaction costs associated with hired labor will be increased and those of capital will be reduced. Thus, the polarization will induce substitution of capital for labor and encourage the development of labor-saving technology, despite a growing abundance of labor relative to land. Employment opportunities and wage rates in the rural sector will be lower in the polarization case than in the peasant stratification case.

Moreover, if the rural economy moves toward polarization, class conflicts will intentify, and the resulting instability in the rural sector will discourage investments in agricultural production and jeopardize long-term efforts to reduce the population pressure on limited land resources.

According to our observations, peasant stratification has been the more dominant form of agrarian change in Southeast Asia. To that extent, social interactions in peasant communities bound by traditional moral principles have been effective in blocking the route to polarization. How long will such a trend continue? Might not the growing stratification and inequality eventually reach a threshold point beyond which the peasant communities begin to be polarized and the personalized village system begins to be replaced by the impersonal market relationship? As income and asset distributions become more skewed in the course of peasant stratification, elites at the top of the social strata in village communities may become so powerful in alliance with external legal and political forces that the utility they derive from the goodwill and loyalty of their poorer neighbors is substantially reduced. At the same time the penetration of the market will increase their desire for modern goods and services relative to their desire for their neighbors' goodwill. Those forces may combine to create the threshold from which the peasant stratification process evolves into the polarization process. Reformist policies unfounded on hard realism but based on ideological preconceptions merely enhance the probability of this evolution by undermining the comparative advantage of the personalized village system. Self-sustaining growth of the rural economy in developing countries of Asia cannot be expected without a policy designed to make positive use of indigenous community institutions and organizational principles as a basis for modern rural development institutions.

Agarian Problems of India:
An East and Southeast Asian View*

Yujiro Hayami

The perspective developed in this book is mainly based on the authors' experience in East and Southeast Asia. We tried to incorporate information on South Asia through a review of the literature and a broad comparison based on macro statistics (Chapter 3). However, our efforts have likely been insufficient to correct the East and Southeast Asian bias inherent in our perspective.

When the manuscript of this volume was about to go to press, an opportunity was granted to me to visit India for about three months. During my stay in India, I was able to make a few field trips to rural areas, including Haryana, Karataka, Kerala and Uttar Pradesh. Time spent in the field was less than four weeks all together. Considering the enormous size and diversity of rural India, my observation is nothing but a drop of water in a vast ocean. The impressions that I present here may well be similar to those of the blind man who touched the nose of an elephant and believed it to be a snake-like animal. Nevertheless, I have dared to prepare this note, which is highly impressionistic and

* This note was prepared during my association with the Institute of Economic Growth, Delhi, for January 20–March 4, 1981; an earlier version was published in the *Economic and Political Weekly* (Hayami, 1981b). My trips to rural India, on which this paper is based, were kindly arranged by Director P. C. Joshi of the Institute. The Indian Institute of Management, Ahmedabad, the Institute for Social and Economic Change, Bangalore, and the Center for Development Studies, Trivandrum, were cordial hosts and helped me to make local arrangements. S. N. Mishra, Vir Narain, N. G. Hanumappa, P. R. G. Nair and T. A. Varghese were excellent guides in my field visits. I owe much to J. N. Sinha for guidance in the search for and the interpretation of macro statistics on rural employment and wages. Discussions with Y. K. Alagh, G. S. Bhalla, A. Bose, G. K. Chadha, A. K. Dasgupta, M. L. Dantwala, G. K. Kadekodi, S. Mundle, S. Navlakha, K. N. Raj, C. H. Hanumantha Rao, S. K. Ray, L. S. Venkatramanan, P. Visaria and V. S. Vyas contributed much to the formation of my perspective.

227

without the support of hard data, in the hope that my very limited observation in India, when contrasted with my experience in East and Southeast Asia, might suggest directions for the formation of a more comprehensive and meaningful view of agrarian problems in Asia as a whole.

Agricultural Growth Performance

Everywhere I saw signs of genuine progress in agricultural production. My impression might be biased due to the fact that my visits were made towards the end of the 1980–81 crop year, which is expected to show a record grain output of 130 million tons. Yet the agricultural output growth rate of about 2.5% per year for the past two decades in India is not a poor performance at all, compared with performances in Southeast Asia today or those of East Asian countries such as Japan and Taiwan in their earlier development stages.[1]

I was especially impressed by the development of irrigation systems, both public and private. The dramatic growth of Haryana-Punjab agriculture is based on extensive utilization of underground water. Even in backward areas such as East Uttar Pradesh, private investments in pumps have been made in large numbers, side by side with government investments in gravity systems.

Whenever water becomes available, farmers miss no opportunity to utilize it efficiently by changing cropping patterns, introducing modern varieties and applying more fertilizers. I was impressed by the very rational calculation of small farmers in an East U.P. village concerning the purchase of irrigation water from tubewell owners—they do not seem to miss a *paisa* in the complex calculation involving many crops and soil types.

I saw a village in Karnataka, along the route from Bangalore to Mysore, which is developing a highly intensive agriculture based on tank irrigation. Since the government built a tank to serve this area some 30 years ago, this village has shifted from single-season dry farming to a very intensive multiple cropping system: in elevated areas where water does not reach they continue to plant traditional crops, millets and pulses; in lower-lying portions commercial crops such as sugarcane and mulberry are combined with rice; and in the lowest portion they plant

[1] The output growth rate in India was about the same as in Indonesia but was lower than in the Philippines and Thailand by nearly one percentage point. However, because the population growth rates in those countries were higher (about 3% as compared with 2.2% in India), the rates of increase in per-capita availability of food from domestic sources was about the same.

coconuts with bananas and peppers—garden crops that did not exist in this area a few decades ago. Villagers process their cane to produce gur and reel silk from cocoons, thereby increasing nonagricultural employment and income. An impressive aspect of this shift is that it is not a one-shot change but a process of successive intensification which is still progressing. This village case seems to suggest the possibility that, even on barren land in the Decan Plateau, highly intensive agriculture comparable to that of Japan and Java can be developed with irrigation investment and farmers' ingenuity.

In contrast, it does not appear that much progress has been made in dryland and rainfed agriculture. No significant breakthrough in technology for dryland and flooding water conditions seems to be in sight, at least at the field level. Research efforts must be further strengthened on this front.

Up to the present, however, water resources in India have been exploited far below their potential capacity, as reflected by the ratio of irrigated area (including poorly irrigated areas) to total arable area: less than one quarter. Thus the potential for future production increase is large. I personally feel that the acceleration of agricultural output growth rate from the present 2.5% level to the Sixth Plan target of 4% is quite possible, not within the Plan period but in the medium term of a decade or two, simply by reinforcing present efforts in irrigation and agricultural research.

I saw no major institutional barrier to achieving such acceleration in agricultural output increase. I saw both large and small farmers, both owner and tenant cultivators, adopting new technology and applying modern inputs whenever water was available.[2]

Of course, there are a number of weak points which prevent agricultural growth potential from being more fully exploited. A major problem seems to be the weakness in organizing collective action at the local community level. While water from private pumps is very efficiently allocated, it is a common observation that water from canal irrigation systems which require coordination within a larger group is less efficiently utilized: for example, abuses by farmers upstream result in water shortages in downstream areas. Agricultural cooperatives act merely as channels of government-supplied credit and inputs to farm producers; they rarely act as local self-help organizations to mobilize savings among members to finance their production activities or to improve marketing of their produce.

[2] Irrigation pumps tend to be concentrated in the hands of large holders. However, I saw an increasing number of smallholders who had installed pumps, either sharing water with other cultivators or selling surplus water.

Inefficiency in local organization seems related to excessive intervention of government in the market. Prohibition of usury or control of interest rates, for example, not only dampens private financial activities but also excludes the possibility of local resource mobilization by cooperatives.

Inefficiency due to government market intervention seems widespread. Institutional credit at low interest rates is stimulating mechanization where labor is abundant relative to capital. Land reform regulations on tenancy contracts are inducing shifts from labor-intensive cropping patterns to labor-saving cropping patterns such as that for coconuts.

It is easy to enumerate other policy and institutional problems. Those problems are largely similar to those of countries in Southeast Asia, although they do represent the major weakness in South and Southeast Asia as compared with East Asia. My feeling is that, despite such weaknesses, a major acceleration of agricultural output growth in India is quite possible.

Poverty and Inequality

In terms of agricultural production performance and its future potential, I see no major difference between India and Southeast Asia: basically I am optimistic.

However, when it comes to the problem of rural poverty and inequality, I found the situation in India much more serious than that in Southeast Asia. Of course, the basic causes of poverty and inequality are the same for the two regions: (a) low rates of return to labor due to low levels of technology and scarce endowments of land and capital relative to labor; and (b) unequal distribution of assets, especially land. Of the two I consider the first strategically more critical. In South and Southeast Asia today, strong population pressure on limited land resources is resulting in a decline in the rates of return to labor relative to that of land: as a larger amount of labor is applied per unit of land for constant technology the marginal product of labor declines relative to that of land. In the real world the decreasing return to labor has been, to some extent, counteracted by improvements in irrigation and technology but not quite fully compensated for. The decreasing return to labor means the pauperization of the landless and near-landless population whose subsistence depends on their labor wage earnings. The increased return to land, which is a more unequally distributed factor relative to labor, has the effect of skewing income distribution by itself. Further, the increased returns to land work as an incentive for the rich to accumulate more land, thereby resulting in greater concentration of land.[3]

According to the perspective developed from my experience in East and Southeast Asia, the best cure for the growing poverty and inequality due to population pressure is to augment land by investing in irrigation systems and developing land-saving and labor-using technologies. Japan and Taiwan were successful in mitigating the problem of rural poverty and inequality by taking this approach until industrialization reached the stage in which labor became scarce and real wage rates rose sharply.

In my view, land reforms in Japan and Taiwan were successful because the reform efforts were paralleled by efforts to decrease the relative return to land. Without reversing the trend of increasing return to land relative to labor, land reform is likely to be infeasible and futile, if carried out, in solving the problem of poverty and inequality.

You may call my position a "technocratic approach" as opposed to a "reformist approach" which considers major asset redistribution (such as redistributive land reform) a precondition to solving the problem of rural poverty and inequality. After my observations on economic and social environments, including local power structure and government administrative capacity, in Southeast Asia, I was convinced that the technocratic approach is the only practical approach for this region if major bloodshed, like that experienced in Kampuchea, is to be avoided.

I believe that my basic perspective will apply to India, too, in the long run. However, as I observed agrarian conditions in India, I became skeptical about whether the technocratic approach is the right way to cope with the agrarian problem in India for the medium run. My skepticism arose from observations on the major difference in social class structure between India and countries in Southeast Asia. Before I elaborate on this point, I would like to summarize the characteristics of agrarian structure in India today, as I observed them.

Emerging Pattern of Agrarian Structure

Although land reform in India since Independence has been subject to criticism for loopholes and ineffective implementation, it has achieved major changes in agrarian structure. Feudalistic non-cultivating landlords, typically *zamindars,* have lost their dominant position on the

[3] Drastic redistribution of land assets, of course, solves the problem of inequality. However, aside from its political difficulty, asset redistribution by itself cannot solve the problem of growing poverty under the growing population pressure on land.

rural scene, although many of them still maintain sizable holdings. The relations between these feudalistic landlords and poor tenants no longer represent the major source of inequality in rural India except for some pockets in the eastern states.

Instead, the growing gap between the middle to upper peasantry and landless laborers has become the core of the poverty and inequality problem. Everywhere I saw signs that the economic and social position of the middle to upper peasantry has been rising. Some of them are ex-tenants under the *zamindari* system. They are eager to improve their farming by introducing new technology and applying modern inputs. They are the major beneficiaries of government programs of irrigation and institutional credit. They try to climb the social ladder by adding more land to their operational holdings within landholding limits imposed by the land reform laws; often the additional land is purchased from non-resident ex-landlords who find farm management troublesome under strict regulations on tenancy contracts, or is leased from marginal farmers who find their holdings too small to utilize capital (such as a bullock team) efficiently.[4]

Some successful peasants become capitalist farmers, but the expansion of their scale of operation seems to be limited partly because of the landholding ceilings and partly because of fragmentation of holdings through inheritance among heirs. Although I saw a number of prosperous capitalistic farms operated by ex-*zamindars* and "gentlemen farmers" with urban occupations, I had the impression that the class which is concentrating both economic and political power in rural India is the middle to upper peasantry.

In contrast, the economic lot of landless laborers and marginal farmers seems to be declining. Except for Haryana and Punjab where technological progress has been especially rapid (and Kerala, which I will discuss later), real wage rates do not seem to be rising. In a number of well-irrigated areas that I have seen, where farmers' incomes have risen several fold, wage earnings of laborers have improved only marginally.[5] In the areas without irrigation, their earnings have been declining, on a per-capita basis at least.

Such observation is consistent with macro statistics. During the past two decades agricultural output and income in India increased at the rate of about 2.5% per year. Since the share of hired laborers' wage earnings in total agricultural income remained virtually constant, the

[4] Cases were frequently found in Haryana where larger holders leased land from smallholders, whereas the reverse seemed more common in East U.P.

[5] In most areas real wage rates seem to have remained largely constant at a level equivalent to 2 to 3 kg of food grains, even though wage earnings increased due to increased employment opportunities.

rates of growth in both cultivators' and agricultural laborers' incomes should have increased at about the same rate as the total output growth rate.[6] Meanwhile, the number of agricultural laborers increased at a rate as fast as 4% per year, in contrast to a slow growth in the number of cultivators at a rate on the order of 1%.[7] Those statistics imply that the per-capita income of cultivators increased at a rate of about 1.5%, whereas that of agricultural laborers decreased by about 1.5% per year; the income position of the landless class declined both relatively and absolutely.

Castes and Labor Relations

The growing income gap between middle to upper peasants and landless agricultural laborers is not unique to India; it is common in Southeast Asia, too. The basic cause of the increasing inequality is nothing but the increase in the return to land relative to the return to labor; the major benefit of the increased land rent has been captured mainly by the middle to upper peasantry since the abolition of feudalistic landlordism —zamindari in India and hacienda in the Philippines.

Since it is extremely difficult, both politically and administratively, to redistribute land from self-cultivating peasants to landless laborers, the technocratic approach to maximizing labor demand by improving irrigation and developing land-saving and labor-using technologies seems to be most appropriate for the solution of the poverty and inequality problem. If such efforts are successful in increasing labor demand faster than labor supply, real wage rates will rise and laborers' lots will improve.

An important condition for the technocratic approach to reducing

[6] According to the estimates of the Central Statistical Organization (*National Accounts Statistics*, 1980), the share of employees' compensation in total agricultural income stayed virtually constant at 20%.

[7] From the 1961 to 1971 census period, the agricultural labor force, including cultivators and agricultural laborers, increased at a rate of 2.3% per year; the number of laborers increased much faster at a rate of 6%, compared with the number of cultivators which grew only 1% per annum. Consequently the share of agricultural laborers in the total agricultural labor force increased from 24 to 31%. These data must be taken with reservations because of differences in definitions between the two censuses. Probably more reliable would be the data from the Labour Bureau's *Rural Labour Inquiry*, which indicate that the annual growth rate in the number of agricultural laborers from 1964–65 to 1974–75 was about 4%. It is most likely that the number of agricultural laborers increased much faster than that of cultivators, and the share of landless laborers in the total agricultural labor population has continued to increase during the past two decades. However, the growth rates of 1 and 4% are conjectural figures adopted here mainly for the purpose of illustrating the nature and magnitude of the growing income gap between cultivators and agricultural laborers.

inequality is that a large portion of increased agricultural income due to better irrigation and technology be transferred to laborers through increased employment opportunities. Such a situation seems to exist in many parts of Southeast Asia in the form of patron-client relationships in village communities. The traditional moral principle of mutual help and income sharing in Southeast Asian villages and its erosion due to modernization forces are often exaggerated, but there is no denying that the principle does exist and is surviving, as is discussed in detail in this book. To violate the principle involves cost in the form of social opprobrium. Therefore, better-off members of a community tend to patronize poorer members by giving them working opportunities for their subsistence. It is a common observation in the Philippines and Indonesia that even small peasants employ a large amount of hired labor and that they further increase their use of hired labor by reducing family labor in response to increases in their income (see Parts II and III). After all, village communities in Southeast Asia are relatively homogeneous socially, if not economically. Many landless laborers are relatives, even sons, of peasant cultivators. Since employers and employees are tied in an enduring and multi-stranded patron-client bond of mutual trust, the transaction cost of labor employment—the cost of negotiating and enforcing labor contracts—is relatively modest (see Chapter 2).

The situation in India seems sharply different from that in Southeast Asia in this respect. Typically, cultivators and agricultural laborers belong to different castes. Division of labor is strictly established. Those who belong to the cultivating castes do not usually engage in hired wage work. In an East U.P. village I met a young man. He and his brother, both married, form a joint family with nine members, who subsist on two acres of unirrigated land (of which one acre is rented under a sharecropping arrangement). Clearly, their family labor capacity exceeds the demand for cultivating their small holding. Yet this man said that he and his family do not seek hired wage employment within the village or nearby towns, because to do so would be humiliating to his caste status. Such an attitude is rarely found among small and marginal farmers in Southeast Asia. Unlike Southeast Asian villages, where cultivators and agricultural laborers are in a continuous spectrum in the same peasant community, they form different communities in India even if they live in the same village.

To my great surprise, the patron-client relationship that characterizes labor employment relations in rural areas of Southeast Asia was rarely found in the Indian villages that I visited. Cultivators employ laborers who belong to the scheduled castes more or less casually, task by task. Typically, the labor contract involves a single transaction for one task in one spot of time. I did not observe a relationship in which a certain laborer worked for a certain cultivator on a number of tasks, often including domestic work, over time under an implicit contract or a tacit mutual understanding. Of course, there are permanent laborers who are employed on a seasonal or an annual basis. But their employment arrangement is like an urban employment contract, with their obligations and compensation clearly specified for a certain period, rather than a patron-client relationship involving a complex of unspecified transactions for which the balance will be cleared over an indefinite period of time.[8] While the patron-client relationship is much weaker in India than in Southeast Asia, mutual-help relations, such as labor and bullock exchanges among cultivators, seem more common in India.[9]

In short, it is my impression that the relation between farmer employers and agricultural laborers now prevailing in India is more like an urban market type than a patron-client type; this somewhat impersonal, market-like relationship in Indian villages is ingrained by caste prejudice, making class conflict so much the more sharp and explosive.[10]

As might be expected, class conflict between employers and employees appeared to me much more tense and sharply felt than in South-

[8] According to a large-scale sample survey in West Bengal conducted by Pranab Bardhan and Ashok Rudra (1980), the proportion of purely casual laborers in the total number of labor families was as much as 84%, while those of attached (permanent) and semi-attached laborers were 11 and 5%, respectively. The employment relation apparently similar to that common in Southeast Asia is the one called "Semi-attached, Type III: laborers are obliged to work for the employer for an unrestricted number of days over an indefinite period" by Bardhan and Rudra. Less than 2% of laborers in their sample belonged to this category. I am not certain, however, that the "Semi-attached, Type III" that Bardhan and Rudra observed in West Bengal is, in substance, the same as the patron-client relationship in Southeast Asia that is ingrained by the traditional moral principle of mutual help and income-sharing within a peasant community—to my eye, villages in India are not peasant communities but "plural" societies consisting of cultivators and laborers, both considering themselves to belong to different communities.

[9] The patron-client relationship might also be common within the same social group. A relation somewhat similar to the patron-client relationship in Southeast Asia was observed in Kerala between a farmer owning 10 acres of rubber plantation and a rubber tapper, both Muslims. This young laborer helps the plantation owner with a number of small chores without specifically receiving wages (perhaps receiving meals and occasional gifts), despite the fact that he belongs to a labor union. Both the employer and the employee deny that there is any agreement for the latter to help the former with those chores. A multi-stranded, continuous relationship without any *explicit* agreement or contract is the very nature of the patron-client relationship.

[10] This caste-based class conflict may have the effect of weakening the conflict between the rich and the poor. Although many small and marginal cultivators are no richer—in fact, some of them are poorer—than *harijan* laborers, it is unlikely that they will unite to fight against the middle to upper peasantry. Instead, it appears that the poor cultivators act as a spearhead against the *harijan* laborers in the caste war, like the poor whites in the U.S. South acted against the blacks.

east Asia.[11] People in scheduled castes told me openly how miserable their lives were relative to their farmer employers and clamored for social justice such as land redistribution. On the other hand, cultivators complained about how unreliable laborers were and how high their wages were relative to their contributions.

I suspect that such attitudes are recent phenomena. In the old days, people in the lower castes would have accepted their fate as the result of misconduct in their earlier life according to the Hindu belief in incarnation. Not to render faithful service to the upper castes would have been considered a sin. Upper caste people would have not hesitated to impose physical penalties on lower caste laborers if they shirked or resisted. At the same time, they would have acted as benevolent patrons so far as the low caste people remained obedient and docile animals. In such a social environment, the caste system would have worked as an efficient mechanism to supply reliable labor or to reduce labor transaction costs. Since Independence, the social environment has changed rapidly. Government support and the spread of education have developed the modern concept of human rights in the mind of scheduled caste people. They no longer accept their status as an inexorable fate. They have learned to assert themselves against the upper castes. The caste system, which was once a mechanism for reducing labor transaction costs, now works to increase labor conflicts and, hence, labor transaction costs.[12]

In any event, it appears to me that the labor transaction costs relative to the wages explicitly paid to laborers are substantially higher in rural India than in Southeast Asia. The result is a strong drive among the middle to upper peasantry for mechanization. This tendency was most clearly visible in East U.P. where the class conflict appears most tense, despite the fact that the wage rate is lowest among the areas that I visited; there I saw a number of farmers holding a little over 10 irrigated acres who own riding tractors, despite male wage rates of only about Rs. 5 to 6 per day, barely half of the Punjab-Haryana level. I also observed a drive among large holders to shift from labor-intensive crop

[11] This does not imply that rural Southeast Asia is free from class conflicts. On the contrary, serious conflicts exist, as evidenced by the bloody suppression of communists in Indonesia in 1965 and the earlier Huk movement or the present New People's Army in the Philippines. However, the nature and the form of class conflicts in Southeast Asia seem to me critically different from those in India, because there is no sharp class differentiation between peasant cultivators and agricultural laborers as in India.

[12] Labor transaction costs include not only the direct costs of labor management but also the expected costs of possible damages and income foregone due to labor disputes.

rotation systems to simpler systems that require less labor management effort, such as sugarcane and orchards.[13]

If my limited observation in any way represents the Indian situation, the technocratic approach would likely be much less effective here in solving the problem of poverty and inequality than in Southeast Asia. In Southeast Asia, a large portion of increased agricultural income due to irrigation and new technology is expected to spill over to landless laborers through increased labor employment under conditions of relative ease of labor management for the middle to upper peasantry within the patron-client relationship. In India, with high labor transaction costs due to the sharp class conflicts among cultivators and agricultural laborers under the caste system, increased labor demand from irrigation and new technology might induce mechanization without creating employment opportunities. If that is the case, the technocratic approach may not contribute much to the solution of poverty and inequality or may even aggravate the problem, at least for the medium run.

The Kerala Experiment: A Reformist Approach

If the technocratic approach is not effective in solving the problem of poverty and inequality, is there a chance for the reformist approach to succeed? The experience of Kerala seems to give a clue to the answer.

It is well known that Kerala State under a communist regime has experimented with a reformist approach, redistributing assets and income by land reform and unionization of agricultural laborers on a scale and with a thoroughness uncomparable with other states in India. I have no preparation to discuss the social and political conditions that enabled Kerala to take such a strong reformist approach; similar conditions do not seem to exist in other states. Here I try to make inferences on the possible consequences of the reformist approach, based mainly on my casual observations of the rural labor market in Kerala.

It is clear that the agricultural wage rate in Kerala is very high and has increased in real terms for the past decade or two, in magnitudes comparable to Punjab and Haryana, despite the fact that labor demand for agriculture has not increased as much as in Punjab and Haryana. The high wage rate in Kerala is associated with a high unemployment rate.[14]

One may be tempted to interpret those phenomena as the effects of

[13] In addition to the difficulty of labor management, the landholding ceiling seems to underlie the shifts from annual crops to perennial plants.

[14] According to National Sample Survey data, the rural unemployment rate in Kerala is distinctively higher than in other states; in 1972–73 it was as high as 24%; the next highest unemployment rate was 12% in Tamil Nadu, and those of Haryana and Punjab were only 3 and 4%, respectively.

unionization in creating an excess supply of labor at an institutionally fixed wage rate above market equilibrium. The unionization has had appreciable effects, as is evident from the much higher wage rate for fully unionized rubber tapping than for non-unionized casual labor— about Rs. 12 to 15 for a half day's work for the former as opposed to Rs. 10 to 12 for a full day's work for the latter. However, as I saw it, the high agricultural wage rate is, to a large extent, supported by the contraction of labor supply to agriculture, despite the fact that potential laborers still stand idle in rural areas, looking for nonagricultural employment.

This curious phenomenon may be partly explained by a high level of education in Kerala that has made rural youths dislike drudgery in agriculture; this effect seems to have been reinforced by a high expected income from nonagricultural occupations for which wage rates are kept high with unionization, even if the probability of actually obtaining a job of that kind is low.

In fact, nonagricultural employment has been expanding in such sectors as construction and services, partly because of large-scale public works and also, more importantly, because of the income multiplier effect of remittances both from abroad and from the rest of India outside the State. In a number of villages I visited, a significant number of people had gone out for work to the Middle East, Singapore and Malaysia. A significant portion of their remittances has been spent for housing construction, spilling over to other economic activities, especially service activities.

With the multiplier effect of foreign remittance, the Kerala economy has been booming for the past several years. Laborers seem to have enjoyed a larger share of the increased economic pie, supported by the reformist policy. However, it is not at all certain how much of the increase in laborers' income is due to the reformist policy and how much is due to other factors. Nor is it certain whether the improved economic status of the labor class can be maintained without transfer income from outside the State.

The disquieting aspect is that there is no sign of increases in productive investments to guarantee the self-sustaining growth of employment and income. Instead, flights of industrial capital from Kerala to other states appear rather pervasive. Farmers are shifting from labor-intensive crops like rice to labor-extensive crops like coconuts.[15] It is not

---

[15] Such a movement is reflected in changes in the price of hillside garden-crop land relative to the price of lowland paddyfield. From what I gathered, the price of garden-crop land was lower than that of lowland paddyfield until about 10 years ago but is now substantially higher. One factor underlying the relative increase in

difficult to imagine that, once the inflow of foreign remittance is stopped, the economic pie will begin to shrink and class conflicts over the share of a reduced pie will intensify. Already the ultrarightist R.S.S. (*Rashtriya Swayam Sevak Sangh:* National Self-Help Organization) has been gaining power, supported by small manufacturers and traders. It might not be just a nightmare that a major disruption will result from sharpened class conflicts when the total economic pie stops growing.

The reformist policy in Kerala has contributed much to the welfare of poor people. The dire poverty manifested by beggers and child laborers which is commonly observed in India is rarely seen, which in itself is a great achievement. However, I wonder if the hasty replication of the Kerala experiment on an all-India scale, without due preparation of the productivity basis, might not result in disaster.

Problems Ahead

In summary, I am optimistic about the growth potential of agricultural production in India. By simply reinforcing the present efforts of investing in irrigation, agricultural research and modern inputs, a major acceleration of agricultural output growth rate seems possible. If government policies are reoriented to reduce excess intervention in the market mechanism and to assist collective action by rural people to promote their own initiatives, agricultural growth performance will further improve significantly.

A more serious problem seems to be that of poverty and inequality. The technocratic approach to increasing labor employment and wage earnings, by intensifying agricultural production based on the development of irrigation systems and of land-saving and labor-using technologies, might not be as effective in India as in Southeast Asia, because of sharp class conflicts between cultivators and agricultural laborers. It is possible that the technocratic approach may induce mechanization under conditions of high labor transaction costs, thereby aggravating the situation.

The reformist approach geared to redistribution of income and assets does seem to have little scope for success, given the social and political conditions of India. Considering the fact that it is not absentee landlords but cultivating peasants who are now dominant in rural India, the redistribution of land to landless laborers on a significant scale

---

garden-crop land prices, besides high wage rates and difficulty of labor management, was the increased demand for residential use corresponding to the housing construction boom based on overseas remittance.

appears almost impossible, except in a few Eastern states.[16] The Kerala experiment in strengthening the bargaining position of laborers, though yet to be analyzed in greater detail, does appear to involve a self-defeating element in the absence of a sufficient productivity basis.

Naturally, the sensible solution is to combine the two approaches. However, it is an extremely difficult task to find the right combination in actual policy design. The two approaches are complementary in some aspects and contradictory in others; the consequences of their complex interactions are hard to calculate *ex ante*. Moreover, the right policy combination must take into consideration the political and administrative constraints that often twist original policy intentions. For example, it is not uncommon to observe that some reformist policies, such as prohibition of tenancy and control of land rent, result in tenant eviction and shifts from labor-intensive crops to labor-extensive crops such as orchards or even to forestry.

To prevent widening inequality and class conflicts, while creating a productivity base for sufficient increases in agricultural income and employment, will require extreme skill in political and administrative maneuvering as well as in policy formulation, which is simply beyond my imagination. I hope Indian wisdom will make this almost impossible task possible so that caste war and bloodshed will not become a regular feature of rural India in the future.

. . . .

During my travels through India, I had an opportunity to visit the Gandhi Ashram in Ahmedabad, where the great Mahatma began his career as a liberator. This visit was not planned originally. The change was created unexpectedly when my field trip to Gujarati villages was suddenly cancelled because of a serious riot triggered by the issue of special seat reservations for scheduled caste students in medical colleges. In the peaceful ashram along the Sabarmati River it was difficult to believe that a caste war was raging in the same city. My mind was absorbed by a phrase on the wall:

[16] Substantial scope for improving the distribution of landholdings seems to exist in the Eastern States through strengthening the implementation of existing land reform laws alone. However, land reform programs must be reoriented with a sharp focus based on rational calculations. The ceilings on landholding (not only ownership but also operational holding) must be strictly enforced by closing loopholes such as registering titles under the names of family members separately and exemption of land under perennial planting. On the other hand, regulations on tenancy forms and land rent must be removed. The regulations on tenancy contracts not only reduce efficiency in resource allocation but also are detrimental to welfare of the poor by closing off the chances of agricultural laborers and small farmers to lease land and by encouraging the adoption of labor-saving technologies by large holders.

If blood be shed, let it be our own.
Let us cultivate calm courage to die without killing.

Does this phrase sound so beautiful because Mahatma asked an impossible thing? Or is it because he believed that the impossible is possible?

Appendix A: Mathematical Analysis of Changes in Factor Shares

The Case of Constant Technology

Let us assume a linear homogeneous production function relating value added (Y) to two production factors, land (A) and labor (L):

$$Y = F(A, L). \tag{1}$$

Assume that the function is concave and twice differentiable with the conditions that $F_A, F_L > 0$ and that the factor markets are perfectly competitive so that $r = F_A$ and $w = F_L$. F_A and F_L are the first partial derivatives of the production function, and r and w are the rates of land rent and wages, respectively. The rent and the wage rates are measured by the units of output.

The problem here is to analyze changes in the income share of labor in response to changes in the factor endowments under constant technology.

In equilibrium, the relative income share of labor ($\theta = wL/Y$) is

$$\theta = \frac{F_L L}{Y}. \tag{2}$$

From equation (2),

$$G(\theta) = G(F_L) + G(L) - G(Y) \tag{3}$$

where $G(X) = (dX/dt)/X$ for any variable X.

Because the production function is assumed homogeneous of degree one, the following relations hold:

$$F_A A + F_L L = Y$$
$$F_{AA} A + F_{AL} L = 0 \qquad (4)$$
$$F_{LA} A + F_{LL} L = 0$$

where $F_A A$, $F_A L$ and $F_L L$ are the second partial derivatives of the production function. The elasticity of substitution (σ) can be expressed as

$$\sigma = \frac{1}{Y} \frac{F_A F_L}{F_{AL}}. \qquad (5)$$

Using equations (4) and (5) and noting $(F_A A / Y) = (1 - \theta)$:

$$G(F_L) = \frac{F_{AL} dA + F_{LL} dL}{F_L}$$

$$= \frac{1 - \theta}{\sigma} [G(A) - G(L)]. \qquad (6)$$

Similarly,

$$G(Y) = (1 - \theta) G(A) + \theta G(L). \qquad (7)$$

Substituting equations (6) and (7) for equation (3), we obtain

$$G(\theta) = (1 - \theta) \frac{\sigma - 1}{\sigma} [G(L) - G(A)]. \qquad (8)$$

If $G(L) - G(A) > 0$,

$$G(\theta) \gtreqless 0 \text{ according to } \sigma \gtreqless 1.$$

Therefore, under constant technology, if the supply of labor increases faster than that of land resulting in an increase in the man/land ratio (L/A), the relative income share of labor declines, provided that the elasticity of substitution is less than unity.

The rate of change in the absolute income of labor (wL) is expressed as

$$G(wL) = G(F_L L) = G(F_L) + G(L). \qquad (9)$$

Substitution of equation (6) into equation (9) results in

$$G(wL) = \frac{\sigma - (1 - \theta)}{\sigma} G(L) + \frac{1 - \theta}{\sigma} G(A). \qquad (10)$$

Assuming the land area is fixed, *i.e.*, $G(A) = 0$, for the sake of simplicity, equation (10) reduces to

$$G(wL) = \frac{\sigma - (1 - \theta)}{\sigma} G(L) \qquad (11)$$

which implies that labor's income declines absolutely in the economy in which the growing labor force presses hard on a fixed land area to such an extent that the elasticity of substitution (σ) becomes smaller than the relative income share of land ($1 - \theta$).

The Case of Technological Progress

We now try to analyze the case in which technological changes occur together with changes in factor endowments. Assuming the technological progress of a factor-augmenting type, the production function can be expressed as

$$Y = F[\alpha(t)A, \beta(t)L] \qquad (12)$$

where $\alpha(t)$ and $\beta(t)$ are land- and labor- augmenting factors, respectively, which are assumed as the functions of time.

Applying to equation (12) the same operations as for equation (4) through (8), we obtain

$$G(\theta) = (1 - \theta)\left(\frac{\sigma - 1}{\sigma}\right)\{[G(L) - G(A)] - [G(\alpha) - G(\beta)]\} \qquad (13)$$

where t is omitted for the sake of simplicity (Ferguson 1969, pp. 241–244). Equation (13) reduces to equation (8) if technological progress is Hicks' neutral, *i.e.*, $G(\alpha) = G(\beta)$.

If $G(L) - G(A) > G(\alpha) - G(\beta)$, $G(\theta) \gtreqless 0$ according to $\sigma \gtreqless 1$, and if $G(L) - G(A) < G(\alpha) - G(\beta)$, $G(\theta) \gtreqless 0$ according to $\sigma \lesseqgtr 1$.

If the pace of land augmentation is sufficiently rapid so that $G(L) - G(A) < G(\alpha) - G(\beta)$, the relative income share of labor increases with technological progress under the condition of $\sigma < 1$.

The rate of change in the absolute income of labor can be expressed as

$$G(wL) = \frac{\sigma - (1 - \theta)}{\sigma} [G(\beta) + G(L)] + \frac{1 - \theta}{\sigma} [G(\alpha) + G(A)] \quad (14)$$

Assuming that the land area is fixed, *i.e.*, $G(A) = 0$ and that technological progress is purely land-augmenting, *i.e.*, $G(\alpha) > 0$ and $G(\beta) = 0$, equation (14) reduces to

$$G(wL) = \frac{\sigma - (1 - \theta)}{\sigma} G(L) + \frac{1 - \theta}{\sigma} G(\alpha). \quad (15)$$

By comparing equation (15) with equation (11), it is clear that, *ceteris paribus*, a rise in the absolute income of labor is larger for a faster rate of land-augmenting technological progress. Even if the elasticity of substitution (σ) is smaller than the share of land $(1 - \theta)$, the absolute income of labor can rise if $G(\alpha)$ is sufficiently large so that the second term in equation (15) is larger than the first term. On the other hand, if the rate of labor augmentation, $G(\beta)$, is high due to the development of labor-displacing technologies such as tractors and herbicides, the chance is large that labor's absolute income declines where $\sigma < (1 - \theta)$.

Appendix B

Distribution of different rice harvesting systems by municipality in the central plain of Luzon, Philippines, based on a survey in February and July 1978

Province and municipality	Sample size	Number of adopters[a]							
		1968				1978			
		T	M	H	G	T	M	H	G
Nueva Ecija									
Lupao	3	3				3			
San Jose City	6	6				3		2	1
Nampicuan	1	1					1		
Muñoz	6	6				1		5	
Bongabon	1	1						1	
Palayan City	1	1						1	
Talavera	5	5						5	
Cabanatuan City	6	5		1				5	1
San Leonardo	5	5						3	2
Gapan	5	3		1			1	3	1
Total	39	36		2		7	2	25	5
Bulacan									
San Miguel	5	5						3	2
San Ildefonso	1	1						1	
San Rafael	1			1				1	
Pulilan	1	1						1	
Plaridel	1			1				1	
Guiguinto	2			1				2	
Total	11	7		3				9	2
Pampanga									
Sta. Ana	1	1							1
San Simon	1			1				1	
Minalin	1			1				1	
Apalit	4			4				3	1
Total	7	1		6				5	2

Province and municipality	Sample size	Number of adopters[a]							
		1968				1978			
		T	M	H	G	T	M	H	G
Pangasinan									
Sison	1			1				1	
Pozorrubio	2			1	1				2
Calasiao	1			1				1	
San Jacinto	1			1				1	
Sta. Maria	1	1				1			
Tayug	3	2				3			
Villasis	1	1					1		
Umingan	3	3				2		1	
Total	13	7		4	1	6	1	4	2
Tarlac									
San Manuel	2	2				2			
Moncada	4	2				3		1	
Mayantoc	6	6				6			
Tarlac	3	3				1	1	1	
La Paz	1	1					1		
Capaz	2	2					1	1	
Conception	1	1					1		
Total	19	17				12	3	4	
Laguna									
San Pedro	1				1				1
Biñan	3		3				3		
Cabuyao	1		1						1
Calamba	2		2						2
Los Baños	1		1						1
Bay	1			1					1
Calauan	1		1						1
Pila	1			1					1
Total	11		8	3					11

[a]/T = *tilyadora*, M = mixture, H = *hunusan*, G = *gama*.

Distribution of different rice harvesting systems by village in Java, Indonesia, based on a survey in August and December 1978.

Sample no.[a]	Location			Harvesting system		Variety[d]	Tool[e]
	Kabupaten	Kecamatan	Desa	Bawon type[b]	Tebasan[c]		
West Java							
A-1	Garut	Limbangan	Ciwangi	LI		M(67)	S(67)
A-2	Sumedang	Situraja	Sukaambit	LS		M(76)	S(76)
D-1	Cianjur	Warungkondang	Gekbrong	OV	T	L	A
D-2	Cianjur	Bojong Picung	Jati	OM		M(77)	AS(77)
D-3	Subang	Subang	Cidahu	LS&OM[f]		M(76)	AS(76)
D-4	Subang	Binong	Mariuk	PO		M(76)	AS(77)
D-5	Subang	Ciasam	Simpang Bedeng	PO		M(76)	S(76)
D-6	Indramayu	Losarang	Krimun	OV		M(75)	AS(76)
D-7	Indramayu	Kertasemaya	Tenajar	LS&PO		M(76)	AS(76)
D-8	Cirebon	Gegesik	Gegesik Kidul	LS&PO		M(76)	AS(76)
D-9	Cirebon	Babakan	Gebanghilir	LS		M(71)	A
D-12	Cirebon	Waled	Cikalak	LS		M(71)	AS(76)
D-13	Majalenka	Sumber Jaya	Cisambeng	LS		M(72)	AS(75)
D-14	Sumedang	Tomo	Tolengas	LS&OV		M(70)	AS(76)
D-15	Sumedang	Congeang	Paseh	LI		M(72)	A
D-16	Sumedang	Cimalaka	Mamdaherang	OM		L	A
D-17	Sumedang	Cikeruh	Cipacing	OM		M(76)	AS(76)

Distribution of different rice harvesting systems by village in Java, Indonesia, based on a survey in August and December 1978.

Sample no.[a]	Location			Harvesting system		Variety[d]	Tool[e]
	Kabupaten	Kecamatan	Desa	Bawon type[b]	Tebasan[c]		
D–18	Subang	Segalaherang	Tambakan	OV		L	A
D–19	Bandung	Cipatat	Mandalawangi	OM		M(73)	AS(73)
D–20	Cianjur	Cugemang	Cicedil	OM	T	L	A
D–21	Bekasi	Cibitung	Talaga Murni	LS&PO		M(71)	AS(71)
D–22	Bekasi	Cikarang	Gedung Waringin	PO		M(70)	AS(75)
D–23	Subang	Pabuaram	Ciberes	LS&PO[f]		M(69)	AS(75)
D–24	Purwakarta	Campaka	Cibatu	LS&OM[f]		M(75)	AS(75)
D–25	Krawang	Klari	Pancawati	LS&PO[f]		M(69)	AS(76)
D–26	Krawang	Klari	Angganita	PO		M(70)	AS(76)
D–27	Bogor	Cibunbulang	Cemplang	LS		M(71)	A
Central Java							
A–3	Pemalang	Pemalang	Beji	OM	T	M(73)	AS(75)
A–4	Pekalongan	Batang	Kedung Miring	OM	T	M(73)	AS(73)
A–5	Kendal	Brangsong	Brangsong	OM[g]	T	M(74)	S(74)
A–6	Semarang	Jambu	Gondrio	OV	T	M(76)	A
A–7	Magelang	Cetang	Sempuh	OM	T	M(77)	A
A–8	Sleman	Ngaglik	Sardono Harjo	LI	T	M(72)	A
A–9	Yogyakarta	Prambanan	Candisari	LI	T	M(74)	A
A–10	Karanganyar	Tawangmanyar	Ngalapabak	OV		L	A
A–11	Karanganyar	Matesih	Kuncung	OV		M(76)	AS(77)

A–12	Karanganyar	Tasikmadu	Papahan	LI		M(76)	AS(77)
A–13	Klaten	Ketandan	Karang Nlese	OM	T	M(68)	AS(75)
A–14	Bantul	Pinunggang	Serimulyo	OM	T	M(73)	A(78)[f]
A–15	Sleman	Kalasan	Kemiten	OM	T	M(68)	AS(76)[j]
A–16	Klaten	Kebon Arum	Jetis	OM	T	M(70)	A(75)[k]
A–18	Sragen	Sambungmacan	Sambungmacan	OM		M(71)	A(77)[l]
A–19	Sragen	Sidoarjo	Jetakpabrik	OM		M(74)	AS(76)
A–20	Boyolali	Banyudono	Banyudono	OM		M(68)	S(76)
A–21	Semarang	Banyubiru	Sentul-Rowodoni	LI	T	M(73)	A
D–10	Berebes	Bulakamba	Bulakamba	PO	T	M(73)	AS(77)
D–11	Tegal	Surodadi	Sidouarjo	PO	T	M(75)	AS(77)
East Java							
A–17	Ngawi	Kadungalar	Gemarang	LI[h]		M(69)	S(76)

[a] A — August survey observations, D — December survey observations.

[b] PO — Purely open, OV — Open to villagers only, OM — Open with maximum limits, LI — Limited to invitees, LS — Limited to those performing extra services.

[c] T — *Tebasan* existed.

[d] M — Modern variety, L — Local variety; inside parentheses are the years of M-adoption.

[e] A — *Ani-ani*, S — sickle, AS — both *ani-ani* and sickle; inside parentheses are the years of S-adoption.

[f] LS became more dominant in the past 10 years.

[g] PO in 1968.

[h] OM in 1968.

[i] AS in *tebasan*.

[j] S in *tebasan*

[k] AS in *tebasan*

[l] AS in *tebasan*

Appendix D

Standard rates of wages, rentals, interests, and rice prices used for imputation.

Laguna, Philippines		East Laguna Village 1976 wet	South Laguna Village 1977 dry
Wages:			
Land preparation	₱/day	13.00	12.00
Transplanting	₱/day	8.40	9.00
Fertilizer & chemical application	₱/day	10.00	9.00
Weeding	₱/day	8.00	8.00
Harvesting and threshing	₱/day	11.00	12.00
Hauling of paddy	₱/day	5.00	5.00
Water control	₱/day	5.00	8.00
Clearing dike	₱/day	10.50	9.00
Repairing dike	₱/day	11.50	9.00
Seedbed preparation	₱/day	5.00	8.00
Rentals:			
Hand tractor	₱/day	65.00	70.00
Carabao	₱/day	15.00	15.00
Threshing machine	% of output	4.0	4.0
Blower	% of output	2.0	n.a.
Interest rate	%/season	40	40
Rice price	₱/kg	1.02	1.09

Subang, Indonesia		South Subang Village		North Subang Village		
		1968–71	1978 dry	1968–71	1978/79 wet	1979 dry
Wages:						
Land preparation	Rp./hour	23	69	19	94	100
Transplanting	Rp./hour	20	60	17	75	88
Fertilizer & chemical application	Rp./hour	23	69	19	94	100
Weeding	Rp./hour	20	60	17	75	88
Harvesting & threshing	Rp./hour	—	60	—	100	94
Hauling of paddy	Rp./hour	23	60	19	75	75
Water control	Rp./hour	23	60	19	75	75
Clearing & repairing dike	Rp./hour	23	69	19	94	100
Seedbed preparation	Rp./hour	23	69	19	94	100
Pulling seedlings	Rp./hour	23	69	19	94	100
Rentals:						
Carabao/cattle	Rp./day	120	620	170	950	n.a.
Sprayer	Rp./hour	n.a.	n.a.	n.a.	50	50
Interest rate	%/season	n.a.	40	n.a.	50	50
Rice price	Rp./kg	19.4	65.0	19.3	66.0	69.0

References

Adams, Dale W. (1977). "Policy Issues in Rural Finance and Development," Paper presented at the conference on *Rural Finance Research* sponsored by the Agricultural Development Council and the American Agricultural Economics Association, held at San Diego, July 28–August 1, 1977.

―――― and Graham, Douglas H. (1980). "A Critique of Traditional Agricultural Credit Projects and Policies," Economics and Sociology Occasional Paper No. 621 (Columbus, Ohio: Ohio State University Department of Agricultural Economics and Rural Sociology).

Africa, Angel A. (1920). "A Preliminary Survey of the Comparative Costs of Different Methods of Harvesting Rice," *Philippine Agriculturist*, Vol. 8 (March–April), pp. 277–292.

Ahmed, Ifmkhar (1976). "Employment Effects of the Green Revolution," *Bangladesh Development Studies,* Vol. 4 (January), pp. 115–128.

Akerlof, George A. (1970). "The Market for 'Lemons': Quality Uncertainty and the Market Mechanism," *Quarterly Journal of Economics*, Vol. 84 (August), pp. 488–500.

Alchian, Armen A. and Demsetz, Harold (1972). "Production, Information Costs and Economic Organization," *American Economic Review*, Vol. 62 (December), pp. 777–795.

―――― (1973). "The Property Right Paradigm," *Journal of Economic History*, Vol. 16 (March), pp. 16–27.

Anderson, James N. (1964). "Land and Society in a Pangasinan Society," in *Social Foundations of Community Development*, eds. Socorro C. Espiritu and Chester L. Hunt (Manila: R. M. Garcia Publishing Co.), pp. 171–193.

―――― (1969). "Buy-and-Sell and Economic Personalism: Foundations for Philippine Entrepreneurship," *Asian Survey*, Vol. 9 (September), pp. 641–668.

Anderson, Terry L. and Hill, P. J. (1975). "The Evolution of Property Rights: A Study of the American West," *Journal of Law and Economics,* Vol. 18 (April), pp. 163–179.

Asian Development Bank (1978). *Rural Asia: Challenge and Opportunity* (New York: Praeger Publishers).

Azam, K. M. (1973). "The Future of the Green Revolution in West Pakistan:

A Choice of Strategy," *International Journal of Agrarian Affairs*, Vol. 5 (March), pp. 404–429.

Bairoch, Paul (1975). *The Economic Development of the Third World since 1900*. English translation by Cynthia Postan (London: Methusen).

Bardhan, Pranab K. (1970). "Green Revolution and Agricultural Laborers," *Economic and Political Weekly*, Vol. 5 (July), pp. 1239–1246.

—— (1977 a). "Variations in Extent and Forms of Agricultural Tenancy: Analysis of Indian Data across Regions and over Time," *Economic and Political Weekly*, Vol. 11 (September), pp. 1505–1511.

—— (1977 b)."Variations in Forms of Tenancy in a Peasant Economy," *Journal of Development Economics*, Vol. 4 (June), pp. 105–118.

—— (1979 a). "Agricultural Development and Land Tenancy in a Peasant Economy: A Theoretical and Emperical Analysis," *American Journal of Agricultural Economics*, Vol. 61 (February), pp. 48–56.

—— (1979 b). "Wages and Unemployment in a Poor Agrarian Economy: A Theoretical and Empirical Analysis," *Journal of Political Economy*, Vol. 87 (June), pp. 479–500.

—— (1980). "Interlocking Factor Markets and Agrarian Development: A Review of Issues," *Oxford Economic Papers*, Vol. 32 (March), pp. 82–98.

—— and Rudra, Ashok (1980). "Types of Labor Attachment in Agriculture: Results of a Survey in West Bengal, 1979," *Economic and Political Weekly*, Vol. 15 (August 30), pp. 1477–1484.

—— and Srinivasan, T. N. (1971). "Cropsharing Tenancy in Agriculture: A Theoretical and Empirical Analysis," *American Economic Review*, Vol. 61 (March), pp. 48–64.

Barker, Randolph (1978). "Barriers to Efficient Capital Investment in Agriculture," in *Distortions of Agricultural Incentives*, ed. Theodore W. Schultz (Bloomington and London: Indiana University Press), pp. 140–160.

—— and Cordova, Violeta G. (1978). "Labor Utilization in Rice Production," in International Rice Research Institute, *Economic Consequences of the New Rice Technology* (Los Baños, Philippines), pp. 113–136.

——; Meyers, W. H.; Crisostomo, Cristina; and Duff, Bart (1972). "Employment and Technological Change in Philippine Agriculture," *International Labor Review*, Vol. 106 (August-September), pp. 111–139.

Bartsch, William G. (1973). *Employment Effects of Alternative Technologies and Techniques in Asian Crop Production: A Survey of Evidence* (Geneva: International Labor Office).

Bautista, Germelino (1977). "Socio-Economic Conditions of the Landless Rice Workers in the Philippines: The Landless of Barrio Sta. Lucia as a Case in Point," in *Hired Labor in Rural Asia*, ed. Shigemochi Hirashima (Tokyo: Institute of Developing Economies).

Bauzon, Leslie E. (1979). "Comparative Rural History: Japan and Southeast Asia." in *A Comparative Study of Paddy-Growing Communities in Southeast Asia and Japan*, eds. Masuo Kuchiba and Leslie E. Bauzon (Tokyo: Toyota Foundation).

Becker, Gary S. (1974). "A Theory of Social Interactions," *Journal of Political Economy*, Vol. 82 (November-December), pp. 1063–1093.

—— (1976). "Altruism, Egoism, and Genetic Fitness: Economics and Sociobiology," *Journal of Economic Literature*, Vol. 14 (September), pp. 817–826.

Bell, Clive (1977). "Alternative Theories of Sharecropping: Some Tests Using Evidence from Northeast India," *Journal of Development Studies*, Vol. 13 (July), pp. 317–346.

——— and Zusman, Pinhas (1976). "A Bargaining Theoretic Approach to Crop-sharing Contracts, "*American Economic Review*, Vol. 66 (September), pp. 578–588.

Ben-Porath, Yoram (1980). "The F- Conception: Families, Friends, and the Organization of Exchange," *Population and Development Review*, Vol. 6 (March), pp. 1–30.

Berry, R. Albert and Cline, William R. (1979). *Agrarian Structure and Productivity in Developing Countries* (Baltimore and London: John Hopkins University Press).

Bhagwati, Jagdish N. and Chakravarty, Sukhamoy (1969). "Contributions to Indian Economic Analysis: A Survey," *American Economic Review*, Vol. 59 (September: Supplement), pp. 2–73.

Binswanger, Hans P. (1978). *The Economics of Tractors in South Asia* (New York: Agricultural Development Council; and Hyderabad, India: International Crops Research Institute for the Semi-Arid Tropics).

Boeke, Julius S. (1953). *Economics and Economic Policy of Dual Societies as Exemplified by Indonesia* (New York: Institute of Pacific Relations).

Brewster, John M. (1950). "The Machine Process in Agriculture and Industry," *Journal of Farm Economics*, Vol. 32 (February), pp. 69–81.

Burke, Robert V. (1979). "Green Revolution Technologies and Farm Class in Mexico," *Economic Development and Cultural Change*, Vol. 28 (October), pp. 135–154.

Chakravarty, Aparajita and Rudra, Ashok (1973). "Economic Effects of Tenancy: Some Negative Results," *Economic and Political Weekly*, Vol. 8 (July No. 28), pp. 1239–1246.

Chambers, J. D. and Mingay, G. E. (1966). *The Agricultural Revolution 1750–1880* (London: Batsford).

Chayanov (Tschajanov), Alexander V. (1966; original publication, 1926). *The Theory of Peasant Economy*, ed. Daniel Thorner, B. Kerblay, R.E.F. Smith (Homewood, Ill.: Richard D. Irwin).

Cheung, Steven N. S. (1968). "Private Property Rights and Share-cropping," *Journal of Political Economy*, Vol. 76 (November/December). pp. 1107–1122.

——— (1969 a). "Transaction Costs, Risk Aversion, and the Choice of Contractual Arrangements," *Journal of Law and Economics*, Vol. 12 (April), pp. 23–41.

——— (1969 b). *The Theory of Share Tenancy* (Chicago and London: University of Chicago Press).

Clay, Edward J. (1976). "Institutional Change and Agricultural Wages in Bangladesh," *Bangladesh Development Studies*, Vol. 4 (October), pp. 423–440.

Cleaver, Harry M. (1972). "The Contributions of the Green Revolution," *American Economic Review*, Vol. 72 (May), pp. 177–188.

Coase, Ronald H. (1937). "The Nature of the Firm," *Economica*, Vol. 4, pp. 386–405.

——— (1960). "The Problem of Social Cost," *Journal of Law and Economics*, Vol. 3 (October), pp. 1–44.

Collier, William L. (1977). *Agricultural Evolution in Java: The Decline of Shared Poverty*, mimeographed.

———; Wiradi, Gunawan; and Soentoro (1973). "Recent Changes in Rice Harvesting Methods," *Bulletin of Indonesian Economic Studies*, Vol. 9 (July), pp. 36–45.

———; Soentoro; Wiradi, Gunawan; and Makali (1974). "Agricultural Technology and Institutional Change in Java," *Food Research Institute Studies*, Vol. 13 (No. 2), pp. 169–194.

Dalisay, Amando M. (1937). "Types of Tenancy Contracts on Rice Farms of Nueva Ecija," *Philippine Agriculturist*, Vol. 26 (July), pp. 159–198.

Dalrymple, Dana G. (1978). *Development and Spread of High-Yielding Varieties of Wheat and Rice in the Less Developed Nations*, Sixth ed., Foreign Agricultural Economic Report No. 95 (Washington D. C.: U. S. Department of Agriculture).

Dasgupta, Biplab (1977). *Agrarian Change and the New Technology in India* (Geneva: United Nations Research Institute for Social Development).

Davis, Lance and North, Douglass (1970). "Institutional Change and American Economic Growth: A First Step towards a Theory of Institutional Innovation," *Journal of Economic History*, Vol. 30 (March), pp. 131–149.

Day, Richard H. (1967). "The Economics of Technological Change and the Demise of the Sharecropper," *American Economic Review*, Vol. 57 (June), pp. 427–449.

de los Reyes, Basilio N. (1972). "Can Land Reform Succeed?" *Philippine Sociological Review*, Vol. 20 (January-April), pp. 79–92.

Demsetz, Harold (1967). "Toward a Theory of Property Rights," *American Economic Review*, Vol. 57 (May), pp. 347–359.

Dewey, Alice G. (1962). *Peasant Marketing in Java* (New York: Free Press).

Duff, J. Bart (1978). "Mechanization and Use of Modern Rice Varieties," in International Rice Research Institute, *Economic Consequences of the New Rice Technology* (Los Baños, Philippines), pp. 145–164.

Dutt, Kalyan (1977). "Changes in Land Relations in West Bengal," *Economic and Political Weekly*, Vol. 12 (December), pp. A106–110.

Eisenstadt, Samuel N. (1968). "Social Institutions," in *International Encyclopedia of the Social Sciences*, ed. David L. Sills, Vol. 14 (London and New York: Macmillan and Free Press), pp. 406–429.

Embree, John F. (1950). "Thailand—A Loosely Structured Social System," *American Anthropologist*, Vol. 52 (April-June), pp. 181–193.

Evers, Hans-Dieter, ed. (1969). *Loosely Structured Social Systems: Thailand in Comparative Perspective*, Yale University Southeast Asia Studies Cultural Report Series No. 17 (New Haven, Conn.).

Falcon, Walter P. (1970). "The Green Revolution: Generations of Problems," *American Journal of Agricultural Economics*, Vol. 52 (December), pp. 698–710.

Fatami Ali, M. S. (1972). "The Green Revolution: An Appraisal," *Monthly Review*, Vol. 2 (June), pp. 112–120.

Feeny, David (1977). "From Property Rights in Man to Property Rights in Land: Institutional Change in Thai Agriculture, 1850–1940," McMaster University Department of Economics Working Paper No. 77–12 (Hamilton, Ontario, Canada).

Ferguson, C. E. (1969). *The Neoclassical Theory of Production and Distribution* (London: The Syndics of the Cambridge University Press).

Frankel, Francine R. (1971). *India's Green Revolution: Economic Gains and Political Costs* (Princeton: Princeton University Press).

Furnival, John S. (1944). *Netherlands India: A Study of Plural Economy* (Cambridge: Cambridge University Press).

——— (1948). *Colonial Policy and Practice: A Comparative Study of Burma and Netherlands India* (Cambridge: Cambridge University Press).

Furubotn, Erik and Pejovich, Svetozar (1972). "Property Rights and Economic

Theory: A Survey of Recent Literature," *Journal of Economic Literature*, Vol. 10 (December), pp. 1137–1162.

Furushima, Toshio (1941). *Nihon Hoken Nogyo Shi* (Agricultural History of Feudal Japan) (Tokyo: Shakai Shobo).

—— (1943). *Kinsei Nihon Nogyo no Kozo* (Structure of Japanese Agriculture in the Late Medieval Age) (Tokyo: Nihon Hyoronsha).

—— (1947 and 1949). *Nihon Nogyo Gijutsu Shi* (History of Agricultural Technology in Japan), 2 vols. (Tokyo: Jichosha).

Gafsi, Salem and Roe, Terry (1979). "Adoption of Unlike High-Yielding Wheat Varieties in Tunisia," *Economic Development and Cultural Change*, Vol. 28 (October), pp. 119–133.

Geertz, Clifford (1959). "The Javanese Village," in *Local, Ethnic, and National Loyalties in Village Indonesia: A Symposium*, ed. G. William Skinner, Yale University Southeast Asia Studies Cultural Report Series, (New Haven, Conn.), pp. 34–41.

—— (1970). *Agricultural Involution: The Process of Ecological Change in Indonesia*, (Berkeley and Los Angeles: University of California Press).

—— (1978). "The Bazaar Economy: Information and Search in Peasant Marketing," *American Economic Review*, Vol. 68 (May), pp. 28–32.

Griffin, Keith (1974). *The Political Economy of Agrarian Change: An Essay on the Green Revolution*. (Cambridge: Harvard University Press).

Hallagan, William (1978). "Self-selection by Contractual Choice and the Theory of Sharecropping," *Bell Journal of Economics*, Vol. 9 (Autumn), pp. 344–354.

Hardie, Robert S. (1952). *Philippine Land Tenure Reform: Analysis and Recommendations* (Manila: Special Technical and Economic Mission, United States Mutual Security Agency).

Hayami, Yujiro (1980). "Economic Approach to Village Community and Institution," *Journal of Rural Economics*, Vol. 3 (June), pp. 27–50.

—— (1981a). "Agrarian Problems of India from an East and Southeast Asian Perspective," *Economic and Political Weekly*, Vol. 16, No. 16 (April 18), pp. 707–712.

—— (1981b). "Induced Innovation, Green Revolution and Income Distribution," *Economic Development and Cultural Change*, Vol. 30 (October).

—— and Hafid, Anwar (1979). "Rice Harvesting and Welfare in Rural Java," *Bulletin of Indonesian Economic Studies*, Vol. 15 (July), pp. 94–112.

—— and Herdt, Robert W. (1977). "Market Price Effects of Technological Change on Income Distribution in Semisubsistence Agriculture," *American Journal of Agricultural Economics*, Vol. 59 (May), pp. 245–256.

—— and Ruttan, Vernon W. (1971). *Agricultural Development: An International Perspective* (Baltimore and London: Johns Hopkins University Press).

——; Maligalig, Luisa; and Fortuna, Nelly (1975). *Socio-Economic Characteristics of a Rice Village in Southern Luzon*, Agricultural Economics Department Paper No. 75-10 (Los Baños, Philippines: International Rice Research Institute).

——, in association with Akino, Masakatsu; Shintani, Masahiko; and Yamada, Saburo (1975). *A Century of Agricultural Growth in Japan* (Minneapolis: University of Minnesota Press; and Tokyo: University of Tokyo Press).

——, in association with Kikuchi, Masao; Moya, Piedad F.; Bambo, Luisa M.; and Marciano, Esther B. (1978). *Anatomy of a Peasant Economy: A Rice Village in the Philippines* (Los Baños, Philippines: International Rice Research Institute).

Heady, Earl O. (1947). "Economics of Farm Leasing Systems," *Journal of Farm Economics*, Vol. 29 (August), pp. 659–678.

Hester, Evett D. and Mabbun, Pablo, et al. (1924). "Some Economic and Social Aspects of Philippine Tenancies," *Philippine Agriculturist*, Vol. 12 (February), pp. 367–444.

Higgins, Benjamin (1955–56). "The Dualistic Theory of Underdeveloped Areas," *Economic Development and Cultural Change*, Vol. 4, pp. 99–115.

Hoffmann, Richard C. (1975). "Medieval Origins of the Common Fields," in *European Peasants and Their Markets*, ed. William N. Parker and Eric L. Jones (Princeton, New Jersey: Princeton University Press), pp. 23–71.

Hsiao, James C. (1975). "The Theory of Share Tenancy Revisited," *Journal of Political Economy*, Vol. 83 (October), pp. 1023–1031.

Husken, Frans (1979). "Landlords, Sharecroppers and Agricultural Laborers: Changing Labor Relations in Rural Java," *Journal of Contemporary Asia*, Vol. 9 (No. 2), pp. 140–151.

Ikehata, Setsuho (1971). "Tonan Ajia Kiso Shakai no Ichi Keitai: Philippine no Barangai Shakai ni Tsuite" (A Contribution to Southeast Asian Infrastructure: Analysis of Pre-Spanish Philippine Society), *The Memoir of the Institute of Oriental Culture*, University of Tokyo, Vol. 54 (March), pp. 83–163.

International Labor Organization (1977). *Poverty and Landlessness in Rural Asia* (Geneva, Switzerland).

International Rice Research Institute (1975). *Changes in Rice Farming in Selected Areas of Asia* (Los Baños, Philippines).

———— (1978). *Interpretive Analysis of Selected Papers from Changes in Rice Farming in Selected Areas of Asia* (Los Baños, Philippines).

Ishikawa, Shigeru (1975). "Peasant Families and the Agrarian Community in the Process of Economic Development," in *Agriculture in Development Theory*, ed. Lloyd G. Reynolds (New Haven and London: Yale University Press), pp. 451–496.

Jha, Dayanatha (1974). "Agricultural Growth, Technology and Equity," *Indian Journal of Agricultural Economics*, Vol. 29 (July-September), pp. 207–216.

Johnson, D. Gale (1950). "Resource Allocation under Share Contracts," *Journal of Political Economy*, Vol. 58 (April), pp. 111–123.

Johnston, Bruce F. and Cownie, John (1969). "The Seed-Fertilizer Revolution and Labor Force Absorption," *American Economic Review*, Vol. 59 (September), pp. 569–582.

Jorgenson, Dale W. (1961). "The Development of a Dual Economy," *Economic Journal*, Vol. 71 (June), pp. 309–334.

Joshi, P. C. (1970). "Land Reform in India and Pakistan," *Economic and Political Weekly*, Vol. 5 (December), pp. 145–152.

Kano, Hiroyoshi (1977). *Land Tenure System and the Desa Community in Nineteenth-Century Java,* IDE Special Paper No. 5 (Tokyo: Institute of Developing Economies).

———— (1979). *Pagelaran: Tobu Java Noson no Tomi to Hinkon* (Pagelaran: Wealth and Poverty in an East Java Village) (Tokyo: Institute of Developing Economies).

———— (1980). "The Economic History of Javanese Rural Society: A Reinterpretation," *The Developing Economies*, Vol. 18 (March), pp. 3–22.

Kerkvliet, Benedict J. (1971). "Peasant Society and Unrest Prior to the Huk Revolution in the Philippines," *Asian Studies*, Vol. 9 (August), pp. 164–213.

—— (1977). *The Huk Rebellion: A Study of Peasant Revolt in the Philippines* (Berkeley: University of California Press).

Khan, M. H. (1975). *Economics of the Green Revolution* (Chicago: Praeger).

Khusro, A. M. (1964). "Returns to Scale in Indian Agriculture," *Indian Journal of Agricultural Economics*, Vol. 19 (October-December), pp. 51–80.

Kikuchi, Masao and Hayami, Yujiro (1980a). "Inducements to Institutional Innovations in an Agrarian Community," *Economic Development and Cultural Change*, Vol. 29 (Oct.), pp. 21–36.

—— (1980b). "Polarization of an Agrarian Community: A Dilemma of the Philippine Land Reform," *Land Economics*, Vol. 56 (August), pp. 350–365.

—— (1980c). "Technology and Labor Contract: Two Systems of Rice Harvesting in the Philippines," *Journal of Comparative Economics*, Vol. 4 (December), pp. 357–377.

——; Cordova, Violeta G.; Marciano, Esther B.; and Hayami, Yujiro (1979). *Changes in Rice Harvesting Systems in Central Luzon and Laguna*, IRRI Research Paper Series No. 31 (Los Baños, Philippines: International Rice Research Institute).

——; Hafid, Anwar; Saleh, Chaerul; Hartoyo, Sri; and Hayami, Yujiro (1980a). "Class Differentiation, Labor Employment and Income Distribution in a West Java Village," *The Developing Economies*, Vol. 18 (March), pp. 45–64.

—— (1980b). *Changes in Community Institutions and Income Distribution in a West Java Village*, IRRI Research Paper Series No. 50 (Los Baños, Philippines: International Rice Research Institute).

——; Yusuf, Abrar; Hafid, Anwar; and Hayami, Yujiro (1980). *Technological Progress and Income Distribution in a Rice Village in Java*, IRRI Research Paper Series No. 55 (Los Banos, Philippines: International Rice Research Institute).

Kirk, Dudley (1979). "World Population and Birth Rates: Agreements and Disagreements," *Population and Development Review*, Vol. 5 (September), pp. 387–403.

Kitamura, Toshio (1950 and 1973). *Nihon Kangai Suiri Kanko no Shiteki Kenkyu* (The Historical Study of Customary Rules on the Utilization of Irrigation Water in Japan), 2 vols. (Tokyo: Iwanami).

Krishna, Raj (1975). "Measurement of the Direct and Indirect Employment Effects of Agricultural Growth with Technical Change," in *Externalities in the Transformation of Agriculture*, eds. Earl O. Heady and Larry R. Whiting (Ames, Iowa: Iowa State University Press).

Kuchiba, Masuo (1975). "*Tonan Ajia ni okeru Sonraku no Kozo*" (A Note on the Village Structure in Southeast Asia), *Tonan Ajia Kenkyu* (Southeast Asian Studies), Vol. 9 (March), pp. 478–488.

——, (1979). "Problems and Approach From Comparative Perspective," in *A Comparative Study of Paddy-Growing Communities in South and Southeast Asia and Japan*, eds. Masuo Kuchiba and Leslie E. Bauzon (Tokyo: Toyota Foundation).

——; Tsubouchi, Yoshihiro; and Maeda, Naribumi, eds. (1979). *Three Malay Villages: A Sociology of Paddy Growers in West Malaysia* (Honolulu: University Press of Hawaii).

Kurien, C. T. (1980). "Dynamics of Rural Transformation: A Case Study of Tamil Nadu," *Economic and Political Weekly*, Vol. 15 (February), pp. 365–390.

Kuznets, Simon (1966). *Modern Economic Growth* (New Haven and London: Yale University Press).

Lal, Deepak (1976). "Agricultural Growth, Real Wages, and the Rural Poor in India," *Economic and Political Weekly*, Vol. 11 (June 1976), pp. 47–61.

Larkin, John A. (1972). *The Pampangans: Colonial Society in a Philippine Province* (Berkeley, Los Angeles and London: University of California Press).

Ledesma, Antonio J. (1976). "The Agrarian Problem and the Unrepresented Minorities during the Commonwealth," *Philippine Journal of Public Administration*, Vol. 11 (July), pp. 216–229.

—— (1980). *Landless Workers and Rice Farmers: Peasant Subclasses under Agrarian Reform in Two Philippine Villages*. Ph. D. Dissertation (Madison: University of Wisconsin).

Lenin, Vladimir I. (1960; original publication, 1899). *The Development of Capitalism in Russia: The Process of Formation of a Home Market for Large-scale Industry*. Vol. 3, pp. 23–607, in Lenin, *Collected Works*, 4th ed. (Moscow: Foreign Languages Publishing House).

Lewis, Arthur W. (1954). "Economic Development with Unlimited Supplies of Labor," *Manchester School of Economics and Social Studies*, Vol. 22 (May), pp. 139–191.

Lewis, Harry T. (1971). *Ilocano Rice Farmers: A Comparative Study of Two Philippine Barrios* (Honolulu: University Press of Hawaii).

Lucas, Robert E. B. (1979). "Sharing, Monitoring, and Incentives:Marshallian Misallocation Reassessed," *Journal of Political Economy*, Vol. 87 (June), pp. 501–521.

Mangahas, Mahar; Miralaro, Virginia A.; and de los Reyes, Romana P. (1974). *Tenants, Lessees, Owners: Welfare Implications of Tenure Change* (Quezon City, Philippines: Ateneo de Manila University Press).

Marx, Karl (1913; original Publication, 1859). *A Contribution to the Critique of Political Economy* (Chicago: Kerr).

—— (1925; original Publication, 1867). *Capital: A Critique of Political Economy, Vol. 1: The Process of Capital Production* (Chicago: Kerr).

—— (1960). *Economic and Philosophical Manuscripts of 1844* (Moscow: Foreign Language Publishing House).

Mauldin, W. Parker and Berelson, Bernard (1978). "Conditions of Fertility Decline in Developing Countries, 1965–75," *Studies in Family Planning*, Vol. 9 (May), pp. 89–147.

Mazumdar, D. (1963). "On the Economics of Relative Efficiency of Small Farmers," *Economic Weekly*, Vol. 15 (July), pp. 1259–1263.

McCloskey, Donald N. (1975). "The Economics of Enclosure: A Market Analysis," in *European Peasants and Their Markets*, ed. William N. Parker and Eric L. Jones (Princeton, New Jersey: Princeton University Press), pp. 123–160.

McLennan, Marshall S. (1969). "Land and Tenancy in the Central Luzon Plain," *Philippine Studies*, Vol. 17 (October), pp. 651–682.

Mehra, S. (1976). Occasional Paper No. 88 (Ithaca: Cornell University).

Mellor, J. W. and Lele, Uma J. (1973). "Growth Linkages with the New Food Grain Technologies," *Indian Journal of Agricultural Economics*, Vol. 28 (January-March), pp. 35–55.

Migdal, Joel S. (1974). *Peasants, Politics, and Revolution* (Princeton, New Jersey: Princeton University Press).

Mitrany, David (1951). *Marx Against the Peasant* (Durham: University of North Carolina Press).

Mizuno, Koichi (1978). "The Social Organization of Rice-Growing Villages," in *Thailand: A Rice-Growing Society*, ed. Yoneo Ishii (Honolulu: The University Press of Hawaii), pp. 83–114.

Mueller, Dennis C. (1976). "Public Choice: A Survey," *Journal of Economic Literature*, Vol. 14 (June), pp. 395–433.
——— (1979). *Public Choice* (London: Cambridge University Press).
Muqtada, M. (1975). "The Seed-Fertilizer Technology and Surplus Labor in Bangladesh Agriculture," *Bangladesh Development Studies*, Vol. 3 (October), pp. 403–426.
Murray, Francis J. (1972). "Land Reform in the Philippines: An Overview," *Philippine Sociological Review*, Vol. 20 (January-April), pp. 151–168.
Narain, Dharm and Joshi, P. C. (1969). "Magnitude of Agricultural Tenancy," *Economic and Political Weekly*, Vol. 4 (September), pp. 139–142.
Nash, James M. (1950). "The Bargaining Problem," *Econometrica*, Vol. 18 (April), pp. 155–162.
Newbery, David M. G. (1975). "The Choice of Rental of Contract in Peasant Agriculture," in *Agriculture in Development Theory*, ed. Lloyd G. Reynolds (New Haven and London: Yale University Press, 1975), pp. 109–137.
——— (1977). "Risk Sharing, Sharecropping and Uncertain Labor Markets," *Review of Economic Studies*, Vol. 64 (October), pp. 585–594.
Nitisastro, Widjojo (1970). *Population Trends in Indonesia* (Ithaca and London: Cornell University Press).
North, Douglass C. and Thomas, Robert P. (1971). "The Rise and Fall of the Manorial System: A Theoretical Approach," *Journal of Economic History*, Vol. 31 (December), pp. 777–803.
——— (1973). *The Rise of the Western World: A New Economic History* (Cambridge, England: Cambridge University Press).
Olson, Mancur (1965). *The Logic of Collective Action* (Cambridge, Mass.: Harvard University Press).
Palmer, Ingrid (1976a). *The New Rice in Asia: Conclusions from Four Country Studies* (Geneva: United Nations Research Institute for Social Development).
——— (1976b). *The New Rice in Indonesia* (Geneva: United Nations Research Institute for Social Development).
Pejovich, Svetozar (1972). "Towards an Economic Theory of the Creation and Specification of Property Rights," *Review of Social Economy*, Vol. 30 (September), pp. 309–325.
Pelzer, Karl J. (1948). *Pioneer Settlement in the Asiatic Tropics* (New York: American Geographical Society).
——— (1971). "The Agricultural Foundation," in *The Economy of Indonesia*, ed. Bruce Glassburner (Ithaca and London: Cornell University Press), pp. 128–161.
Penny, David H. (1969). "Indonesia," in *Agricultural Development in Asia*, ed. Richard T. Shand (Canberra: Australian National University Press), pp. 251–279.
Phelan, John L. (1959). *The Hispanization of the Philippines: Spanish and Filipino Responses, 1965–1700* (Madison: University of Wisconsin Press).
Polanyi, Karl (1957). *The Great Transformation* (New York: Reinholt and Co.).
Popkin, Samuel L. (1979). *The Rational Peasant* (Berkeley, Los Angeles and London: University of California Press).
Posner, Richard A. (1980). "A Theory of Primitive Society, with Special Reference to Law," *Journal of Law and Economics*, Vol. 23 (April), pp. 1–53.
Raffles, T. Stamford (1830). *The History of Java* (London: John Murray), 2 volumes.
Raj, K. N. (1976). "Trends in Rural Unemployment in India: An Analysis with Reference to Conceptual and Measurement Problems," *Economic and Political Weekly*, Vol. 11 (August), pp. 1281–1292.
Ranade, Chandra G. and Herdt, Robert W. (1978). "Shares of Farm Earnings from

Rice Production," in International Rice Research Institute, *Economic Consequences of the New Rice Technology* (Los Baños, Philippines), pp. 87–104.

Ranis, Gustav and Fei, John C. H. (1961). "A Theory of Economic Development," *American Economic Review*, Vol. 51 (September), pp. 533–565.

Rao, A. P. (1967). "Size of Holdings and Productivity," *Economic and Political Weekly*, Vol. 2 (November), pp. 1989–1991.

Rao, C. H. Hanumantha (1966). "Alternative Explanations of the Inverse Relationship between Farm Size and Output per Acre in India," *Indian Economic Review*, New Series Vol. 1 (October), pp. 1–12.

—— (1970). "Farm Size and Credit Policy," *Economic and Political Weekly*, Vol. 5 (December), pp. 157–160.

—— (1971). "Uncertainty, Entrepreneurship, and Sharecropping in India," *Journal of Political Economy*, Vol. 79 (May-June), pp. 578–595.

—— (1975). *Technological Change and Distribution of Gains in Indian Agriculture* (Delhi: Macmillan Company of India).

Reid, Joseph D. (1973). "Sharecropping as an Understandable Market Response: The Post-Bellum South," *Journal of Economic History*, Vol. 33 (March), pp. 106–130.

—— (1977). "The Theory of Share Tenancy Revisited Again," *Journal of Political Economy*, Vol. 85 (April), pp. 403–407.

Ricardo, David (1951; original publication, 1817). *On the Principle of Political Economy and Taxation*, 3rd ed., ed. by Piero Sraffa (Cambridge: Cambridge University Press).

Rivera, Generoso E. and McMillan, Robert T. (1954). *An Economic and Social Survey of Rural Households in Central Luzon* (Manila: Cooperative Research Project of the Philippine Council for United States Aid and the United States of America Operations Mission to the Philippines).

Rosenzweig, Mark R. (1978). "Rural Wages, Labor Supply, and Land Reform: A Theoretical and Empirical Analysis," *American Economic Review*, Vol. 68 (December), pp. 847–860.

Roumasset, James A. (1979). "Sharecropping, Production Externalities and the Theory of Contracts," *American Journal of Agricultural Economics*, Vol. 61 (November), pp. 643–647.

Ruttan, Vernon W. (1964). "Equity and Productivity Objectives in Agrarian Reform Legislation: Perspectives on the New Philippine Land Reform Code," *Indian Journal of Agricultural Economics*, Vol. 19 (July-December), pp. 115–130.

—— (1966). "Tenure and Productivity of Philippine Rice Producing Farms," *Philippine Economic Journal*, Vol. 5 (First Semester), pp. 42–63.

—— (1977). "The Green Revolution: Seven Generalizations," *International Development Review*, Vol. 19 (August), pp. 16–23.

—— (1978a). "Institutional Innovations," in *Distortions of Agricultural Incentives*, ed. Theodore W. Schultz (Bloomington and London: Indiana University Press), pp. 290–304.

—— (1978b). "A Postscript on Alternative Paths of Induced Institutional Change," in *Induced Innovation*, ed. Vernon W. Ruttan and Hans P. Binswanger (Baltimore and London: Johns Hopkins University Press), pp. 409–413.

Sairin, Sjafri (1976). "*Beberapa Masalah Derep: Studi Kasus Yogyakarta*" (Some Problems Concerning Rice Harvesting Methods: The Case of Yogyakarta), *Prisma*, Vol. 5 (September), pp. 59–67.

Sajogyo and Collier, William L. (1973). "Adoption of New High Yielding Rice Varieties by Java's Farmers," in *Technical Change in Asian Agriculture*, ed. Richard T. Shand (Canberra: Australian National University), pp. 80–107.

Schickele, Rainer (1941). "Effect of Tenure Systems on Agricultural Efficiency," *Journal of Farm Economics*, Vol. 23 (February), pp. 185–207.

Schultz, Theodore W. (1964). *Transforming Traditional Agriculture* (New Haven and London: Yale University Press).

—— (1975). "The Value of the Ability to Deal with Disequilibria," *Journal of Economic Literature*, Vol. 13 (September), pp. 827–846.

Scott, James C. (1972). "The Erosion of Patron-Client Bonds and Social Change in Rural Southeast Asia," *Journal of Asian Studies*, Vol. 33 (November), pp. 5–37.

—— (1976). *The Moral Economy of the Peasant* (New Haven and London: Yale University Press).

Sen, Amartya K. (1964). "Size of Holdings and Productivity," *Economic Weekly*, Vol. 16 (February), pp. 323–326.

Sen, Bandhudas (1974). *The Green Revolution in India: A Perspective* (New Delhi: Wiley Eastern).

Shanin, Teodor, ed. (1971). *Peasants and Peasant Societies* (Harmondsworth, England: Penguin Books).

Sidhu, Surjit S. (1974). "Economics of Technical Change in Wheat Production in the Indian Punjab," *American Journal of Agricultural Economics*, Vol. 56 (May), pp. 217–226.

Sinaga, Rudolf S. and Collier, William L. (1975). "Social and Regional Implications of Agricultural Development," *Prisma*, Vol. 1 (November), pp. 24–35.

Smith, Joyotee and Gascon, Fe (1979). *The Effect of the New Rice Technology on Family Labor Utilization in Laguna*, IRRI Research Paper Series No. 42 (Los Baños, Philippines: International Rice Research Institute).

Smith, Thomas C. (1959). *Agrarian Origins of Modern Japan* (Stanford: Stanford University Press).

Soejono, Irlan (1976). "Growth and Distributional Changes in Paddy Farm Income in Central Java," *Bulletin of Indonesian Economic Studies,* Vol. 12 (July), pp. 80–89.

Soentoro (1973). *Sistim Perburuhan Ngepak-Ngedok di 6 Desa Sample di Jawa* (The Ngepak-Ngedok Labor System in Six Sample Villages in Java) (Bogor, Indonesia: Agro-Economic Survey).

——; Collier, William L.; and Hidayat, Kliwon (1980). "Land Markets in Rural Java." A Paper prepared for AES-IRRI Joint Workshop on *Village Economy and Institutions* held at the International Rice Research Institute, Los Baños, Philippines. August 25–27.

Sriswasdilek, Jerachone (1973). *The Yield Performance and Economic Benefits of the High Yielding Rice Varieties in Don Chedi, Suphan Buri, Thailand*, M. S. Thesis, University of the Philippines at Los Baños, Philippines.

Stiglitz, Joseph E. (1974). "Incentives and Risk Sharing in Sharecropping," *Review of Economic Studies*, Vol. 61 (April), pp. 219–255.

Stoler, Ann L. (1977). "Rice Harvesting in Kali Loro," *American Ethnologist*, Vol. 4 (No. 4), pp. 678–698.

Sturgess, N. H., and Wijaya, Hesti (1979). "Land Leasing in East Java," *Bulletin of Indonesian Economic Studies*, Vol. 15 (July), pp. 75–93.

Suh, Wan Soo (1976). *Factors Affecting the Rate of Adoption of Tongil Rice Variety in Selected Locations of Korea*, M. S. Thesis, University of the Philippines at Los Baños, Philippines.

Takahashi, Akira (1969). *Land and Peasants in Central Luzon: Socio-Economic Structure of Bulacan Village* (Tokyo: The Institute of Developing Economies).

Takaya, Yoshikazu (1975). *"Inasakuken no Rekishi"* (A History of the Rice-Growing Region), in *Ine to Nomin* (Rice and Peasants), ed. Shinichi Ichimura (Kyoto: Kyoto University Center for Southeast Asian Studies), pp. 28–57.

───── (1977). "Rice-Growing Societies of Asia: An Ecological Approach," *South East Asian Studies*, Vol. 15 (December), pp. 442–451.

Takigawa, Tsutomu (1976). *Sengo Philippine Nochi Kaikaku Ron* (Treatise on Postwar Philippine Land Reform) (Tokyo: Institute of Developing Economies).

Timmer, C. Peter (1969). "The Turnip, the New Husbandry, and the English Agricultural Revolution," *Quarterly Journal of Economics*, Vol. 83 (August), pp. 375–395.

Umehara, Hiromitsu (1967). "Philippine no Beisaku Noson (Rice Village in the Philippines)," in *Ajia no Tochi Seido to Noson Shakai Kozo* (Land Tenure System and Rural Social Structure in Asia), Vol. 2, eds. Tsutomu Takigawa and Hitoshi Saito (Tokyo: Institute of Developing Economies, 1967), pp. 141–206.

───── (1974). *A Hacienda Barrio in Central Luzon: A Case Study of a Philippine Village* (Tokyo: The Institute of Developing Economies).

───── (1976). "Philippine ni okeru Shiteki Tochi Shoyuken Tenkai ni Kansuru Ichi Kosatsu" (A Study on the Development of Private Land Ownership in the Philippines), in *Ajia Tochi Seisakuron Josetsu* (Introduction to Land Tenure Systems in Asia), ed. Hitoshi Saito (Tokyo: Institute of Developing Economies).

Utami, Widya and Ihalauw, John (1973). "Some Consequences of Small Farm Size," *Bulletin of Indonesian Economic Studies*, Vol. 9 (July), pp. 46–56.

Utrecht, E. (1969). "Land Reform in Indonesia," *Bulletin of Indonesian Economic Studies*, Vol. 5 (November), pp. 71–88.

van der Kolff, G. H. (1936). *The Historical Development of the Labor Relationships in a Remote Corner of Java as They Apply to the Cultivation of Rice* (New York: Institute of Pacific Studies).

Warriner, Doreen (1969). *Land Reform in Principle and Practice* (Oxford: Clarendon Press).

───── (1973). "Results of Land Reform in Asian and Latin American Countries," *Food Research Institute Studies*, Vol. 12 (No. 2), pp. 115–131.

Wharton, Clifton R. (1969). "The Green Revolution: Cornucopia or Pandora's Box," *Foreign Affairs*, Vol. 47 (April), pp. 464–476.

White, Benjamin (1976). "Population, Involution and Employment in Rural Java," *Development and Change*, Vol. 7 (No. 3), pp. 267–290.

Williamson, Oliver E. (1975). *Market and Hierarchies: Analysis and Antitrust Implications* (New York: Free Press).

Wiradi, Gunawan (1978). *Rural Development and Rural Institutions: A Study of Institutional Changes in West Java*, Rural Dynamics Series No. 6 (Bogor, Indonesia: Agro Economic Survey).

Wolf, Eric (1966). *Peasants* (Englewood Cliffs, New Jersey: Prentice-Hall).

───── (1969). *Peasant Wars of the Twentieth Century* (New York, Evanston, and London: Harper and Row).

Wurfel, David (1958). "Philippine Agrarian Reform under Magsaysay," *Far Eastern Survey*, Vol. 27 (January and February), pp. 7–15 and 23–30.

Yamklinfung, Prasert (1979). "Japanese Paddy-Growing Communities from a Thai Viewpoint," in *A Comparative Study of Paddy-Growing Communities in Southeast Asia and Japan*, eds. Masuo Kuchiba and Leslie E. Bauzon (Tokyo: Toyota Foundation).

Index